ENHANCED A+ LAB MANUAL

FOR GUIDE TO MANAGING AND MAINTAINING YOUR PC

ENHANCED THIRD EDITION

CLINT SAXTON, A+, MCSE, MCT

Australia • Canada • Mexico • Singapore • Spain • United Kingdom • United States

Enhanced A+ Lab Manual for Guide to Managing and Maintaining Your PC, Enhanced Third Edition, is published by Course Technology.

Senior Product Manager
Lisa Egan
Managing Editor
Stephen Solomon
Senior Vice President, Publisher
Kristen Duerr
Production Editor
Jennifer Goguen

Developmental Editor
Jill Batistick
Associate Product Manager
Laura Hildebrand, Elizabeth Wessen
Editorial Assistant
Elizabeth Wessen, Janet Aras
Manuscript Quality Assurance
John Bosco

Manuscript Quality Engineer
Nicole Ashton
Marketing Manager
Toby Shelton
Text Designer
GEX Publishing Services
Cover Designer
Abby Scholz

Printed in America

4 5 BM 05 04 03 02 01

For more information, contact Course Technology, 25 Thomson Place, Boston, MA 02210; or find us on the World Wide Web at www.course.com.

Disclaimer

Course Technology reserves the right to revise this publication and make changes from time to time in its content without notice.

The Web addresses in this book are subject to change from time to time as necessary without notice.

ISBN 0-619-03435-1

Table of Contents

A+ Core Objectives

This book maps to CompTIA's newly revised A+ Certification Exams. This A+ Table of Contents enables you to find all of the A+ content quickly.

A+ OS Objectives

Objectives	Chapters
1.1 Identify the operating system's functions, structure, and major system files to navigate the operating system and how to get to needed technical information.	1, 4, 12-14
1.2 Identify basic concepts and procedures for creating, viewing and managing files and directories, including procedures for changing file attributes and the ramifications of those changes (for example, security issues).	1, 12-14
1.3 Identify the procedures for basic disk management.	6, 12, 14
2.1 Identify the procedures for installing Windows 9x, and Windows 2000 for bringing the software to a basic operational level.	6, 12, 14
2.2 Identify steps to perform an operating system upgrade.	12, 14
2.3 Identify the basic system boot sequences and boot methods, including the steps to create an emergency boot disk with utilities installed for Windows 9x, Windows NT, and Windows 2000.	8, 12-14
2.4 Identify procedures for loading/adding and configuring device drivers, applications and the necessary software for certain devices.	14, 17, 18
3.1 Recognize and interpret the meaning of common error codes and startup messages from the boot sequence, and identify steps to correct the problems.	4, 8, 12, 13
3.2 Recognize common problems and determine how to resolve them.	2, 4, 6, 8, 12-14, 17, 19, 20
4.1 Identify the networking capabilities of Windows including procedures for connecting to the network.	13, 14, 16
4.2 Identify concepts and capabilities relating to the Internet and basic procedures for setting up a system for Internet access.	14, 16

PREFACE

Use this Lab Manual as a dynamic tool to gain direct experience setting up and repairing personal computers. Designed for use in conjunction with *Enhanced A+ Guide to Managing and Maintaining Your PC, Enhanced Third Edition* by Jean Andrews, this lab manual merges tutorial and lab experiences for complete understanding of PC maintenance and thorough preparation for the A+ service technician exams. Inside this manual you will discover 80 exciting labs tailored to provide simulated real-life experience through hands-on exercises. After completing all 80 lab exercises, you will have not only practiced each A+ objective in a hands-on environment, but also will have gained valuable DOS, Windows 9x, Windows NT, and Windows 2000 installation and configuration skills, all of which are vital in the quickly evolving PC industry.

This book provides comprehensive preparation for the revised A+ Certification examinations offered through the Computer Technology Industry Association (CompTIA). Because the popularity of this certification credential is quickly growing among employers, obtaining certification increases your ability to gain employment, improve your salary, and enhance your career. To find more information about A+ Certification and its sponsoring organization, CompTIA, see their Web site at *www.comptia.org*.

Uniquely designed with you in mind, this lab manual is written from the "show-me" perspective—instead of simply describing a procedure or task, this manual shows you how to complete it, step by step. Each lab will allow you to interact with a PC, provide you the freedom to make mistakes, and most importantly, enable you to recover and LEARN from those mistakes in a safe environment. Whether your goal is to become an A+ certified technician, develop an understanding of operating systems, or become a PC hardware technician, the *A+ Lab Manual*, along with the *Enhanced A+ Guide to Managing and Maintaining Your PC* textbook, will take you there!

Features

In order to ensure a successful experience for both instructors and students, this book includes the following pedagogical features:

- **Objectives**—Every lab opens with a list of learning objectives that sets the stage for students to absorb the lessons of the lab.
- **Materials Required**—This feature outlines all the materials students need to complete the lab successfully.

- **Lab Setup & Safety Tips**—This quick list summarizes any safety precautions or preliminary steps instructors and students should take before beginning a lab.

- **Activity**—Every lab activity is broken down into manageable sections to ensure the student understands each step of the lab.

- **Lab Notes**—These notes provide the key definitions and acronyms that complement the information in the body of the lab.
- **Review Questions**—Exercises at the end of each lab let students test their understanding of the lab material.
- **A+ Table of Contents**—The A+ Table of Contents is a unique feature that allows you to find coverage for all A+ Certification objectives quickly. This Table of Contents is found directly after the primary Table of Contents in the front of the book.
- **Web Site**—For updates to this book and information about other A+ and PC Repair products, go to www.course.com/pcrepair.

Acknowledgments

I would like to give special thanks to Amanda Hart, for her patience, support and encouragement throughout this entire project.

I would also like to extend my sincere appreciation to Jill Batistick, Lisa Egan, and all the Course Technology staff for their instrumental roles in the development of this lab manual.

Many thanks also to the reviewers for their insights and valuable input. A sincere thank you to:

Donald Hofmann	Grayson County College
Bruce Lane	Blue Feather Technologies
David Mansheffer	Brown University

CLASSROOM SETUP

Lab activities have been designed to explore many different types of hardware and software technologies while maintaining a readily available list of hardware and software components.

Most labs take 30 to 45 minutes; a few may take a little longer. Most schools teaching Windows 2000 should have computers that meet or exceed the Modern Configuration requirements.

Your classroom should be networked, and at a minimum, each lab workstation must meet the Simple Configuration requirements:

Simple Configuration

- 90 Mhz or better Pentium-compatible computer
- 16 MB of RAM
- 540 MB hard drive
- 1 NIC (Network Interface Card)

The majority of the lab activities can be completed with the Simple Configuration hardware; however, some labs will require the following:

Typical Configuration

- 166 Mhz or better Pentium-compatible computer
- 24 MB of RAM
- 800 MB hard drive
- CD-ROM drive
- 1 NIC (Network Interface Card)

Modern Configuration

- 200 Mhz or better Pentium-compatible computer
- 64 MB of RAM
- 2 GB hard drive
- CD-ROM drive
- 1 NIC (Network Interface Card)
- 1 sound card

Activities requiring the Typical or Modern configurations focus on Windows NT, Windows 2000, and specialty hardware.

LAB SETUP INSTRUCTIONS

Configuration Type and Operating Systems

Configure your lab workstation with the required components. Before beginning a lab activity, verify that each lab workstation meets the requirements of the configuration specified (Simple, Typical, or Modern). Then, make sure that the proper operating system is installed and in good health. Note that some labs don't require an operating system to be installed prior to the lab activity. Check the Lab Setup and Safety Tips section for the lab.

Additional Devices

Identify and locate any additional devices that are required for the lab activity. Additional devices are typically hardware, software, or documentation that may, or may not, be required for completing the lab activities.

Lab Setup and Safety Tips

Before beginning any lab, be sure to read the Lab Setup and Safety Tips section and configure your lab workstation as described. Specific activity requirements are specified in this section and are often critical to the success of the lab activities. Don't skip this step!

THE TECHNICIAN'S WORK AREA

Although many computer problems are associated with software, there are still times when you must get out your screwdriver and open the computer's case. In those situations, it is important to have the proper tools and be properly grounded to ensure that you don't cause more damage than you repair. Now, let's take a look at the components of a technician's ideal work area:

- Grounding mat (with grounding wire properly grounded)
- Grounding wrist strap (attached to the grounding mat)
- Non-carpet flooring
- A clean work area (no clutter)
- A set of screwdrivers
- ¼" Torx bit screwdriver
- ⅛" Torx bit screwdriver
- Needle-nose pliers
- A PLCC (Plastic Leadless Chip Carrier)
- Pen light (flashlight)
- Several new antistatic bags (for transporting and storing hardware)

At miminum, you must have at least two key items. The first key item is a grounding strap. If a grounding mat isn't available, you can attach the grounding strap to the computer's chassis, and in most cases, provide sufficient grounding for handling hardware components inside the computer case. The second key item is, of course, a screwdriver. You won't be able to open most chassis without some type of screwdriver.

Protect Yourself, Your Hardware, and Your Software

When you work on a computer, it is possible to harm both the computer and yourself. The most common accident that happens when attempting to fix a computer problem is the erasing of software or data. Experimenting without knowing what you are doing can cause damage. To prevent these sorts of accidents, as well as the physically dangerous ones, take a few safety precautions. The text below describes the potential sources of damage to computers and how to protect against them.

Power to the Computer

To protect both yourself and the equipment when working inside a computer, turn off the power, unplug the computer, and always use a grounding bracelet. Consider the monitor and the power supply to be "black boxes." Never remove the cover or put your hands inside this equipment unless you know about the hazards of charged capacitors. Both the power supply and the monitor can hold a dangerous level of electricity even after they are turned off and disconnected from a power source.

Static Electricity, or ESD

Electrostatic discharge (ESD), commonly known as static electricity, is an electrical charge at rest. A static charge can build up on the surface of a nongrounded conductor and on nonconductive surfaces such as clothing or plastic. When two objects with dissimilar electrical charges touch, static electricity passes between them until the dissimilar charges are made equal. To see how this works, turn off the lights in a room, scuff your feet on the carpet, and touch another person. Occasionally you may see and feel the charge in your fingers. If you can feel the charge, then you discharged at least 3,000 volts of static electricity. If you hear the discharge, then you released at least 6,000 volts. If you see the discharge, then you released at least 8,000 volts of ESD. A charge of less than 3,000 volts can damage most electronic components. You can touch a chip on an expansion card or system board and damage the chip with ESD and never feel, hear, or see the discharge.

There are two types of damage that ESD can cause in an electronic component: catastrophic failures and upset failures. A catastrophic failure destroys the component beyond use. An upset failure damages the component so that it does not perform well, even though it may still function to some degree. Upset failures are the most difficult to detect because they are not easily observed.

Protect Against ESD

To protect the computer against ESD, always ground yourself before touching electronic components, including the hard drive, system board, expansion cards, processors, and memory modules. Ground yourself and the computer parts, using one or more of the following static control devices or methods:

- ***Ground bracelet or static strap:*** A ground bracelet is a strap you wear around your wrist. The other end is attached to a grounded conductor such as the computer case or a ground mat, or it can plug into a wall outlet (only the ground prong makes a connection!).
- ***Grounding mats:*** Grounding mats can come equipped with a cord to plug into a wall outlet to provide a grounded surface on which to work. Remember, if you lift the component off the mat, it is no longer grounded and it is susceptible to ESD.
- ***Static shielding bags:*** New components come shipped in static shielding bags. Save the bags to store other devices that are not currently installed in a PC.

The best solution to protect against ESD is to use a ground bracelet together with a ground mat. Consider a ground bracelet to be essential equipment when working on a computer. However, if you find yourself in a situation where you must work without one, touch the computer case before you touch a component. When passing a chip to another person, ground yourself. Leave components inside their protective bags until ready to use. Work on hard floors, not carpet, or use antistatic spray on the carpets.

Besides using a grounding mat, you can also create a ground for the computer case by leaving the power cord to the case plugged into the wall outlet. This is safe enough because the power is turned off when you work inside the case. However, if you happen to touch an exposed area of the power switch inside the case, it is possible to get a shock. Because of this risk, in this book, you are directed to unplug the power cord to the PC before you work inside the case.

There is an exception to the ground-yourself rule. Inside a monitor case, the electricity stored in capacitors poses a substantial danger. When working inside a monitor, you *don't* want to be grounded, as you would provide a conduit for the voltage to discharge through your body. In this situation, be careful *not* to ground yourself.

When handling system boards and expansion cards, don't touch the chips on the boards. Don't stack boards on top of each other, which could accidentally dislodge a chip. Hold cards by the edges, but don't touch the edge connections on the card.

After you unpack a new device or software that has been wrapped in cellophane, remove the cellophane from the work area quickly. Don't allow anyone who is not properly grounded to touch components. Do not store expansion cards within one foot of a monitor, because the monitor can discharge as much as 29,000 volts of ESD onto the screen.

Hold an expansion card by the edges. Don't touch any of the soldered components on a card. If you need to put an electronic device down, place it on a grounded mat or on a static shielding bag. Keep components away from your hair and clothing.

Protect Hard Drives and Disks

Always turn off a computer before moving it to protect the hard drive, which is always spinning when the computer is turned on (unless the drive has a sleep mode). Never jar a computer while the hard disk is running. Avoid placing a PC on the floor, where the user can accidentally kick it.

Follow the usual precautions to protect disks. Keep them away from magnetic fields, heat, and extreme cold. Don't open the floppy shuttle window or touch the surface of the disk inside the housing. Treat disks with care and they'll generally last for years.

CHAPTER

1

How Computers Work

Labs Included in This Chapter

- ♦ Lab 1.1 Components of a Personal Computer System
- ♦ Lab 1.2 Operating a DOS-Based PC
- ♦ Lab 1.3 Operating a Windows 95/98-Based PC
- ♦ Lab 1.4 Operating a Windows 2000-Based PC
- ♦ Lab 1.5 Operating a Linux-Based PC

Lab 1.1 Components of a Personal Computer System

Objective

The objective of this lab is to introduce you to the components of a personal computer (PC) system, which include: monitor, keyboard, mouse, printer, printer cable, power cables, and system unit. After completing this lab exercise, you will be able to:

- Identify the various components of a PC system.
- Describe the functionality of the various PC system components.
- Attach each of the most commonly used devices.
- Properly perform basic cleaning and maintenance procedures for each of the most commonly used PC components.

Materials Required

- Operating system: Windows 9x
- Lab workgroup size: 2–4 students
- Configuration type: simple

Simple Configuration

- 90 Mhz or better Pentium-compatible computer
- 16 MB of RAM
- 540 MB hard drive
- 1 NIC (Network Interface Card)

Additional Devices

- Labels for each group of students
- Paper towels for each group of students
- At least two spray bottles filled with a cleaning solution of either water and ammonia or plain water
- One demonstration PC with each of the following components properly attached and labeled:
  - Monitor
  - Keyboard
  - Mouse
  - Printer
  - Printer cable
  - Power cables
  - System unit

Lab Setup & Safety Tips

Each group of students should have all of the following PC components unattached:

- Monitor
- Keyboard
- Mouse
- Power cables
- System unit

Lab Activity

ACTIVITY

Attaching your lab workstation's devices

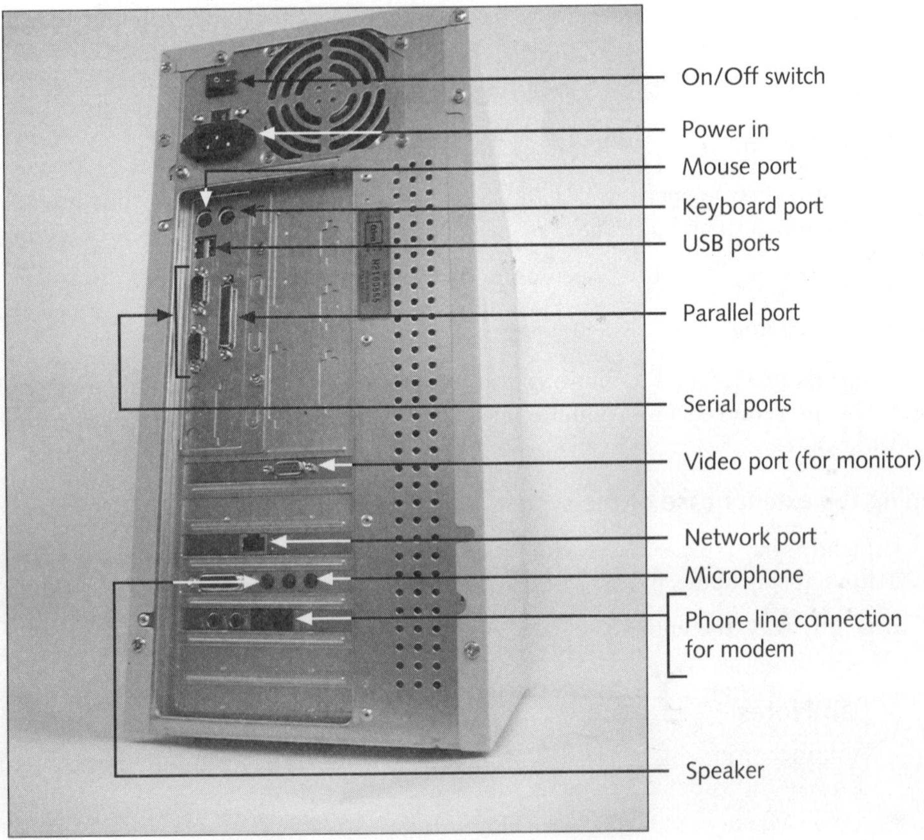

Figure 1-1 Input/output devices connect to the computer case by ports usually found on the back of the case

1. Observe the configuration of your instructor's demonstration PC. A sample case backing is shown in Figure 1-1.
2. Write down the name and function of each device labeled on your instructor's demonstration PC.

    ____

    ____

    ____

    ____

    ____

3. Attach your lab workstation's components in the same manner as on your instructor's demonstration PC.
4. Power on your lab workstation to verify that each component has been properly connected.
5. Allow your instructor to verify proper operation of the lab workstation.
6. Click the **Start** button and click **Shutdown**.
7. Click the **Shutdown this computer** toggle button, and click the **OK** button.
8. After the lab workstation has properly shut down, power off the computer.

Cleaning your mouse

1. Turn the mouse upside down.
2. Locate and remove the cover of the mouse ball.
3. Remove the mouse ball.
4. Inside the housing of the mouse ball, you will find several rollers. Clear these rollers of debris.
5. After clearing any debris from the rollers, replace the mouse ball and its cover.

Cleaning your monitor

1. Lightly spray a paper towel with water or a manufacturer-recommended cleaning solution from a spray bottle. (Never spray anything directly on the screen of your monitor.)
2. Gently wipe the entire screen using the slightly damp paper towel.

Clearing a stuck key

Most keyboards are designed to allow you to remove the keys by gently pulling or prying the key upward. This procedure is most commonly used when debris has become jammed underneath a particular key.

Cleaning the exterior case of the system unit

1. Lightly spray a paper towel with water or a manufacturer-recommended cleaning solution from a spray bottle. (Never spray anything directly on the exterior of your system unit case.)
2. Gently wipe the entire case using the slightly damp paper towel.

Lab Notes

Although every PC has different peripherals and types of devices, all PCs require some of the same components, which are listed below:

- Monitor
- Keyboard
- Mouse
- Power cables
- System unit

Review Questions

Circle True or False.

1. A monitor requires one cord and one cable to function properly. True / False
2. Most keyboards have their own power source. True / False
3. Providing that a keyboard and mouse connector physically appear the same, they are considered electronically interchangeable by the computer. True / False

____

____

____

____

____

4. You are a desktop support technician at the PC Store. Matt, one of your customers, has called you with a problem. He explains that he just finished moving his PC and reconnecting all the cables, but now he is getting error messages and both the keyboard and mouse won't work. What is the most likely cause of Matt's problem?

5. Another customer, Judy, also just finished moving her PC, and now the monitor screen is blank. She explains that the power light for the monitor is turned on and that the system unit power light also is on. Which cables would you ask Judy to check first?

6. Describe how to clean a mouse.

Lab 1.2 Operating a DOS-Based PC

Objective

The objective of this lab is to provide you with the experience of creating files and directories in the DOS environment. After completing this lab exercise, you will be able to:

- Start a DOS computer.
- Start a DOS application.
- Create a DOS system disk.
- Create a directory.
- Create and save a text file.
- Describe the purpose of a system disk.
- Delete files and directories.
- View the contents of a directory.
- Properly shut down your DOS lab workstation.

Materials Required

- Operating system: DOS
- Lab workgroup size: 2–4 students
- Configuration type: simple

Simple Configuration

- 90 Mhz or better Pentium-compatible computer
- 16 MB of RAM
- 540 MB hard drive
- 1 NIC (Network Interface Card)

Additional Devices

- Two unformatted floppy disks for each lab workstation

Lab Setup & Safety Tips

- This lab assumes that the DOS operating system is installed in a directory called DOS.
- Each lab workstation should have MS-DOS 5.0 or greater installed and functioning properly.
- After completing this lab exercise, be sure to keep your system disk in a safe place; you will use it in future labs.

Activity

Creating a DOS system disk

1. Power on your lab workstation, and allow it to boot into the DOS environment.
2. Place the blank floppy disk in drive A.
3. At the C prompt, type **FORMAT A:**.
4. Press **Enter** and respond to the formatting prompts.

5. After the disk has been formatted, type **SYS A:**.
6. Press **Enter**.
7. Type **CD DOS** and press **Enter**.
8. Type **COPY FDISK.EXE A:** and press **Enter**.
9. Type **COPY FORMAT.COM A:** and press **Enter**.
10. Type **COPY SCANDISK.EXE A:** and press **Enter**.
11. Type **COPY DEFRAG.EXE A:** and press **Enter**.

Understanding a DOS system disk

1. Place the system disk in drive A.
2. Turn on the PC.
3. Record the results: ______________________________
4. Turn off the PC.
5. Place a blank disk in drive A.
6. Turn on the PC.
7. Record the results: ______________________________
8. Turn off the PC.
9. Remove the floppy disk from drive A.

Creating a file using DOS EDIT

1. Turn on the PC, and allow it to boot into the DOS environment.
2. At the C prompt, type **EDIT** and then press **ESC**.
3. Type **This is a test file.** in the Edit program.
4. Press **Alt** + **F** (hold down the Alt key and at the same time, press the letter F).
5. Press the down arrow [↓] key to select **Save As** from the File menu.
6. At the top of the Save As dialog box, locate the **File Name** section.
7. Type **C:\Test.txt** as the filename.
8. Press **Enter**.
9. Press **Alt** + **F**.
10. Press the down arrow [↓] key to select **Exit** from the File menu.

Creating a directory

1. Figure 1-2 shows the logic behind directories. At the C prompt, type **MD C:\LAB1.2** and press **Enter**. Your lab workstation should respond by returning you to a C prompt.
2. Type **CD LAB1.2** and press **Enter**. Your lab workstation should respond with the following prompt: **C:\LAB.1.2>**. This means that you are now in the **LAB1.2** directory.
3. Change back to the root directory by typing **CD ..** (.. is an abbreviation for the previous or parent directory). Your lab workstation should return to the C prompt (C:\>) or root directory.

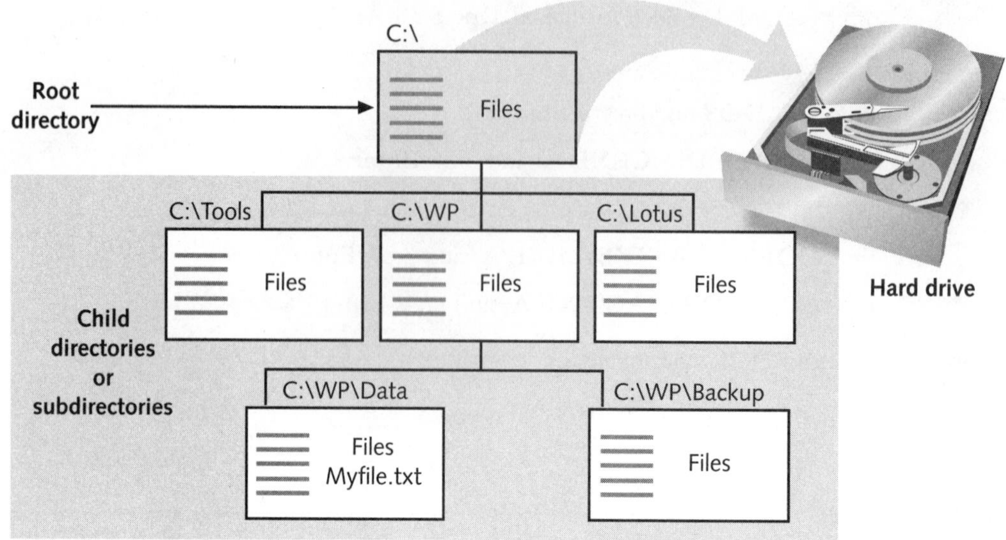

Figure 1-2 A hard drive is organized into groups of files stored in directories. The first directory is called the root directory. All directories can have sub- or child directories. Under Windows, a directory is called a folder.

Viewing the contents of a directory

1. At the C prompt (C:\>), type **DIR** (directory listing).
2. Press **Enter**.
3. You will see the default output format of the **DIR** command, as shown below. (Additional directories may appear on your computer.) Beginning from left to right, the **DIR** command displays an object's name, extension (note that directories do not have extensions), type (note that files do not have a type), creation date, creation time, and the object's full name. The first two object names, "." and "..", represent the current directory and the parent directory, respectively.

```
.          <DIR>       06-24-00     2:02p  .
..         <DIR>       06-24-00     2:02p  ..
DOS        <DIR>       06-24-00     2:02p  dos
test       txt         06-24-00     2:02p  test.txt
```

Deleting a file

1. At the C prompt, type **DIR**.
2. Press **Enter**.
3. Record the results: ______________________________

   ____

   ____

   ____

   ____

4. At the C prompt, type **DEL C:\TEST.TXT**.
5. Press **Enter**.
6. At the C prompt, type **DIR**.

7. Press **Enter**.
8. Record the results: ______________________________

Deleting a directory

1. At the C prompt, type **DIR**.
2. Press **Enter**.
3. Record the results: ______________________________

____

____

____

____

4. At the C prompt, type **RMDIR C:\LAB.1.2**, which removes the directory.
5. Press **Enter**.
6. At the C prompt, type **DIR**.
7. Press **Enter**.
8. Record the results: ______________________________

Lab Notes

EDIT—The Edit program is a DOS text editor that lets you create and modify text files in the DOS environment.

DOS system disk—A DOS system disk is a bootable disk that boots a PC using a minimal amount of DOS system files. The following files are required for a DOS system disk to function properly: COMMAND.COM, IO.SYS, and MSDOS.SYS.

MD—The MD, or Make Directory command, is used to create a directory in the DOS environment.

DIR—The **DIR** DOS command allows you to view the contents of a directory and provides limited search capabilities.

RMDIR—The **RMDIR** DOS command allows you to remove empty directories.

How do I shut down DOS?—DOS is one of the simplest operating systems to shut down; you simply power off the PC.

Review Questions

Circle True or False.

1. All DOS system disks are bootable. True / False
2. When viewing a directory list with the DIR command, the "." represents the parent directory. True / False
3. A DOS system disk cannot function properly without the IO.SYS file. True / False
4. You can use the Edit program to create DOS system disks. True / False

5. What files are required for a DOS system disk to function properly?

6. You are working as a PC desktop support technician at the Fun Job Corporation. Kyle, one of your customers, just rebooted his PC after copying some files from a disk to his hard drive. Kyle says that he is receiving the error message, "Non-system disk or disk error," and his PC keeps repeating that error no matter what he does. Describe what the problem is and how, Kyle should resolve it.

Lab 1.3 Operating a Windows 95/98-Based PC

Objective

The objective of this lab is to show you how to operate and navigate in the Windows 95/98 environment. After completing this lab exercise, you will be able to:

- Start a Windows 95 or Windows 98 computer.
- Start an application within Windows 95 or Windows 98.
- Create and save a text file in the Windows 95/98 environment.
- Create a directory using Windows Explorer.
- Delete files and directories.
- View the contents of a directory.
- Properly shut down a Windows 95 or 98 computer.

Materials Required

- Operating system: Windows 95 and Windows 98
- Lab workgroup size: 4–6 students
- Configuration type: simple

Simple Configuration

- 90 Mhz or better Pentium-compatible computer
- 16 MB of RAM
- 540 MB hard drive
- 1 NIC (Network Interface Card

Additional Devices: None

Lab Setup & Safety Tips

- The classroom workstations should be divided; half should have Windows 95, and the other half should have Windows 98. Students should work in groups so that each has access to both a Windows 95 and a Windows 98 computer.

Activity

Creating a text file in Windows 95 and Windows 98

1. Power on the lab workstation and allow it to boot into the Windows environment.
2. Click the **Start** button.
3. Point to **Programs**, and then point to **Accessories**.
4. Click **Notepad**.
5. In the Notepad window, type **This is a test file.**.
6. In the upper-left corner of the Notepad window, click the **File** menu, and then click **Save As**.
7. Click the **Save in** drop-down list arrow.
8. Click **Desktop**.

9. In the File name section of the Save As dialog box, type **Test.txt**.
10. Click the **Save** button.
11. In the Notepad window, click **File**, and then click **Exit**.

Creating a folder (directory)

1. Click the **Start** button.
2. Point to **Programs**.
3. Click **Windows Explorer**.
4. Click your **drive C** icon to highlight it.
5. In the upper-left corner of the Windows Explorer, click the **File** menu.
6. Point to **New** and click **Folder**.
7. Type **LAB1.4** and press **Enter**.
8. Click the **File** menu.
9. Click **Close**.

Viewing the contents of a folder (directory)

1. Click the **Start** button.
2. Point to **Programs**.
3. Click **Windows Explorer**.
4. Click your **drive C** icon to highlight it.
5. In the right Windows Explorer pane, double-click the folder **LAB1.4** (the folder will be empty).
6. Click **File** on the menu bar.
7. Click **Close**.

Deleting a file

1. Click the **Start** button.
2. Point to **Programs**.
3. Click **Windows Explorer**.
4. Click the **Desktop** icon to highlight it.
5. In the right Windows Explorer pane, right-click **Test.txt**.
6. Click **Delete** on the menu bar.
7. Click **Yes** when prompted to delete Test.txt.
8. In Windows Explorer, click **File** on the menu bar.
9. Click **Close**.

Deleting a folder (directory)

1. Click the **Start** button.
2. Point to **Programs**.
3. Click **Windows Explorer**.
4. Click your **drive C** icon to highlight it.

5. In the right Windows Explorer pane, click the **LAB1.4** folder to highlight it.
6. Press the **Delete** key on the keyboard.
7. Click **Yes** when prompted to delete the **LAB1.4** folder.
8. In Windows Explorer, click **File** on the menu bar.
9. Click **Close**.

Shutting down Windows 95/98

1. Click the **Start** button.
2. Click **Shut Down**.
3. Select the **Shut Down the computer?** option in the Shut Down Windows dialog box, and then click the **Yes** button.
4. Wait for Windows to completely shut down and tell you that it is safe to turn off your computer.
5. Turn off computer.

Lab Notes

Notepad—Notepad is the Windows 95/98 equivalent of the DOS Edit program. It is simply a text editor you can use to create and modify text files.

Windows Explorer—The Windows Explorer is a Windows-based utility that simplifies file and directory management.

What is the difference between a folder and a directory?—A folder and a directory are the same thing. The difference lies in the operating system you are using. In the DOS environment, the correct term is directory, whereas in the Windows 95/98 environment, the correct term is folder.

What is the difference between Windows 95 and Windows 98?—Windows 98 includes FAT32 support, updated drivers, enhanced security features, and USB support, whereas Windows 95 does not include these features.

What happens when a file is deleted?—In the Windows 9x environment, when a file is deleted, it is moved to the Recycle Bin. The Recycle Bin is the "trash can" icon found on the desktop. The Recycle Bin is a holding area for deleted files. *Warning:* If a file is deleted from a floppy disk or a network drive, the file will not be moved to your Recycle Bin.

Review Questions

Circle True or False.

1. EDIT is the DOS equivalent of the Notepad program. True / False
2. The term folder is another name for a directory. True / False
3. In the Windows 9x environment, the Temp directory is a holding area for deleted files. True / False

4. Al has finished writing a grocery list for himself in Notepad. He usually keeps personal documents in a folder called Personal, which is located on his Desktop. Describe the steps Al must take to save his grocery list in his Personal folder.

5. For what purpose does Windows 98 use the Recycle Bin?

6. You are employed at the Happy Day Corporation. Bill, the manager of your department, has a laptop with Windows 95. He is new to the Windows 95 environment and is trying to shut down his computer. List the instructions you would give Bill to properly shut down his Windows 95 laptop.

Lab 1.4 Operating a Windows 2000-Based PC

Objective

The objective of this lab is to show you how to operate and navigate in the Windows 2000 environment. After completing this lab exercise, you will be able to:

- Start a Windows 2000-based computer.
- Start an application within Windows 2000.
- Create and save a text file in the Windows 2000 environment.
- Create a directory using Windows Explorer.
- Delete files and directories.
- View the contents of a directory.
- Properly shut down a Windows 2000 computer.

Materials Required

- Operating system: Windows 2000 Professional
- Lab workgroup size: 2–4 students
- Configuration type: modern

Modern Configuration

- 200 Mhz or better Pentium-compatible computer
- 64 MB of RAM
- 2 GB hard drive
- CD-ROM drive
- 1 NIC (Network Interface Card)
- 1 Sound card

Additional Devices: None

Lab Setup & Safety Tips

- The workstation should be configured so that the students don't have to provide a user name and password each time the system is rebooted.

Activity

Creating a text file in Windows 2000

1. Power on the lab workstation and allow it to boot into the Windows environment.
2. Click the **Start** button.
3. Point to **Programs**, and then point to **Accessories**.
4. Click **Notepad**.
5. In the Notepad window, type **This is a test file.**.
6. In the upper-left corner of the Notepad window, click **File** on the menu bar, and then click **Save As**.
7. Click the **Save in** list arrow.

8. Click **Desktop**.
9. In the File name section of the Save As dialog box, type **Test.txt**.
10. Click the **Save** button.
11. In the Notepad window, click **File**, and then click **Exit**.

Creating a folder (directory)

1. Click the **Start** button.
2. Point to **Programs**, and then point to **Accessories**.
3. Click **Windows Explorer**.
4. Double-click **My Computer**.
5. Click your **drive C** icon to highlight it.
6. In the upper-left corner of Windows Explorer, click **File** on the menu bar.
7. Point to **New**, and then click **Folder**.
8. Type **LAB1.4**, and then press **Enter**.
9. Click **File** on the menu bar.
10. Click **Close**.

Viewing the contents of a folder (directory)

1. Click the **Start** button.
2. Point to **Programs**, and then point to **Accessories**.
3. Click **Windows Explorer**.
4. Double-click **My Computer**.
5. Click your **drive C** icon to highlight it.
6. In the right Windows Explorer pane, double-click the folder **LAB1.4** (the folder will be empty).
7. Click **File** on the menu bar.
8. Click **Close**.

Deleting a file

1. Click the **Start** button.
2. Point to **Programs**, and then point to **Accessories**.
3. Click **Windows Explorer**.
4. Click the **Desktop** icon to highlight it.
5. In the right pane of Windows Explorer, right-click **Test.txt**.
6. Click **Delete** on the menu.
7. Click **Yes** when prompted to delete Test.txt.
8. In Windows Explorer, click **File** on the menu bar.
9. Click **Close**.

Deleting a folder (directory)

1. Click the **Start** button.
2. Point to **Programs**, and then point to **Accessories**.
3. Click **Windows Explorer**.
4. Double-click **My Computer**.
5. Click your **drive C** icon to highlight it.
6. In the right pane of Windows Explorer, click the **LAB1.4** folder to highlight it.
7. Press the **Delete** key on the keyboard.
8. Click **Yes** when prompted to delete the **LAB1.4** folder.
9. In Windows Explorer, click **File** on the menu bar.
10. Click **Close**.

Shutting down Windows 2000

1. Click the **Start** button.
2. Click **Shut Down**.
3. Use the menu to select **Shut down**.
4. Wait for Windows to completely shut down and tell you that it is safe to turn off your computer.
5. Turn off your computer.

Lab Notes

It seems the same! Is Windows 2000 really different than 9x?—Although much of the user interface is the same (for instance, the Recycle Bin) or very similar to the Windows 9x environment, the Windows 2000 operating system mechanics differ significantly from Windows 9x. As you continue through this text, you will explore some of those differences.

The Windows 2000 suite—Windows 2000 is actually a suite of operating systems—each designed for a different size computer system. Windows 2000 is built on the Windows NT architecture and is designed to ultimately replace Windows 9x for low-end systems, and replace Windows NT for mid-range and high-end systems. Windows 2000 includes four operating systems:

- **Windows 2000 Professional**—This OS is designed to ultimately replace both Windows 9x and Windows NT Workstation as a personal computer desktop or notebook OS. It is an improved version of Windows NT Workstation, and uses the same updated technology approach to hardware and software. It also includes all the popular features of Windows 9x, including Plug and Play.
- **Windows 2000 Server**—This OS is the improved version of Windows NT Server and is designed as a network operating system for low-end servers.
- **Windows 2000 Advanced Server**—This network operating system has the same features as Windows 2000 Server, but is designed to run on more powerful servers. It supports many processors and can support up to 64 GB of memory.
- **Windows 2000 Datacenter Server**—This network operating system is another step up from Windows 2000 Advanced Server and is designed to support up to 16 processors. It is intended for large enterprise operations centers.

Review Questions

Circle True or False.

1. Although the design of the Windows 2000 suite was based on Windows NT, it has been created to replace both Windows 9x and Windows NT operating systems. True / False
2. In Windows 2000 the My Computer icon has been replaced with the My Control Center icon, also referred to as the MCC. True / False
3. Windows 2000 still uses the Recycle Bin. True / False
4. Jacob has saved all his work files in a folder named Work which is located on his D: drive. Now, he wants to read a work file called oldtasks.txt. Describe how you would locate Jacob's work file using Windows Explorer, and describe how to open oldtasks.txt.

 ____

 ____

 ____

 ____

 ____

5. Amanda wants to purchase Windows 2000 and install it on her PC at home. Amanda's home computer has the following configuration:

 550 Mhz Pentium III

 256 MB of RAM

 15 GB hard drive

 CD-ROM drive

 Sound card

 Digital camera

 Amanda uses her home computer primarily for homework. To best meet Amanda's needs, what version of Windows 2000 would you recommend for her and why?

 ____

 ____

 ____

 ____

 ____

6. List and briefly describe the operating systems included in the Windows 2000 suite.

 ____

 ____

 ____

 ____

 ____

Lab 1.5 Operating a Linux-Based PC

Objective

The objective of this lab is to show you how to operate and navigate in the Linux environment. After completing this lab exercise, you will be able to:

- Start a Windows Linux-based computer.
- Start a Linux application.
- Create and save a plain text file using VI.
- Create a directory.
- Delete files and directories.
- View the contents of a directory.
- Properly shut down a Linux computer.

Materials Required

- Operating system: Linux
- Lab workgroup size: 2–4 students
- Configuration type: simple

Simple Configuration

- 90 Mhz or better Pentium-compatible computer
- 16 MB of RAM
- 540 MB hard drive
- 1 NIC (Network Interface Card)

Additional Devices: None

Lab Setup & Safety Tips

- Each group of students should have a logon with root access to their lab workstation.
- Each lab workstation should be configured to automatically start the GUI at boot time.
- Each lab workstation must have the VI Editor installed.

Activity

Creating a plain-text file using VI

1. Power on the lab workstation and allow it to boot into the Linux environment.
2. Log on with the user name and password provided by your instructor.
3. In the terminal window, type **vi** and press **Enter**.
4. Press the **ESC** key on the keyboard, which confirms that you are in command mode.
5. Press the **I** key on the keyboard (you are now in insert mode).
6. Type **This is a text file that I created using VI.**.
7. Press the **Esc** key on the keyboard, which will return you to command mode.
8. Type **:wq! /testfile**. This writes data to a file and quits VI.

Creating a directory

1. In the terminal window, type **mkdir /mydir**.
2. Press the **Enter** key.

Viewing the contents of the root directory

1. In the terminal window, type **CD /** . This will change the current directory to the root directory.
2. Type **ls –l**, and then press the **Enter** key. This lists the contents of the directory in a manner similar to the DOS dir command.

Deleting a file

1. In the terminal window, type **rm –i /testfile** (-i sends you to interactive mode).
2. Click **Yes** when prompted to delete /testfile.

Deleting a directory

1. In the terminal window, type **rm –i –r /mydir** (-r sends you to recursive mode).
2. Click **Yes** when prompted to delete the /mydir directory.

Shutting down Linux

1. Type **/sbin/shutdown –h now**, and then press the **Return** key (-h indicates halt; now indicates when the shutdown should occur).

Lab Notes

What is a man page?—The term man page refers to the man command which is used to view the manual pages for the Linux commands. Man pages are the Linux equivalent of the Windows Help menu. To view a man page, type man followed by the name of the command or application about which you want more information. For example, man rm would provide a detailed description of the rm command and how it can be invoked.

VI Quick Reference:

- VI starts in command mode.
- Press the letter i to enter Insert mode (allows normal typing).
- Press the Esc key to return to command mode.
- In command mode, type :q! to quit VI without saving changes.
- In command mode, type :wq! to save and quit VI.

Review Questions

Circle True or False.

1. The md command can be used to make a new directory. True / False
2. rm –i –r /mydir/test101 will remove the test101 directory and all of its subdirectories. True / False
3. "man pages" supply detailed information about command usage in the Unix and Linux environment. True / False

4. Emily wants to delete the following file:

   /home/emily/temp.old

   Type the command to delete the temp.old file.

   (Be sure to include the entire path)

   ____

   ____

   ____

   ____

   ____

5. Use the man pages on your Linux lab workstation to identify four flags that can be supplied to the shutdown command. Describe the meaning of each flag.

   ____

   ____

   ____

   ____

   ____

6. Use the man pages on your Linux lab workstation to find out what three options can be used with the ls command. Include a brief description of how the output will be formatted.

   ____

   ____

   ____

   ____

   ____

CHAPTER

2

How Software and Hardware Work Together

LABS INCLUDED IN THIS CHAPTER

Lab 2.1 CMOS Manipulation

Objective

The objective of this lab is to familiarize you with the operation of your lab workstation's complementary metal-oxide semiconductor (CMOS) setup program. After completing this lab exercise, you will be able to:

- Use the CMOS Setup program to customize the operation and configuration of a PC.
- Replace the CMOS battery.

Materials Required

- Operating system: Windows 9x
- Lab workgroup size: 2–4 students
- Configuration type: simple

Simple Configuration

- 90 Mhz or better Pentium-compatible computer
- 16 MB of RAM
- 540 MB hard drive
- 1 NIC (Network Interface Card)

Additional Devices: None

Lab Setup & Safety Tips

- Because there are so many different types of setup programs, it is recommended that you ask for some tips from your instructor before proceeding.
- Removing the CMOS battery will cause CMOS data loss. Be sure to complete a system configuration worksheet before removing the battery.
- Always unplug the power cord and properly ground yourself before touching components inside a computer.
- Note that some CMOS batteries cannot be removed.

Activity

Creating a System Configuration Worksheet

A System Configuration Worksheet is a spreadsheet or other type of document that contains all of your workstation's CMOS configuration parameters. Use the sections below to develop your own System Configuration Worksheet for your lab workstation.

For each of the following system components, record the information currently saved in your lab workstation's CMOS:

CPU ______________________________

Memory ______________________________

IDE 1 ______________________________

IDE 2 ______________________________

IDE 3 ______________________________

IDE 4 ____

SCSI ____

Serial 1 ____

Serial 2 ____

LPT 1 ____

Network card ____

CACHE ____

Changing CMOS Values

1. Review the System Configuration Worksheet provided for your computer.
2. Start your PC.
3. Following the instructions provided on your screen, enter the Setup program.
4. Change the DATE for your computer to **today's date**, in the year 2010.
5. Change the Hard Disk Drive configuration to **NONE**.
6. Save your changes.
7. Shut down your computer, and allow it to reboot.
8. Observe the changes in the startup sequence.
9. Enter the Setup program.
10. Reconfigure your hard drive to match the parameters of your System Configuration Worksheet.
11. Activate the Power Management on your PC.
12. Assign the password of **LAB** in all uppercase letters to your system Setup program.
13. Save your changes.
14. Shut down your computer and allow it to reboot.
15. Observe the changes in the startup sequence.

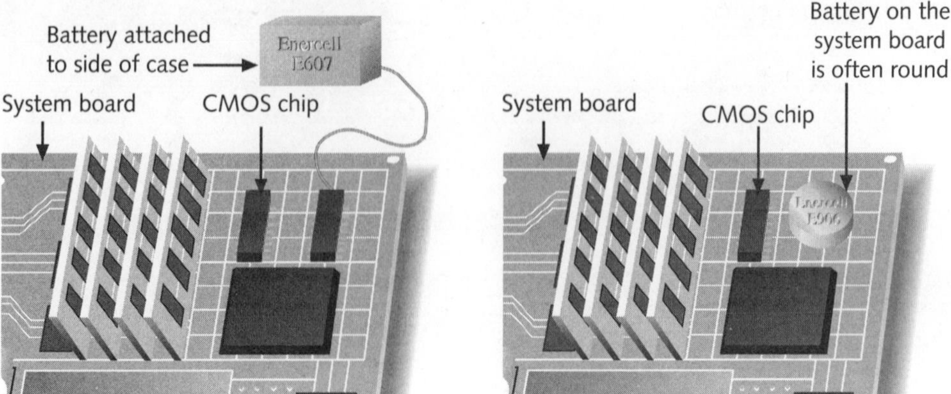

Figure 2-1 The battery that powers the CMOS chip may be on the system board or attached nearby

Removing the CMOS Battery

1. Figure 2-1 shows potential locations for a battery. Power off the lab workstation and unplug the power cord (it is not necessary to unplug all other cords).
2. Remove the case from the lab workstation.
3. Locate the CMOS battery (most look similar to a watch battery).
4. Write down the polarity of the battery side that is facing up.
5. Remove the CMOS battery.

Installing the CMOS Battery

1. Locate the CMOS battery socket.
2. Install and secure the battery.
3. Verify that the polarity facing up matches your notes.
4. Replace the case.

Restoring your lab workstation using the System Configuration Worksheet

1. Enter the Setup program.
2. Refer to the System Configuration Worksheet, and reconfigure all CMOS settings to their original configuration.

Lab Notes

How do I flash the BIOS?—The process of flashing a computer's BIOS is dangerous for the computer. If the BIOS is flashed with the incorrect BIOS update or is interrupted during the flash, the data on the EEPROM chip could be lost or corrupted and render the system BIOS useless. For this reason, there is no lab exercise that allows you to flash a workstation's BIOS.

How is data stored in CMOS?—CMOS configuration data is stored in the CMOS microchip. When the computer is powered off, the chip is able to maintain the configuration data by means of a small battery usually attached directly to the system board. If the onboard CMOS battery is disconnected or suffers a power loss, all the CMOS configuration data will be lost and the system will boot with factory configured defaults.

Review Questions

Circle True or False.

1. A System Configuration Worksheet is used to record your operating system's configuration. True / False
2. The system time and date are configured using the CMOS SETUP program. True / False
3. It is best practice to always record your CMOS settings before making changes. True / False
4. Describe some of the dangers of flashing a BIOS.

   ____

   ____

   ____

   ____

   ____

5. You just finished installing 32 MB of RAM into Umair's computer. You now want to verify that Umair's computer recognizes all 32 MB of RAM. Describe below how you can verify the memory configuration of Umair's computer.

   ____

   ____

   ____

   ____

   ____

6. Describe how replacing a CMOS battery affects a CMOS password and other configured CMOS parameters.

   ____

   ____

   ____

   ____

   ____

Lab 2.2 IRQ and DMA Management

Objective

The objective of this lab is to provide you with the necessary experience of viewing currently installed device drivers, modifying their IRQ, DMA, and I/O address settings, and developing a general understanding of resource allocations. After completing this lab exercise, you will be able to:

- List examples of standard IRQ and DMA usage.
- Explain how to determine which IRQ and DMA channels and addresses are being utilized.
- Explain how to modify IRQ and DMA address settings to resolve resource conflicts.

Materials Required

- Operating system: Windows 9x
- Lab workgroup size: 2–4 students
- Configuration type: simple

Simple Configuration

- 90 Mhz or better Pentium-compatible computer
- 16 MB of RAM
- 540 MB hard drive
- 1 NIC (Network Interface Card)

Additional Devices: None

Lab Setup & Safety Tips

- During this lab exercise you will use Device Manager to view the properties of your lab workstation. It is important that you not change parameters, otherwise your lab workstation may not function properly. (You will modify Device Manager parameters in later labs.)

Activity

Recording your lab workstation's IRQ settings

1. Start your lab workstation, and allow it to boot into Windows 9x.
2. Click the **Start** button.
3. Point to **Settings**.
4. Click **Control Panel**.
5. Double-click the **System** icon.
6. Click the **Device Manager** tab, as shown in Figure 2-2.
7. Click the **Properties** button.

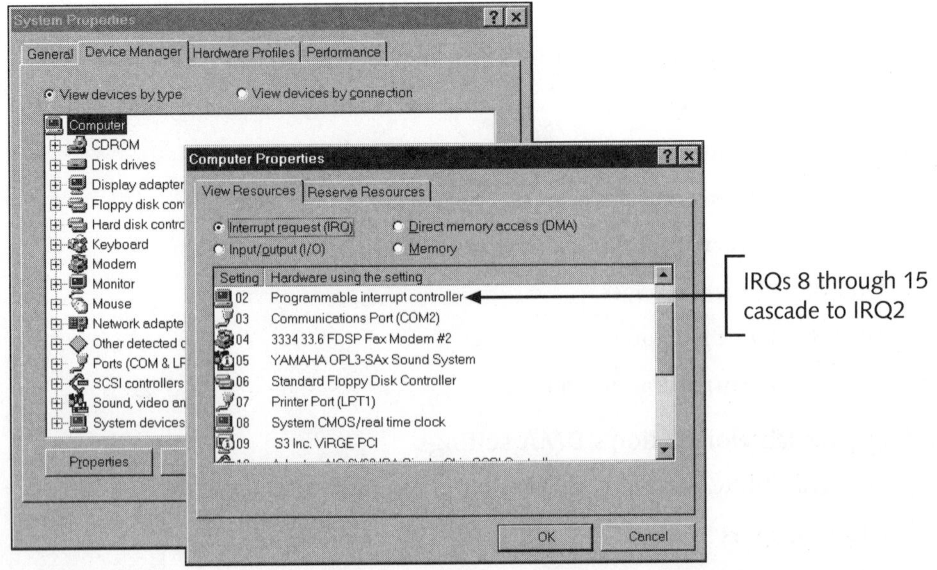

Figure 2-2 Use Device Manager to see how IRQs are used by your system

8. Record the device name for each of the following IRQs:

IRQ 00 ______________________________

IRQ 01 ______________________________

IRQ 02 ______________________________

IRQ 03 ______________________________

IRQ 04 ______________________________

IRQ 05 ______________________________

IRQ 06 ______________________________

IRQ 07 ______________________________

IRQ 08 ______________________________

IRQ 09 ______________________________

IRQ 10 ______________________________

IRQ 11 ______________________________

IRQ 12 ______________________________

IRQ 13 ______________________________

IRQ 14 ______________________________

IRQ 15 ______________________________

Viewing the Edit Interrupt Request window using Device Manager

1. Start your lab workstation, and allow it to boot into Windows 9x.
2. Click the **Start** button.
3. Point to **Settings**.
4. Click **Control Panel**.
5. Double-click the **System** icon.
6. Click the **Device Manager** tab.

7. Double-click **Ports**.
8. Double-click **Printer Port (LPT1)** (options may vary).
9. Click the **Resources** tab.
10. Deselect **Use automatic settings**.
11. Double-click **Interrupt Request**.
12. The **Edit Interrupt Request** window allows IRQ modification.
13. Do not make any changes.
14. Click **Cancel** three times.
15. Close the **Control Panel** window.

Recording your lab workstation's DMA settings

1. Start your lab workstation, and allow it to boot into Windows 9x.
2. Click the **Start** button.
3. Point to **Settings**.
4. Click **Control Panel**.
5. Double-click the **System** icon.
6. Click the **Device Manager** tab.
7. Click the **Properties** button.
8. Click the **Direct Memory Access (DMA)** option button.
9. Record the device name for each of the following DMA channels:

   DMA 01 ______________________________

   DMA 02 ______________________________

   DMA 03 ______________________________

   DMA 04 ______________________________

Lab Notes

Device Manager—Device Manager is a Windows 9x program that displays all the devices that Windows 9x has detected, and the resources each device has been assigned.

Problems in Device Manager—If Windows 9x is having a problem with a device, it will notify you in Device Manager, using one of the following symbols:

- X (Red X)—A red X indicates that the device has been disabled.
- ! (Exclamation point)—The exclamation point indicates a problem. Often, exclamation points indicate resource conflicts or hardware malfunctions. A description of the exact problem can be found by double-clicking the device.
- ? (Question mark)—The question mark indicates an unknown device. Question marks typically note devices that are functioning properly but don't have a driver installed. Most often, a question mark device is found under the Other Device icon.

Lab Notes (continued)

What is an IRQ?—An IRQ (interrupt request number) is a line on a bus that is assigned to a device and is used to signal the CPU for servicing. These lines are assigned a reference number (for example, the normal IRQ for a printer port is IRQ 7).

What is a DMA?—A DMA (direct memory access) controller chip resides on the system board and provides channels that a device may use to bypass the CPU and send data directly to memory.

Review Questions

Circle True or False.

1. Device Manager can be used to view all of the DMA channels and the devices configured to use them. True / False
2. Device Manager is located on the Control Panel and accessed by double-clicking the Add New Hardware icon. True / False
3. IRQ is an acronym for internal response question. True / False
4. DMA is an acronym for direct memory access. True / False
5. You are employed as a hardware technician at Crunchy Com Corporation. One of your coworkers, Todd, just finished installing a modem into a customer's computer. Unfortunately, the modem doesn't seem to be functioning properly. Todd believes there is a resource conflict between the modem and another device. Describe how you could use Device Manager to locate the resource conflict.

   ____
   ____
   ____
   ____
   ____

6. Consult your list of IRQs. For which device is IRQ 15 normally reserved?

   ____
   ____
   ____
   ____
   ____

7. Jacob believes his sound card has been disabled on his Windows 98 laptop. Use Device Manager to describe how Jacob could confirm that his sound card has been disabled.

   ____
   ____
   ____
   ____
   ____

Lab 2.3 I/O Management

Objective

The objective of this lab is to provide you with experience managing I/O addresses. After completing this lab exercise, you will be able to:

- List examples of standard I/O address usage.
- Explain how to determine which I/O addresses are being utilized.
- Explain how to modify I/O address settings to resolve resource conflicts.
- Explain the importance of unique I/O addresses.

Materials Required

- Operating system: Windows 9x
- Lab workgroup size: 2–4 students
- Configuration type: modern

Modern Configuration

- 200 Mhz or better Pentium-compatible computer
- 64 MB of RAM
- 2 GB hard drive
- CD-ROM drive
- 1 NIC (Network Interface Card)
- 1 Sound card

Additional Devices

- 1 I/O expansion card for each lab workgroup

Lab Setup & Safety Tips

- During this lab exercise, you will use Device Manager to view the properties of your lab workstation. It is important that you not change the parameters of Device Manager; otherwise, your lab workstation may not function properly. You will get a chance to modify Device Manager parameters in later labs.

Activity

Recording your lab workstation's I/O Address settings

1. Start your lab workstation, and allow it to boot into Windows 9x.
2. Click the **Start** button.
3. Point to **Settings**.
4. Click **Control Panel**.
5. Double-click the **System** icon.
6. Click the **Device Manager** tab.
7. Click the **Properties** button.
8. Click **Input/output (I/O)**.

9. Record all of the I/O address for each of the following devices:

   Floppy drive ______________________________

   ____

   ____

   ____

   ____

   NIC (Network Interface card) ______________________________

   ____

   ____

   ____

   ____

   Sound Card ______________________________

   ____

   ____

   ____

   ____

   Keyboard ______________________________

   ____

   ____

   ____

   ____

   Printer Port (LPT1) ______________________________

   ____

   ____

   ____

   ____

   Direct memory access controller ______________________________

   ____

   ____

   ____

   ____

10. Close all open windows and dialog boxes.

Viewing the Edit Input/Output Range window using Device Manager

1. Start your lab workstation, and allow it to boot into Windows 9x.
2. Click the **Start** button.
3. Point to **Settings**.
4. Click **Control Panel**.

5. Double-click the **System** icon.
6. Click the **Device Manager** tab.
7. Double-click **Sound, video, and game controllers**.
8. Double-click the installed sound card driver.
9. Click the **Resources** tab.
10. Deselect **Use automatic settings**.
11. Double-click **Input/Output Range**. (*Note:* Some Input/Output ranges may not be configurable. When they are not configurable, double-clicking produces no effect.)
12. The **Edit Input/Output Range** window allows I/O address modification.
13. Do not make any changes.
14. Click **Cancel** three times.
15. Close the **Control Panel** window.

Lab Notes

What is an I/O address?—An I/O address is an address stored in RAM and assigned to the operations of one particular device.

What exactly is an I/O card?—The term I/O card refers to an expansion card that often contains serial, parallel, and game ports on the same adapter board, providing an input/output interface with the CPU.

Which devices most often require I/O addresse manipulation?—Depending on the type of hardware purchased, you may need to manipulate the I/O addresses using Device Manager. Sound cards and network interface cards often require manual I/O configuration, meaning that you cannot use Device Manager at all.

Why are some I/O ranges not configurable in Device Manager?—Depending on the type of hardware device, the I/O address range may be hard-coded into the expansion card. Other expansion cards allow I/O address range configuration via jumpers or DIP switches.

2

Review Questions

Circle True or False.

1. An I/O address is an address stored on the hard drive, and is assigned to the operation of one particular device. True / False
2. All LPT ports require one I/O address. True / False
3. The term I/O card is often used to refer to an expansion card which contains a serial, parallel, and game port. True / False
4. Floppy drives do not require an I/O address assignment. True / False
5. Describe why some I/O ranges are not configurable in Device Manager.

____

____

____

____

____

6. John has configured the jumpers on his NIC (Network interface card) to use I/O address 300. Using Device Manager, what steps must John complete to confirm that I/O address 300 is properly assigned to the NIC?

____

____

____

____

____

Lab 2.4 Understanding the Boot Process

Objective

The objective of this lab is to familiarize you with the boot process of a PC and to provide hands-on troubleshooting experience. After completing this lab exercise, you will be able to:

- Describe, in order, the PC boot process.
- Describe the effect that various defective components have on the boot process.
- Troubleshoot the PC boot process.

Materials Required

- Operating system: Windows 9x
- Lab workgroup size: 2–4 students
- Configuration type: simple

Simple Configuration

- 90 Mhz or better Pentium-compatible computer
- 16 MB of RAM
- 540 MB hard drive
- 1 NIC (Network Interface Card)

Additional Devices: None

Lab Setup & Safety Tips

- Always unplug the power cord and properly ground yourself before touching any component inside a computer.

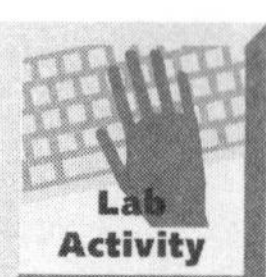

Activity

Observing the boot process

1. Turn on your PC.
2. Note the various startup screens.
3. Shut down your PC.
4. Verify that you are properly grounded.
5. Unplug the power cord from the system unit.
6. Remove the case.
7. Remove all of the SIMMS from your PC.
8. Restart your PC.
9. Record the effect of removing the SIMMS: ______________________________

   ____
10. Shut down your PC.
11. Reinstall the SIMMs that you removed in Step 7.
12. Restart your PC.
13. Note the effect of replacing the SIMMS.

14. Shut down your PC.
15. Reverse the hard drive cable at the system board.
16. Restart your PC.
17. Record the effect of reversing the hard drive cabling: ______________________________

    ____
18. Shut down your PC.
19. Correctly install the hard drive cable at the system board.
20. Remove the hard drive cable from the hard drive.
21. Restart your PC.
22. Record the effect of the uninstalled hard drive cable: ______________________________

    ____
23. Shut down your PC.
24. Reinstall the hard drive cable at the hard drive.
25. Restart your PC.
26. Note the effect of the installed hard drive cable.
27. Shut down your PC.
28. Remove the floppy drive cable from the system board.
29. Restart your PC.
30. Record the effect of the uninstalled floppy drive cable: ______________________________

    ____
31. Shut down your PC.
32. Reinstall the floppy drive cable.
33. Restart your PC.
34. Note the effect of the installed floppy drive cable.
35. Shut down your PC.
36. Remove the keyboard from the PC.
37. Restart your PC.
38. Record the effect of the uninstalled keyboard: ______________________________

    ____
39. Shut down your PC.
40. Reinstall the keyboard.
41. Restart your PC.
42. Note the effect of the installed keyboard.

Lab Notes

What is POST?—POST stands for power-on self-test. POST is a self-diagnostic program used to perform a simple test of the CPU, RAM, and various I/O devices. The POST is performed when the computer is first powered on.

Review Questions

Circle True or False.

1. A PC can function properly without any memory installed. True / False
2. Hard drive data cables are reversible. True / False
3. Floppy drive data cables are not reversible. True / False
4. If a PC is started without a keyboard attached, you will receive an error message during the POST. True / False
5. Write a troubleshooting question using one of the error messages you recorded during the last activity for Lab 2.4. The question must have only one correct answer.

____

____

____

____

____

6. You just finished moving a PC from one building to another. You have not changed any of the PC's hardware configurations, but now when you start the system it gives you a keyboard/mouse error. If the keyboard and mouse are plugged in, what could be the problem?

____

____

____

____

____

CHAPTER

3

THE SYSTEM BOARD

LABS INCLUDED IN THIS CHAPTER

LAB 3.1 COMPONENT IDENTIFICATION

Objective

The objective of this lab is to provide you with the ability to identify various components of the system board from several different generations of personal computers. After completing this lab exercise, you will be able to:

- Identify the major components of system boards from different generations.
- Describe the functions of major system board components from different generations.

Materials Required

- Operating system: Windows 9x
- Lab workgroup size: 2–4 students
- Configuration type: simple

Simple Configuration

- 90 Mhz or better Pentium-compatible computer
- 16 MB of RAM
- 540 MB hard drive
- 1 NIC (Network Interface Card)

Additional Devices

- System board documentation for each of the lab workstations. You should be able to identify the location and purpose of each jumper block on the system board.
- Each group of students will require a packet of labels.
- Any available system boards from each of the following generations:
  - PC
  - PC-AT
  - 286
  - 386
  - 486
  - Pentium
  - Pentium Pro
  - Pentium II
  - Pentium III

Lab Setup & Safety Tips

To create the instructor's display, arrange the available system boards with the following components labeled:

- ISA expansion bus
- PCI expansion bus
- VLB expansion bus
- MCA expansion bus
- EISA expansion bus
- Bus control chip set
- System BIOS
- Keyboard BIOS
- Battery
- DRAM
- SIMMS
- DIMMS
- Keyboard connector
- Mouse connector
- Cache memory
- Integrated IDE controller
- Integrated floppy drive controller
- Integrated I/O connectors
- Power supply
- RAM slots
- CPU socket

Lab Activity

ACTIVITY

Viewing the instructor's display

1. Record at least one unique fact about each of the following system boards:

PC ____________________

PC-AT ____________________

286 ____________________

386 ____________________

486 ____________________

Pentium I ____________________

Pentium Pro ____________________

Pentium II ____________________

Pentium III ____________________

System board diagram

1. In the space provided, make a diagram of your lab workstation's system board. In your diagram, label each of the components depicted in Figure 3-1, and describe each component's function.

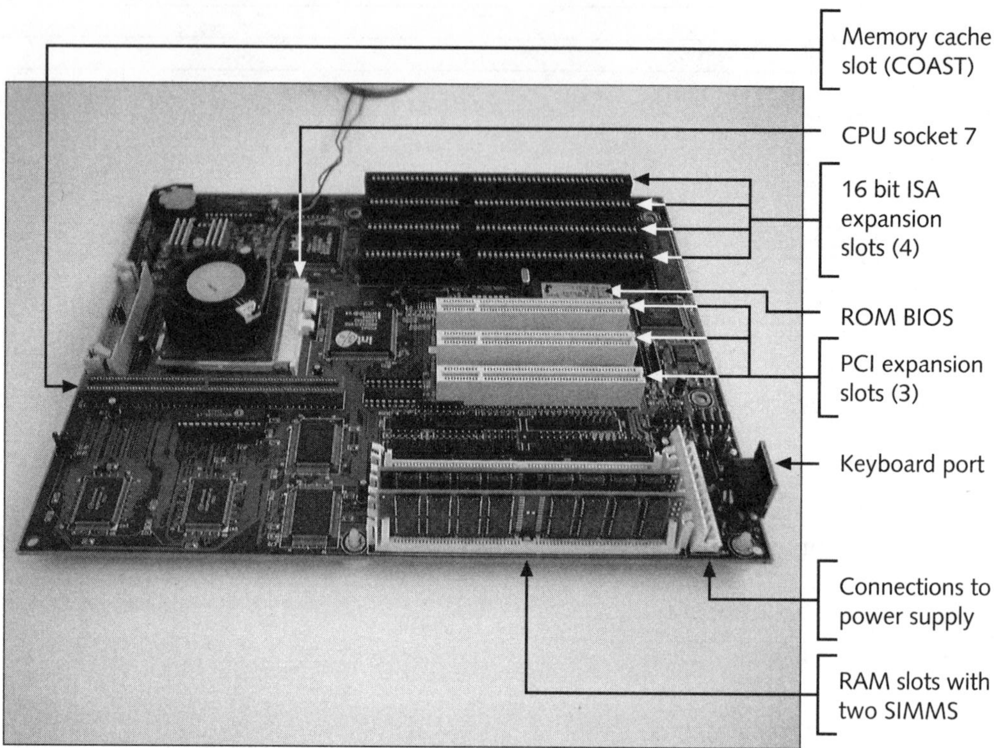

Figure 3-1 A typical AT system board is shown with memory cache and Socket 7 for the Intel Classic Pentium CPU. The CPU with a fan on top is installed as are two SIMM memory modules.

Labeling the jumper blocks

1. Refer to Table 3-1 to find the documentation you need to label each of the jumper blocks found on the system board. (Documentation can be found at each manufacturer's Web site, as listed in Table 3-1.).

Table 3-1 Major manufacturers of system boards

Manufacturer	Web Address
American Megatrends, Inc.	*www.megatrends.com*
ASUS	*www.asus.com*
First International Computer, Inc.	*www.fica.com*
Giga-Byte Technology Co., Ltd.	*www.giga-byte.com*
Intel Corporation	*www.intel.com*
Supermicro Computer, Inc.	*www.supermicro.com*
Tyan Computer Corporation	*www.tyan.com*

Lab Notes

Form Factors—The term form factor refers to the shape and size of a system board.

What is a voltage regulator?—A CPU voltage regulator controls the amount of voltage on the system board. The voltage selections are made by jumper settings on the system board.

What is a chip set?—A chip set is a group of chips on the system board that relieves the CPU of some of the system's processing tasks, providing careful timing of activities and increasing the overall speed and performance of the system. See Table 3-2 for more information on the Intel chip set family.

Table 3-2 The Intel chip set family

Common Name	Model Number	Comments
Intel i800 Series	840	Designed for multiprocessor systems using Pentium II Xeon or Pentium III Xeon processors
	820	Designed for Pentium II and Pentium III systems
	810	First Intel chip set to eliminate the PCI bus as the main device interconnection
Orion	450GX, KX	Supports Pentium Pro (includes support for multiprocessors)
	450NX	Designed for servers with multiple Pentium II or Pentium II Xeon processors
Natoma	440FX	Supports Pentium Pro and Pentium II (Discontinued in January, 1999)
	440BX	Designed for servers and workstations (Pentium II and III)
	440GX	Designed for servers and workstations using the Pentium II Xeon and Pentium III Xeon
	440ZX	Designed for entry-level PCs using Pentium II
	440LX	Designed for Celeron processors
	440MX	Designed for notebook computers (M = mobile)
	440EX	Designed for smaller system boards such as the mini-ATX
Triton III	430VX	Value chip set, supports SDRAM
	430MX	Used for notebooks (M = mobile)
	430TX	Supports SDRAM, ultra DMA; replaced the VX and MX
Triton II	430HX	High performance, supports dual processors
Triton I	430FX	The oldest chip set, no longer produced

Review Questions

Circle True or False.

1. The mouse and keyboard ports are always located directly next to the CPU socket True / False
2. AT-style system boards require two power connectors from the power supply. True / False
3. Different system boards can use different types of memory. True / False
4. Most CPUs are bolted to the system board to prevent them from slipping off and causing the entire PC to crash. True / False
5. Describe the role of a voltage regulator.

____

____

____

____

____

6. Compare the role of a chip set to that of the CPU.

____

____

____

____

____

Lab 3.2 CPU Identification and Installation

Objective

The objective of this lab is to enable you to identify the various central processing units (CPUs), or microprocessors, and their corresponding mounting technologies from different generations of personal computers. After completing this lab exercise, you will be able to:

- Identify the various generations of CPUs, or microprocessors, used in PCs.
- Identify the various generations of CPU mounting technology used in PCs.
- Install and remove a 486 CPU.

Materials Required

- Operating system: Windows 9x
- Lab workgroup size: 2–4 students
- Configuration type: simple

Simple Configuration

- 90 Mhz or better Pentium-compatible computer
- 16 MB of RAM
- 540 MB hard drive
- 1 NIC (Network Interface Card)

Additional Devices

- One chip-pulling tool for each lab workstation
- Any available CPUs from each of the following families:
  - 8088
  - 80286
  - 80386
  - 80486
  - Pentium
  - Pentium Pro
  - Pentium II
  - Pentium III
  - Celeron
  - Pentium II Xeon
  - Pentium III Xeon
  - AMD K-5
  - AMD K-6
  - Athlon
  - Duron

Lab Setup & Safety Tips

- Arrange the CPUs and the matching mounting technology, labeling each so that other students can inspect them.
- Always unplug the power cord and properly ground yourself before touching any component inside a computer.

Activity

Viewing the instructor's display

1. Record the speed and voltage(s) of each CPU provided by your instructor's display. Figure 3-2 shows CPU socket design.

 8088 ______

 80286 ______

 80386 ______

 80486 ______

 Pentium ______

 Pentium Pro ______

 Pentium II ______

 Pentium III ______

 Celeron ______

 Pentium II Xeon ______

 Pentium III Xeon ______

 AMD K-5 ______

 AMD K-6 ______

 Athlon ______

 Duron ______

 Other ______

 Other ______

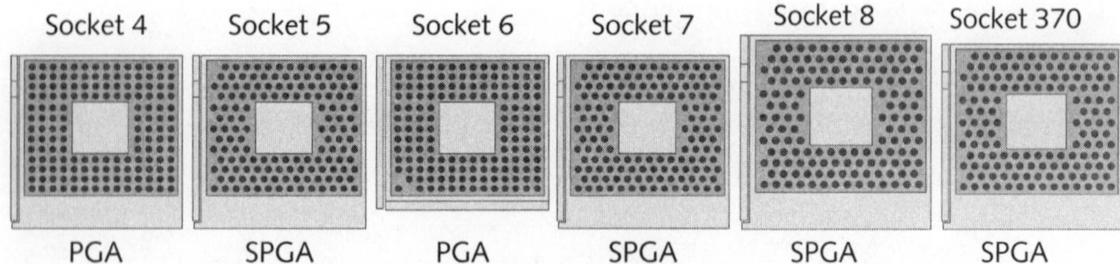

Figure 3-2 CPU sockets use either a PGA or SPGA design; rows of pins are arranged on the socket either in even rows (PGA) or staggered (SPGA)

2. In Table 3-3, note the mounting technology associated with the respective CPUs; also note the characteristics of the mounting technology.

Table 3-3 CPU sockets and slots

Connector Name	Used by CPU	Number of Pins	Voltage
Socket 4	Classic Pentium 60/66	273 pins 21 × 21 PGA grid	5 V
Socket 5	Classic Pentium 75/90/100/120	320 pins 37 × 37 SPGA grid	3.3 V
Socket 6	Not used	235 pins 19 × 19 PGA grid	3.3 V
Socket 7	Pentium MMX, Fast Classic Pentium, AMD K5, AMD K6, Cyrix M	321 pins 37 × 37 SPGA grid	2.5 V to 3.3 V
Super Socket 7	AMD K6-2, AMD K6-III	321 pins 37 × 37 SPGA grid	2.5 V to 3.3 V
Socket 8	Pentium Pro	387 pins 24 × 26 SPGA grid	3.3 V
Socket 370 or PGA370 Socket	Pentium III FC-PGA, Celeron PPGA, Cyrix III	370 pins SPGA grid	1.5 V or 2 V
Slot 1 or SC242	Pentium II, Pentium III	242 pins in 2 rows Rectangular shape	2.8 V and 3.3 V
Slot A	AMD Athlon	242 pins in 2 rows Rectangular shape	1.3 V to 2.05 V
Slot 2 or SC330	Pentium II Xeon, Pentium III Xeon	330 pins in 2 rows Rectangular shape	1.5 V to 3.5 V

Removing your workstation's CPU

1. Power off your lab workstation.
2. Unplug the system unit's power cord.
3. Verify that you are properly grounded.
4. Remove the case from your lab workstation, as shown in Figure 3-3.

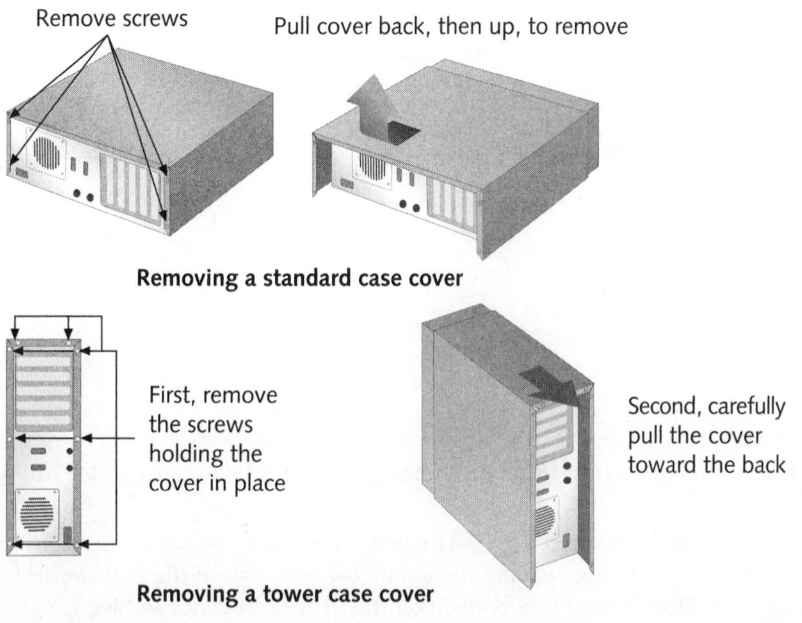

Figure 3-3 Removing the cover

5. Locate the CPU.
6. If the computer's heat sink must be removed, release the heat sink from the top of the CPU (if the heat sink doesn't come off with ease, leave it on top of the CPU).
7. (Slot architecture) Depress the release levers located at the top, on either side of the CPU.
8. (Slot architecture) Gently pull straight up on the CPU.
9. (Socket architecture) Release the ZIF lever.
10. (Socket architecture) Note how the CPU is currently installed. This will be important when you try to reinstall the CPU. Specifically note the orientation of the writing on the CPU.
11. (Socket architecture) Use the chip-pulling tool to remove your CPU. *Warning:* When removing your CPU, pull evenly straight up on the CPU; do not bend it from side to side.
12. Stand clear of the case, and plug in the power cord.
13. Power on the PC.
14. Record the results of starting a PC without a CPU: ______________________________

Reinstalling your workstation's CPU

1. Power off the workstation.
2. Remember which direction the CPU should be facing, and gently slide it back into the correct position.
3. Don't force the CPU. (Socket architecture) If it is not moving into place with ease, check for bent pins on the bottom of the CPU.
4. (Socket architecture) Lock the CPU into position using the ZIF lever.
5. (Slot architecture) Make sure that both latches on either sides of the slot have been locked back into position.
6. If necessary, replace the heat sink on top of the CPU.

7. Test the installation before replacing the case.
8. Stand clear of the case, and plug in the power cord.
9. Power on the PC and verify that the system boots properly.
10. Power off the PC and unplug the power cord.
11. Replace the case.
12. Plug in the system unit.
13. Power on the system unit.
14. Power off the PC.

Lab Notes

CPU form factors—Intel currently has five form factors used to house its processors:

- SEP (Single Edge Processor)—The processor is not completely covered by the black plastic housing, making the circuit board visible at the bottom of the housing. The first Celeron processors used the SEP form factor in Slot 1.
- SECC (Single Edge Contact Cartridge)—The processor is completely covered with a black plastic housing, and a heat sink and fan are attached to the housing. You can't see the circuit board or edge connector in an SECC form factor. The Pentium II and Pentium III use an SECC form factor in Slot 1.
- SECC2 (Single Edge Contact Cartridge, version 2)—The processor SECC2 has a heat sink and fan similar to the SECC, but the edge connector on the processor circuit board is visible at the bottom of the housing. Pentium II and Pentium III use the SECC2 form factor.
- PPGA (Plastic Pin Grid Array)—The processor is housed in a square box designed to fit flat into Socket 370. Pins are on the underside of the flat housing, and heat sinks or fans can be attached to the top of the housing using a thermal plate or heat spreader. Current Celeron processors use this form factor.
- FC-PGA (Flip Chip Pin Grid Array)—This form factor looks like the PPGA form factor and uses Socket 370. Heat sinks or fans can be attached directly to the top of the package. The Pentium III uses FC-PGA as one of its two form factors.

How do I control the CPU settings?—Most CPU's are configured using jumper blocks or DIP switches located directly on the system board.

Do I always need a heat sink?—Any CPU, starting with a 486 and moving up, requires a heat sink to maintain proper CPU temperature.

What is the correct voltage for my CPU?—CPU voltage varies depending on the make, model, and generation of the CPU. Consult both the documentation for your CPU and the following tables:

Table 3-4 The Intel Pentium family of CPUs

Processor	Current Processor Speeds (MHz)	Primary L1 Cache	Secondary L2 Cache	System Bus Speeds (MHz)
Classic Pentium	60, 66, 75, 90, 100, 120, 133, 150, 166, 200	16K	None	66
Pentium MMX	166, 200, 233	32K	None	66
Pentium Pro	150, 166, 180, 200	16K	256K, 512K, or 1 MB	60, 66
Pentium II	233, 266, 300, 333, 350, 366, 400, 450	32K	256K, 512K	66, 100

Table 3-5 Cyrix and AMD competitors of the advanced Pentiums

Processor	Current Clock Speeds (MHz)	Compares to	System Bus Speed (MHz)	Socket or Slot
Cyrix M II	300, 333, 350	Pentium II, Celeron	66, 75, 83, 95, 100	Socket 7
Cyrix III	433, 466, 500, 533	Celeron, Pentium III	66, 100, 133	Socket 370
AMD-K6-2	166, 200, 266, 300, 333, 350, 366, 380, 400, 450, 475, 500, 533, 550	Pentium II, Celeron	66, 95, 100	Socket 7 or Super Socket 7
AMD-K6-III	350, 366, 380, 400, 433, 450	Pentium II	100	Super Socket 7
AMD Athlon	600, 650, 700, 750, 800, 850, 900, 950,	Pentium III	200	Slot A

Review Questions

Circle True or False.

1. All CPUs are the same size. True / False
2. CPU voltage varies depending on the generation and brand name of the CPU. True / False
3. Chip pullers were designed to remove the heat sink from the top of the CPU. True / False
4. ZIF sockets are used to connect the memory to the system board. True / False
5. Which is faster: the 8088 processor or the 486 processor?

____

____

____

____

____

6. You are currently employed as a PC support technician at the Heavenly Palace Factory. Your supervisor wants to upgrade his 486 computer to a Pentium III. He has asked you to tell him the parts that he will need to purchase for this upgrade. List below the minimum parts your supervisor needs to complete this upgrade. (*Reminder:* Don't forget that many of the newer system boards don't support the same type of memory as the older 486 computers.)

____

____

____

____

____

7. You are at your local computer store and are considering upgrading your home PC to a Pentium Pro. Will you be able to use the CPU cooling fan from the 486 you have at home if you purchase the Pentium Pro chip?

____

____

____

____

____

8. What types of CPUs do the following architectures support?

   Slot 1 _______________

   Slot 2 _______________

   Slot A _______________

   Socket 8 _______________

   Socket 7 _______________

   Super Socket 7 _______________

   Socket 370 _______________

9. What CPU form factor did the first Celeron processors use?

____

____

____

____

____

Lab 3.3 Configuring System Board Frequencies

Objective

The objective of this lab is to provide hands-on experience configuring system board frequencies. After completing this lab exercise, you will be able to:

- Describe the relationship between a system board's multiplier and the system board's overall performance.
- Describe how to configure the CPU frequency.
- Describe how to configure a system board multiplier.
- Use manufacturer documentation to calculate the appropriate CPU frequency.
- Use manufacturer documentation to calculate the appropriate multiplier.
- Identify jumper blocks which control the CPU frequency and system board multiplier.

Materials Required

- Operating system: Windows 9x
- Lab workgroup size: 2–4 students
- Configuration type: simple

Simple Configuration

- 90 Mhz or better Pentium-compatible computer
- 16 MB of RAM
- 540 MB hard drive
- 1 NIC (Network Interface Card)

Additional Devices: None

Lab Setup & Safety Tips

- Always unplug the power cord and properly ground yourself before touching any component inside a computer.

Activity

Locating jumper banks

1. Power off your PC.
2. Verify that you are properly grounded.
3. Unplug the system unit's power cord.
4. Remove the top of the case. Your jumper group may resemble that which is shown in Figure 3-4.
5. In the space provided, make a diagram of your system board, depicting the location of each jumper block found. Document your design by recording the jumper number and the function of the jumper block.

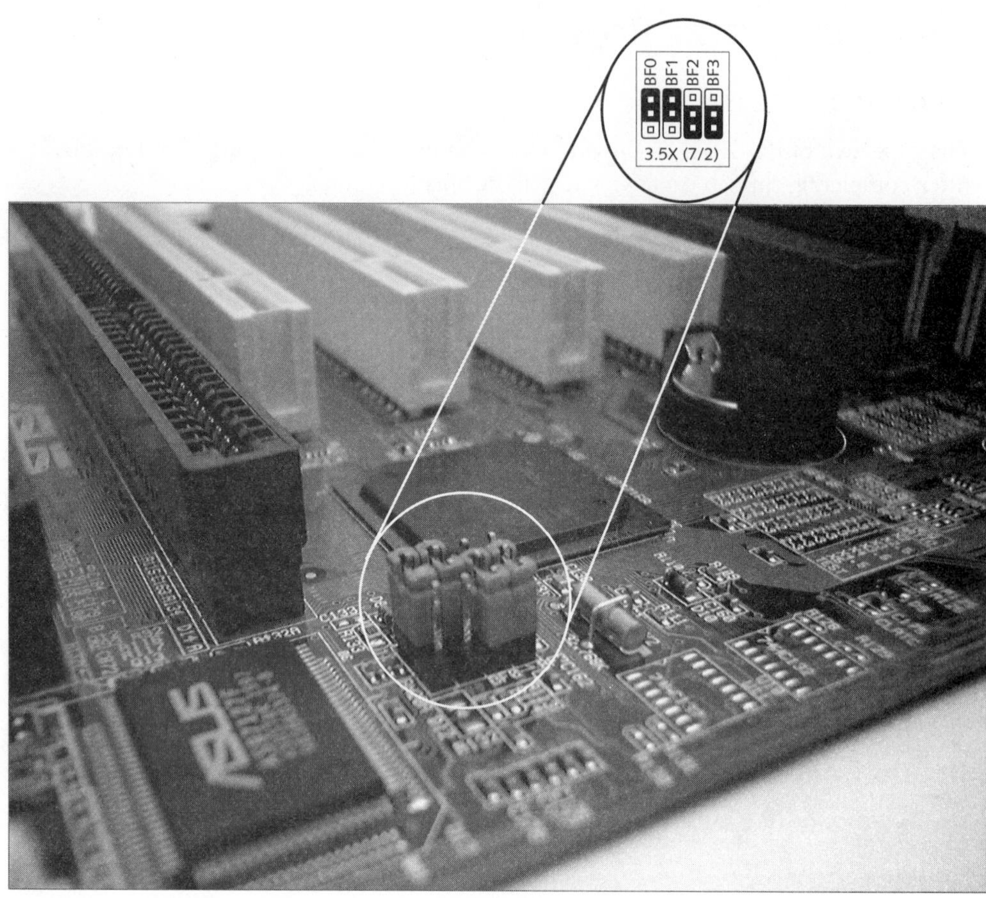

Figure 3-4 Jumper blocks are groups of jumpers

Understanding bus and CPU frequency

❶ Begin with the speed of your CPU
❷ The CPU speed determines the ratio (multiplier)
❸ The CPU speed also determines the bus frequency

Set the jumpers by the Internal speed of your processor as follows:

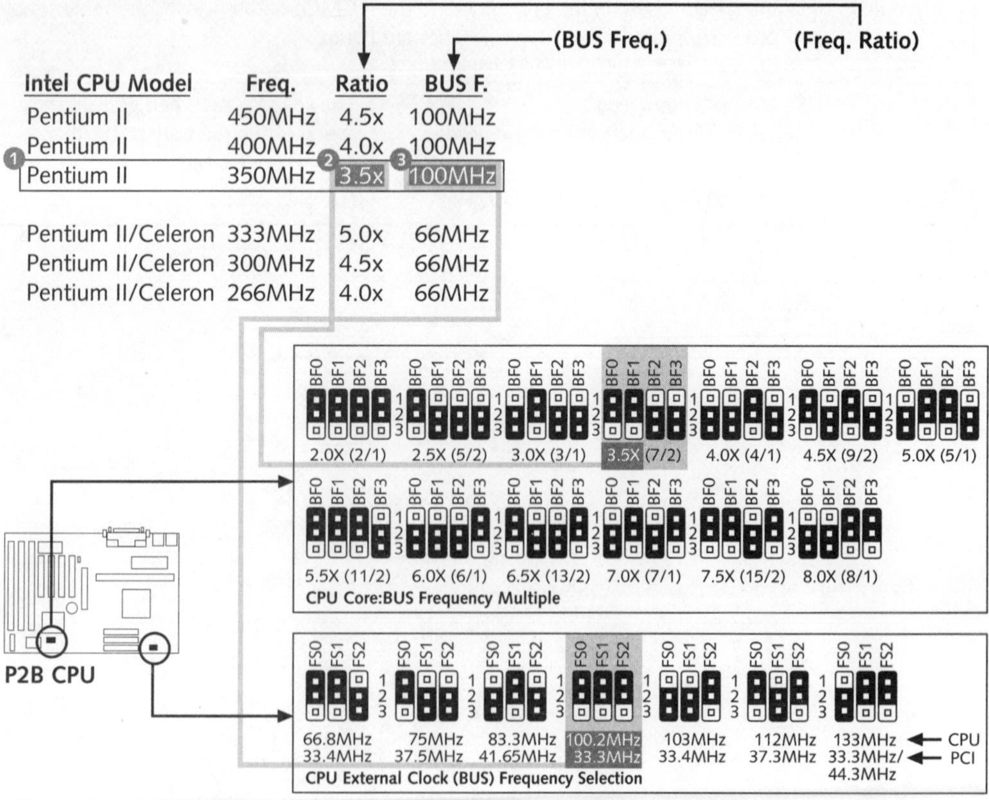

Figure 3-5 Based on the advertised speed of your CPU, select the multiplier and the bus frequency from the table, which then determines the jumper settings to use

(Remember that the term "speed" is often used, rather than "frequency", when referring to a computer's CPU or bus. Speed seems to be easier for people to understand.)

1. Use Figure 3-5 to determine the appropriate multiplier for the following processors:
   - Pentium II 450MHz Multiplier: ____________________
   - Pentium II 400MHz Multiplier: ____________________
   - Pentium II/Celeron 333MHz Multiplier: ____________________
   - Pentium II/Celeron 266MHz Multiplier: ____________________

Lab Notes

Overclocking—The term overclocking refers to running a system board at a frequency higher than is recommended or guaranteed by the CPU or chipset manufacturer. Overclocking a computer can cause damage to the CPU and system board components.

Multiplier—The factor by which the bus speed or frequency is multiplied to get the CPU clock speed. Refer to Table 3-6 for more information.

Table 3-6 System-board speeds and how they are determined

Bus or Device	How Speed Is Determined	How Controlled
CPU	Processor speed = memory bus speed X multiplier. Typical speeds are 350 MHz, 450 MHz, and 500 MHz.	Multiplier is set by jumpers or DIP switches on the system board or in CMOS setup
Memory bus or system bus	System board manufacturer recommends the speed based on the processor and the processor's rated speed. Typical values are 66 MHz, 100 MHz, and 133 MHz.	Set by jumpers, DIP switches, or in CMOS setup. Most commonly set by jumpers.
PCI bus	Memory bus speed / 2 (or for faster boards, it can be divided by 3)	The speed is set when you set the speed of the memory bus; either 33 MHz or 66 MHz.
ISA bus	Runs at only one speed: 8.77 MHz.	NA

Review Questions

Circle True or False.

1. The term CPU frequency and CPU speed are interchangeable. True / False
2. Two common system board bus speeds are 66 Mhz and 100 Mhz. True / False
3. The system board multiplier is really a ratio. True / False
4. Studies have shown that the smaller the multiplier number, the slower the system will perform. True / False
5. To what action does the term overclocking refer, and could it damage your workstation?

   ____
   ____
   ____
   ____
   ____

6. How will a workstation's overall performance be affected if its multiplier is configured with a larger number than it should be? ____

   ____
   ____
   ____
   ____

Lab 3.4 Bus Identification and PCI Expansion Card Installation

Objective

The objective of this lab is to provide a hands-on opportunity to view and identify the different types of PC expansion buses. After completing this lab exercise, you will be able to:

- Identify the various expansion buses used in PCs.
- Describe the various components of the respective expansion buses.
- Install a PCI expansion card.

Materials Required

- Operating system: Windows 9x
- Lab workgroup size: 2–4 students
- Configuration type: simple

Simple Configuration

- 90 Mhz or better Pentium-compatible computer
- 16 MB of RAM
- 540 MB hard drive
- 1 NIC (Network Interface Card)

Additional Devices

- One PCI expansion card of any kind
- Any available system boards from each of the following generations:

- PC	- 386	- Pentium III
- PC-AT	- 486	- Celeron
- IBM PC	- Pentium	- Athlon
- 286	- Pentium II	- Pentium II/III Xeon

Lab Setup & Safety Tips

- Arrange the system boards with their respective expansion buses so that students can inspect them.
- Always unplug the power cord and properly ground yourself before touching any component inside a computer.

Activity

Getting to know expansion buses

1. Examine the bus connections in Figure 3-6, and then inspect and note the characteristics of the following architectures:
   - ISA 8-bit expansion bus
   - ISA 16-bit expansion bus
   - EISA 32-bit expansion bus
   - VLB expansion bus
   - PCI expansion bus
   - MCA expansion bus
   - AGP expansion bus

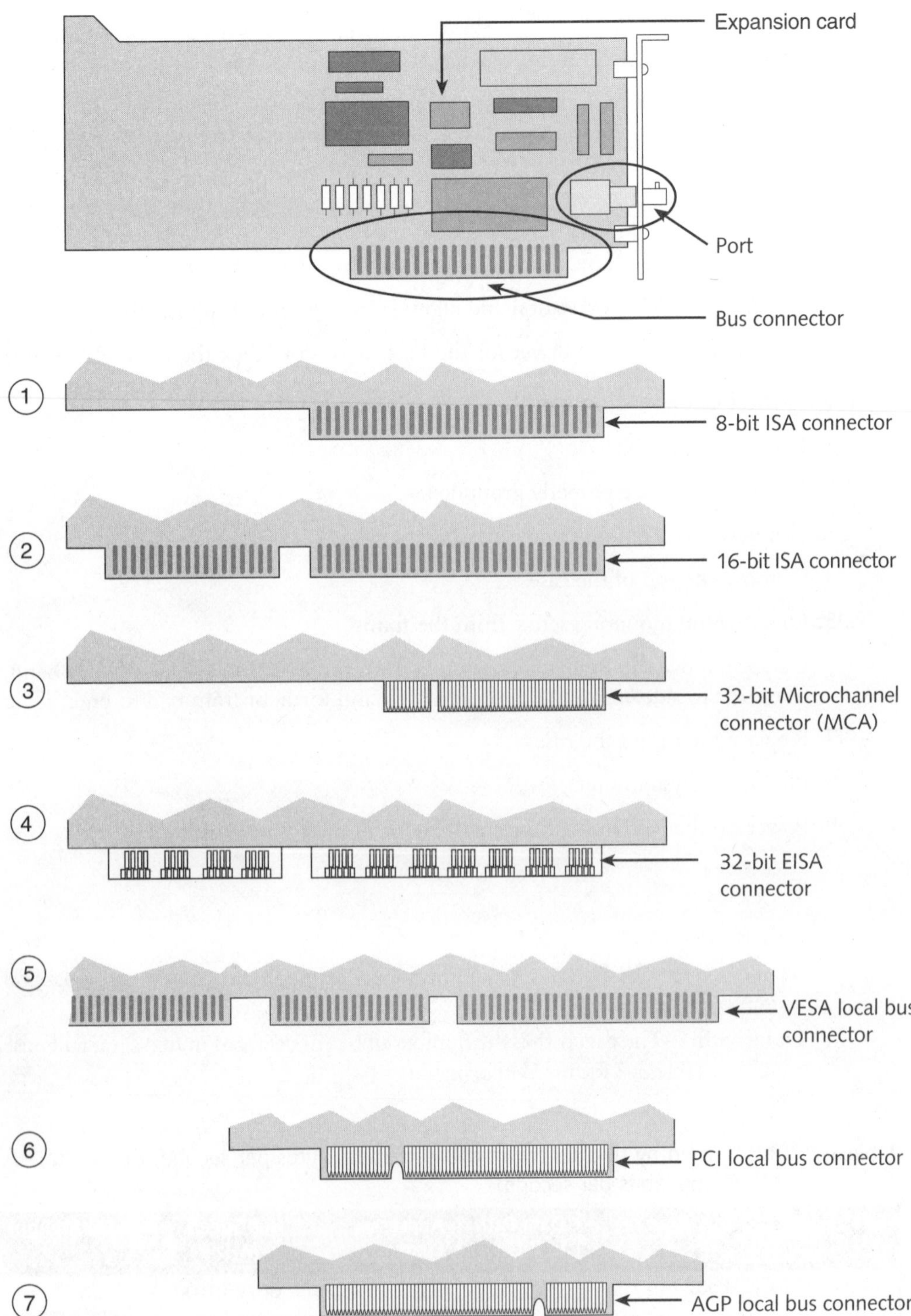

Figure 3-6 Seven bus connections on expansion cards

2. After the labels on the display are removed and then rearranged, match the labels to their corresponding expansion buses.

Installing a PCI expansion card

1. Power off your PC.
2. Verify that you are properly grounded.
3. Unplug the system unit's power cord.

4. Remove the top of the case.
5. Locate the available PCI slot where you plan to install the PCI expansion card.
6. Gently install the PCI expansion card into the slot. *Warning*: Don't bend the card from side to side; move the card only back and forth, or from end to end.
7. Screw the mounting screw into place.
8. Replace the top of the case.
9. Plug in the system unit.
10. Power on the lab workstation and allow it to boot into Windows 9x.
11. If prompted to install a driver for the PCI expansion, click the **Cancel** button.

Removing the PCI expansion card

1. Power off your PC.
2. Verify that you are properly grounded.
3. Unplug the system unit's power cord.
4. Remove the top of the case.
5. Unscrew the mounting screw from the frame.
6. Gently remove the PCI expansion card from the PCI slot. *Warning*: Don't bend the card from side to side; move the card only back and forth, or from end to end.
7. Replace the top of the case.
8. Plug in the system unit.
9. Power on the lab workstation, and allow it to boot into Windows 9x.

Lab Notes

What is bus speed?—Bus speed is the speed or frequency at which the data on the system board is moving.

Data path?—The data path is the number of bits of data transmitted simultaneously on a bus. See Table 3-7 for more information.

Table 3-7 Buses listed by throughput in MB/sec (megabytes per second) or Mbps (megabits per second)

Bus	Bus Type	Data Path in Bits	Address Lines	Bus Speed in MHz	Throughput
Memory bus	Local	64	32	66, 75, 100 ...	Up to 528 MB/sec
AGP	Local video	32	NA	66, 75, 100 ...	Up to 1.07 GB/sec
PCI	Local I/O	32	32	33, 66	Up to 264 MB/sec
VESA or VL Bus	Local video or expansion	32	32	Up to 33	Up to 250 MB/sec

Review Questions

Circle True or False.

1. ISA is always faster than PCI. True / False
2. Microchannel is a 64-bit bus. True / False
3. Microchannel and EISA can use the same expansion slot. True / False
4. An ISA expansion card can be either 8-bit or 16-bit. True / False
5. John wants to add a sound card to his 386. Before purchasing the sound card, he is going to look at his system board to find out what type he should purchase. Below, describe to John how to tell if he has an 8-bit or a 16-bit ISA expansion slot on his system board.

 ____
 ____
 ____
 ____
 ____

6. What is one advantage of using PCI instead of ISA?

 ____
 ____
 ____
 ____
 ____

CHAPTER

4

Understanding and Managing Memory

LABS INCLUDED IN THIS CHAPTER

- ♦ Lab 4.1 Installing RAM and Understanding the CONFIG.SYS File
- ♦ Lab 4.2 Memory Management in DOS
- ♦ Lab 4.3 Memory Management in Windows 9x
- ♦ Lab 4.4 Memory Management in Windows NT
- ♦ Lab 4.5 Memory Management in Windows 2000

Lab 4.1 Installing RAM and Understanding the CONFIG.SYS File

Objective

The objective of this lab is to teach you how to properly install RAM and to understand the differences between the kinds of RAM currently sold on the market. After completing this lab exercise, you will be able to:

- Install and remove RAM.
- Write and modify a CONFIG.SYS file.
- Compare different types of RAM.

Materials Required

- Operating system: Windows 9x
- Lab workgroup size: 2–4 students
- Configuration type: simple

Simple Configuration

- 90 Mhz or better Pentium-compatible computer
- 16 MB of RAM
- 540 MB hard drive
- 1 NIC (Network Interface Card)

Additional Devices: None

Lab Setup & Safety Tips

- Always unplug the power cord and properly ground yourself before touching any component inside a computer.

Activity

Removing RAM (SIMMS)

1. Power off the lab workstation.
2. Unplug the power cord.
3. Remove the case from the lab workstation.
4. Locate the SIMM banks on your system board.
5. On either end of the SIMM, gently pull the metal latches open.
6. Gently and evenly, lean the SIMM forward.
7. Slide the SIMM chip out of the SIMM bank at a 45-degree angle.

Installing RAM (SIMMS)

1. Power off the lab workstation.
2. Unplug the power cord.
3. Remove the case from the lab workstation.
4. Locate the SIMM banks on your system board.

5. Place the SIMM at a 45-degree angle and then gently snap it into place, as shown in Figure 4-1.
6. Plug in the power cord.
7. Power on your lab workstation.
8. Enter the CMOS Setup program.
9. Verify that the Setup program recognizes the correct amount of memory.
10. Save the changes and reboot the workstation.
11. Allow your lab workstation to boot into Windows 9x.
12. Right-click the **My Computer** icon.
13. Select **Properties** from the shortcut menu.
14. On the General tab, locate the Computer heading.
15. Verify that Windows 9x is using all of the installed memory.

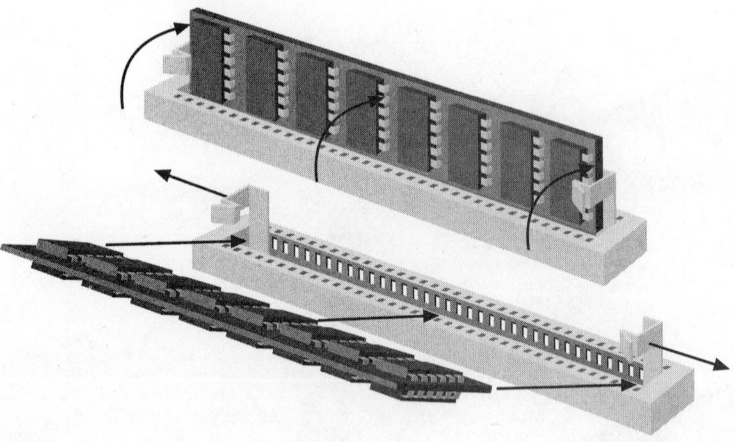

Figure 4-1 Installing a SIMM module

Removing RAM (DIMMS)

1. Power off the lab workstation.
2. Unplug the power cord.
3. Remove the case from the lab workstation.
4. Locate the DIMM banks on your system board.
5. On either end of the DIMM, gently pull the latches open and press down on them until you see the DIMM chip begin to move.
6. Gently and evenly, pull the DIMM chip straight up and free from the system board.
7. Repeat these steps until you have completely emptied the system board.

Installing RAM (DIMMS)

1. Power off the lab workstation.
2. Unplug the power cord.
3. Remove the case from the lab workstation.
4. Locate the DIMM banks on your system board.
5. Gently and evenly slide the DIMM into the bank.

6. Firmly and evenly press on the top edge of the DIMM until it slides into place. (The latches should close when the DIMM is properly installed, as shown in Figure 4-2.)
7. Plug in the power cord.
8. Power on your lab workstation.
9. Enter the CMOS Setup program.
10. Verify that the Setup program recognizes the correct amount of memory.
11. Save the changes and reboot the workstation.
12. Allow your lab workstation to boot into Windows 9x.
13. Right-click the **My Computer** icon.
14. Select **Properties** from the shortcut menu.
15. On the General tab, locate the Computer heading.
16. Verify that Windows 9x is using all of the installed memory.

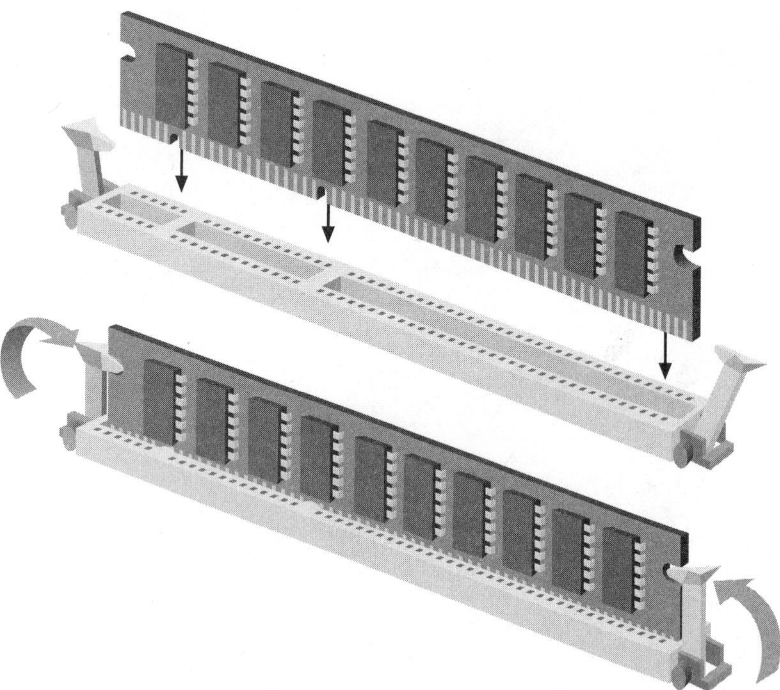

Figure 4-2 Installing a DIMM module

Recording the characteristics of RAM

In the following section, write the full description of each type of RAM; be sure to include the most common usages for each type of memory, typical memory speed, and a brief description of the physical characteristics. You will find the definitions in Chapter 4 of your textbook. Finding and copying the information will help you memorize it; once you are out in the field, you will be expected to know this information from memory.

SRAM ____

____

____

____

____

DRAM ____

____

____

____

____

DIMMS ____

____

____

____

____

Parity RAM ____

____

____

____

____

Nonparity RAM ____

____

____

____

____

EDO RAM ____

____

____

____

____

FPM RAM ____

____

____

____

____

Flash Memory ____

____

____

____

____

SDRAM ____

____

____

____

____

COAST ____

____

____

____

____

Examining the CONFIG.SYS

1. Start your lab workstation in MS-DOS mode.
2. At the command prompt in the root directory, type **EDIT CONFIG.SYS** and press **Enter**. Your lab workstation should respond by launching the EDIT program and opening the CONFIG.SYS file.

On the following lines copy the contents of your CONFIG.SYS; then next to each command, write how your lab workstation should respond. Every CONFIG.SYS can be different; the purpose of this exercise is to teach you how to interpret the commands that you find in the CONFIG.SYS file on your workstation. You will find the command definitions in Chapter 4 of your textbook.

Example:

BUFFERS=40—This command tells DOS how many buffers to maintain when transferring data to and from secondary storage.

____

____

____

____

____

____

____

____

____

____

____

____

____

____

____

____

____

____

____

____

____

Lab Notes

What is conventional memory?—Conventional memory, or base memory, is the first 640K of RAM.

What is upper memory?—Upper memory includes memory addresses starting at 641K and going up to 1024K.

What is extended memory?—Memory addresses above 1024K are referred to as residing in extended memory.

What is expanded memory?—Expanded memory is memory that falls outside the linear memory addressing scheme. Note that expanded memory normally is accessed via upper memory. Refer to your textbook for more information about expanded memory.

What is virtual memory?—Virtual memory is an area of secondary storage that is set aside to be used as an area of RAM. Note that because it is secondary storage the access time is considerably slower than that of RAM.

What is ECC?—ECC (Error checking and correction) is a chip set feature on the system board that checks the integrity of data stored on DIMMs and can correct single-bit errors in a byte. More advanced ECC schemas can detect, but not correct, double-bit errors in a byte.

Review Questions

Circle True or False.

1. When you install memory into a Pentium-class system board that uses 72-pin SIMMs, the memory must always be installed in pairs. True / False
2. Conventional memory includes the first 128K of RAM. True / False
3. EDO stands for extended data output. True / False
4. EDO RAM is faster than FPM RAM. True / False
5. Flash memory is commonly used as a cache for desktop PCs. True / False
6. If the following line were added to your CONFIG.SYS file, what would it tell your computer to do?

   DEVICE=C:\DOS\HIMEM.SYS

   ____

   ____

   ____

   ____

   ____

7. What would the following command tell your PC to do?

   EDIT AUTOEXEC.BAT

   ____

   ____

   ____

   ____

   ____

8. If the following line were added to your CONFIG.SYS file, what would it tell your computer to do?

   Dos=high,umb

   ____

   ____

   ____

   ____

   ____

Lab 4.2 Memory Management in DOS

Objective

The objective of this lab is to make you familiar with some common methods of memory management available in DOS. After completing this lab exercise, you will be able to:

- Load TSRs from AUTOEXEC.BAT.
- Use the MEM command to view your workstation's current memory configuration.

Materials Required

- Operating system: DOS
- Lab workgroup size: 2–4 students
- Configuration type: simple

Simple Configuration

- 90 Mhz or better Pentium-compatible computer
- 16 MB of RAM
- 540 MB hard drive
- 1 NIC (Network Interface Card)

Additional Devices

- One disk for each lab workstation containing a TSR

Lab Setup & Safety Tips

- Your instructor must prepare a TSR for this lab exercise.

Activity

Loading a TSR high

1. Allow your lab workstation to boot to DOS.
2. Insert the TSR disk provided by your instructor.
3. Use the COPY command to copy the TSR from the disk to the root directory of your lab workstation.
4. Make C:\ your current directory.
5. Type **EDIT AUTOEXEC.BAT** and press **Enter**.
6. Add the following to your AUTOEXEC.BAT file: **LH C:\TSR.TSR**. (*Note:* The TSR.TSR should be replaced with the name of the TSR on the disk.)
7. Press the **Alt** key.
8. Use the down arrow [↓] to select **Save** from the File menu.
9. Press the **Alt** key.
10. Use the down arrow [↓] to select **Exit** from the File menu.
11. Reboot your lab workstation.
12. To verify that the TSR loaded, attempt to use its function.

Using the MEM command

1. Allow your lab workstation to boot to DOS.
2. Type **MEM** at the command prompt and press **Enter.**
3. Compare the information provided by the MEM command to Table 4-1.

Table 4-1 Types of memory

Main Memory	Cache Memory
DRAM, needs constant refreshing	SRAM, does not need refreshing
Slower than SRAM because of refreshing time	Faster, but more expensive
Physically housed on DIMMs and SIMMs	Physically housed on the system board on COAST modules, or single chips, or included inside the processor case
Technologies include: • FPM • EDO • BEDO • Synchronous DRAM (SDRAM) • Direct Rambus DRAM • Double Data Rate SDRAM (SDRAM II) • SyncLink SDRAM (SLDRAM)	Technologies include: • Synchronous SRAM • Burst SRAM • Pipelined burst • Asynchronous SRAM • Housed within the processor case (new trend)
Memory addresses are assigned	No memory addresses assigned here

Lab Notes

What is a TSR?—A TSR is any program or device driver that resides in memory even though it is not active. TSR stands for terminate and stay resident.

What is HIMEM.SYS?—HIMEM.SYS is a device driver used to manage expanded memory in the DOS environment. If HIMEM.SYS fails to load, reboot the PC and check your CONFIG.SYS to verify that the path is specified correctly.

Review Questions

Circle True or False.

1. TSR stands for terminate safety return. True / False
2. TSRs are programs that stay in memory even when they are not being used. True / False
3. TSRs can be loaded into memory only via the CONFIG.SYS. True / False
4. You can use the MEM command to view the amount of available hard drive space. True / False
5. The HIMEM.SYS file is used primarily to test conventional memory. True / False
6. If the following line were added to your AUTOEXEC.BAT file, what would it tell your computer to do?

   LH c:\myfile

   ____

   ____

   ____

   ____

   ____

Lab 4.3 Memory Management in Windows 9x

Objective

The objective of this lab is to teach you how to manage and control memory allocation in the Windows 9x environment. After completing this lab exercise, you will be able to:

- Configure the Windows 9x swap file.
- Describe the advantages and disadvantages of using a swap file in Windows 9x.

Materials Required

- Operating system: Windows 9x
- Lab workgroup size: 2–4 students
- Configuration type: simple

Simple Configuration

- 90 Mhz or better Pentium-compatible computer
- 16 MB of RAM
- 540 MB hard drive
- 1 NIC (Network Interface Card)

Additional Devices: None

Lab Setup & Safety Tips

- Reconfiguring your swap file will have a severe impact on your computer's performance.

Activity

Disabling the Windows 9x swap file

1. Allow your lab workstation to boot into Windows 9x.
2. Right-click the **My Computer** icon.
3. Select **Properties** from the shortcut menu.
4. Click the **Performance** tab, as shown in Figure 4-3.

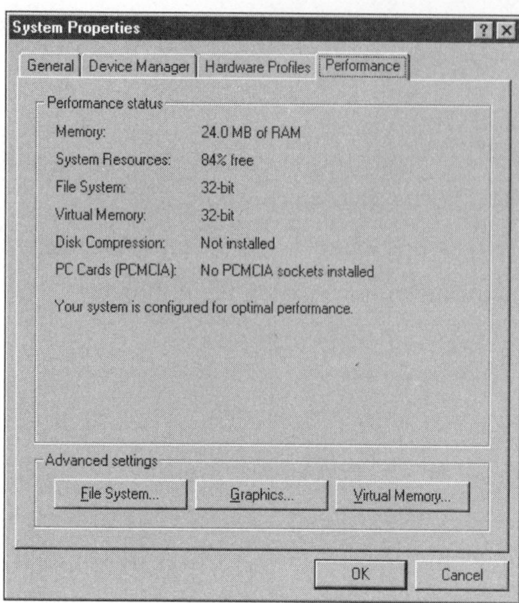

Figure 4-3 System Properties Performance box in Windows 9x

5. Click the **Virtual Memory** button.
6. Click the **Let me specify my own virtual memory settings** option button.
7. Place a check mark in the **Disable virtual memory** check box.
8. Click **OK**.
9. Click the **Yes** button on the confirmation message.
10. Click the **Close** button.
11. Click **Yes** when you are prompted to restart your computer.
12. Observe and describe the performance results: ______________________

____

____

____

____

Specifying a permanent swap file

1. Allow your lab workstation to boot into Windows 9x.
2. Right-click the **My Computer** icon.
3. Select **Properties** from the shortcut menu.
4. Click the **Performance** tab.
5. Click the **Virtual Memory** button.
6. Click the **Let me specify my own virtual memory settings** option button.
7. Clear the check mark from the **Disable virtual memory** check box.
8. Set the minimum swap file size to **150MB**.
9. Set the maximum swap file size to **150MB**.
10. Click **OK**.

11. Click the **Yes** button on the confirmation message.
12. Click **Yes** when you are prompted to restart your computer.
13. Observe and describe the performance results: ______________________________

Allowing Windows to manage its virtual memory

1. Allow your lab workstation to boot into Windows 9x.
2. Right-click the **My Computer** icon.
3. Select **Properties** from the shortcut menu.
4. Click the **Performance** tab.
5. Click the **Virtual Memory** button.
6. Click the **Let Windows manage my virtual memory settings** option button, as shown in Figure 4-4.

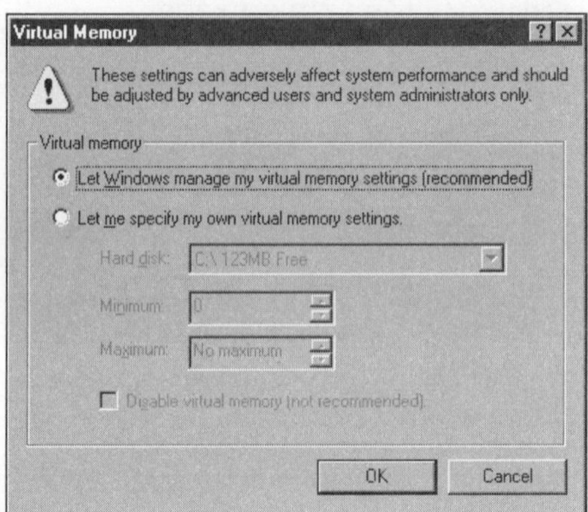

Figure 4-4 Options for managing virtual memory in Windows 9x

7. Click the **OK** button on the Virtual Memory dialog box.
8. Click the **Yes** button if you receive a confirmation message.
9. Click the **Close** button.
10. Click **Yes** when you are prompted to restart your computer.
11. Observe and describe the results: ______________________________

Lab Notes

What is Windows doing when it manages my virtual memory?—By default, Windows 9x will manage your virtual memory. This means that it will size and resize your Swap file as it sees fit. In most circumstances this is the recommended memory-management method.

What are multiple swap files?—Some Microsoft operating systems, such as Windows NT, support multiple swap files to improve the virtual memory management speed and capabilities. However, Windows 95 and Windows 98 do not support that configuration.

What is a memory conflict, and how does it occur?—A memory conflict occurs when two or more applications attempt to use the same memory address or address range.

What is an illegal operation?—These errors vary depending on the situation. You can find out exactly which applications were involved by clicking the Details button. Many times these errors are GPFs (General Protection Fault) and should be handled accordingly.

Review Questions

Circle True or False.

1. Windows 9x has the ability to manage its own swap files. True / False
2. If you have a new computer, it is always recommended that you disable your virtual memory because it isn't needed. True / False
3. The swap file is a folder on the hard drive, and is used by the operating system for virtual memory management. True / False
4. In Windows 9x each program has its own swap file. True / False
5. How many swap files can Windows 9x use at the same time? ____________________
6. You are employed as a desktop PC support technician at the Sweet Town Hot Water Company. Billy, one of your customers, has asked that you show him how to disable the swap file on his Windows 95 laptop. In the space below, write instructions for Billy.

____

____

____

____

____

Lab 4.4 Memory Management in Windows NT

Objective

The objective of this lab is to teach you how to manage and control memory allocations in the Windows NT environment. After completing this lab exercise, you will be able to:

- Properly configure one or multiple Windows NT swap files.
- Describe the optimum virtual memory configuration for the Windows NT operating system.
- Configure the maximum registry size.

Materials Required

- Operating system: Windows NT Workstation
- Lab workgroup size: 2–4 students
- Configuration type: typical

Typical Configuration

- 166 Mhz or better Pentium-compatible computer
- 24 MB of RAM
- 800 MB hard drive
- CD-ROM drive
- 1 NIC (Network Interface Card)

Additional Devices: None

Lab Setup & Safety Tips

- Each lab workstation must be configured with a D partition.

Activity

Configuring the Windows NT swap file

1. Right-click the **My Computer** icon, and then click **Properties**.
2. Click the **Performance** tab.
3. Click the **Change** button.
4. Click in the **Initial Size** box and set the value to **85**.
5. Click in the **Maximum Size** box and set the value to **100**.
6. Click the **Set** button.
7. Click the **OK** button.
8. Click the **Close** button.
9. Click the **Yes** button to restart your lab workstation.

Configuring multiple swap files

1. Right-click the **My Computer** icon, and then click **Properties**.
2. Click the **Performance** tab.

3. Click the **Change** button.
4. At the top of the virtual memory property sheet, select drive **D**.
5. Click in the **Initial Size** box and set the value to **85**.
6. Click in the **Maximum Size** box and set the value to **100**.
7. Click the **Set** button.
8. Click the **OK** button.
9. Click the **Close** button.
10. Click the **Yes** button to restart your lab workstation.

Controlling the Windows NT registry size

1. Right-click the **My Computer** icon, and then click **Properties**.
2. Click the **Performance** tab.
3. Click the **Change** button.
4. Click in the **Maximum Registry Size** box and set the value to **10**.
5. Click the **OK** button.
6. Click the **Close** button.
7. Click the **Yes** button to restart your lab workstation.

Lab Notes

What are the ideal virtual memory settings for Windows NT?—To obtain optimum performance from the Windows NT operating system, Microsoft recommends that you place one swap file (pagefile.sys) on each physical hard drive except the hard drive that contains the Windows NT system directory.

What is the ideal registry size?—For most Windows NT installations, it isn't necessary to modify the registry size parameter. Should it become necessary to adjust the maximum registry size parameter on a Windows NT Workstation, don't allow it to grow larger than 14MB.

Review Questions

Circle True or False.

1. Windows NT supports the use of multiple swap files at the same time. True / False
2. When working in the Windows NT environment, it is recommended that you maintain a 20MB swap file at all times. True / False
3. The largest swap file Windows NT workstation supports is 40MB. True / False
4. In Windows NT you can control the maximum size of the registry. True / False
5. Describe how to configure Windows NT Workstation to use multiple swap files.

____

____

____

____

____

6. Jimmy just installed Windows NT workstation on his PC. He has asked you to explain how he can move his swap file from his drive C to his drive D. In the space below, write the instructions you would give to Jimmy.

____

____

____

____

____

Lab 4.5 Memory Management in Windows 2000

Objective

The objective of this lab is to teach you how to manage and control memory allocations in the Windows 2000 environment. After completing this lab exercise, you will be able to:

- Properly configure one or multiple Windows 2000 swap files.
- Describe the optimum virtual memory configuration for the Windows 2000 operating system.
- Configure the maximum registry size.

Materials Required

- Operating system: Windows 2000 Professional
- Lab workgroup size: 2–4 students
- Configuration type: modern

Modern Configuration

- 200 Mhz or better Pentium-compatible computer
- 64 MB of RAM
- 2 GB hard drive
- CD-ROM drive
- 1 NIC (Network Interface Card)
- 1 Sound card

Additional Devices: None

Lab Setup & Safety Tips

- The workstation should be configured so that the students don't have to provide a user name and password each time the system is rebooted.
- Each lab workstation must be configured with a D drive or partition.

Activity

Configuring the Windows 2000 swap file

1. Right-click the **My Computer** icon, and then click **Properties**.
2. Click the **Advanced** tab.
3. Click the **Performance Options** button.
4. Click the **Change** button.
5. Click in the **Initial Size** box and set the value to **150**.
6. Click in the **Maximum size** box and set the value to **250**.
7. Click the **Set** button.
8. Click the **OK** button on the virtual memory property sheet.
9. Click the **OK** button in the alert window.
10. Click the **OK** button in Performance Options.

11. Click the **OK** button in the System Properties window.
12. Click **Yes** when prompted to restart your lab workstation.

Configuring multiple swap files

1. Right-click the **My Computer** icon, and then click **Properties**.
2. Click the **Advanced** tab.
3. Click the **Performance Options** button.
4. Click the **Change** button.
5. At the top of the virtual memory property sheet, select drive **D**.
6. Click in the **Initial Size** box and set the value to **85**.
7. Click in the **Maximum Size** box and set the value to **100**.
8. Click the **Set** button.
9. Click the **OK** button on the virtual memory property sheet.
10. Click the **OK** button in Performance Options.
11. Click the **OK** button in the System Properties window.
12. Click **Yes** when prompted to restart your lab workstation.

Controlling the Windows 2000 registry size

1. Right-click the **My Computer** icon, and then click **Properties**.
2. Click the **Advanced** tab.
3. Click the **Performance Options** button.
4. Click the **Change** button.
5. Click in the **Maximum Registry Size** box and set the value to **55**.
6. Click the **OK** button.
7. Click the **OK** button in Performance Options.
8. Click the **OK** button in the System Properties window.
9. Click the **Yes** button when prompted to restart your lab workstation.

Lab Notes

What are the ideal virtual memory settings for Windows 2000?—To obtain optimum performance from the Windows 2000 operating system, it is recommended that you place one swap file (pagefile.sys) on each physical hard drive except for the boot volume (unless it is the only physical drive).

Review Questions

Circle True or False.

1. Pagefile.sys is the name of the Windows 2000 swap file. True / False
2. For optimum performance you should always configure a swap file on every partition. True / False
3. The largest swap file Windows 2000 Professional supports is 125MB. True / False
4. The Maximum registry size of Windows 2000 Professional is 5.4 MB. True / False
5. You have just finished installing Windows 2000 Advanced Server for Ronda. Her computer has 3 physical hard drives and 6 logical drives. Windows 2000 is installed on Ronda's first physical drive (C:\). For Ronda's computer to be configured for optimum performance, how many swap files would you configure on her server and why?

   ____

   ____

   ____

   ____

   ____

6. Linda is attempting to install a new application on her Windows 2000 Professional computer, but it isn't working. When Linda attempts the installation, her computer says something about "registry quota too low." Write instructions, in the form of an e-mail to Linda, describing how she can change her registry quota.

   ____

   ____

   ____

   ____

   ____

CHAPTER

5

FLOPPY DRIVES

LABS INCLUDED IN THIS CHAPTER

Lab 5.1 Configuring a Single Floppy Drive

Objective

The objective of this lab is to provide you with the hands-on experience of removing, installing, and configuring a floppy drive. After completing this lab exercise, you will be able to:

- Install a single floppy disk drive in a PC.
- Configure a single floppy disk drive to function properly within a PC system.
- Remove a single floppy disk drive from a PC.

Materials Required

- Operating system: Windows 9x
- Lab workgroup size: 2–4 students
- Configuration type: simple

Simple Configuration

- 90 Mhz or better Pentium-compatible computer
- 16 MB of RAM
- 540 MB hard drive
- 1 NIC (Network Interface Card)

Additional Devices

- Necessary data cable and controller to allow for a 5.25-inch floppy drive installation
- One 3.5-inch floppy drive installed in each lab workstation
- One 5.25-inch floppy drive for each lab workstation
- One 5.25-floppy disk
- Necessary tools to remove the case and to mount/dismount the floppy drives
- Each lab workstation should have one available 5.25-inch bay.

Lab Setup & Safety Tips

- Each group of students should be given one 5.25-inch floppy drive.
- Always unplug the power cord and properly ground yourself before touching any component inside a computer.

Activity

Removing the 3.5-inch floppy drive

1. Power off your PC.
2. Verify that you are properly grounded.
3. Unplug the power cord from the system unit.
4. Remove the top of the case and observe the floppy drive system, as shown in Figure 5-1.
5. Unplug the data cable connected to the 3.5-inch floppy drive.
6. Unplug the power connector for the 3.5-inch floppy drive.
7. Dismount the 3.5-inch floppy drive.

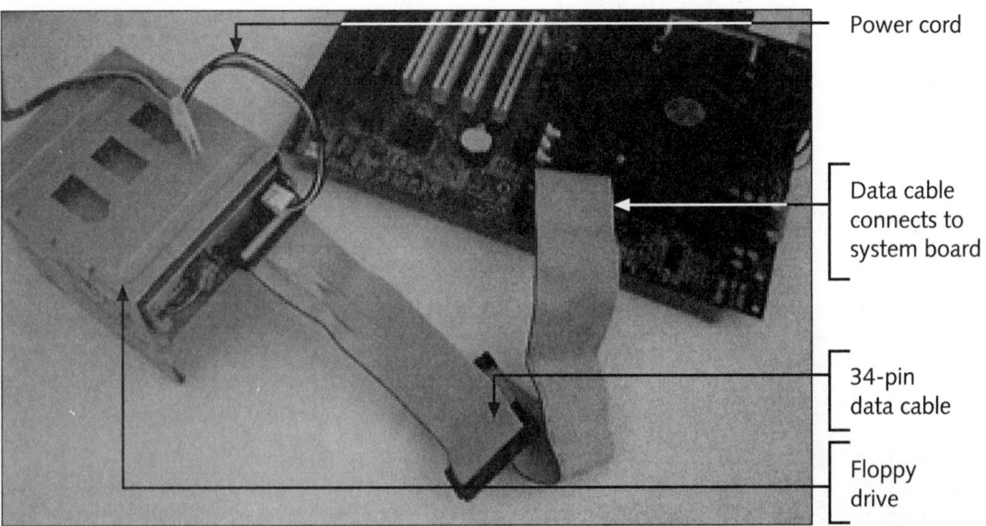

Figure 5-1 Floppy drive subsystem: floppy drive, data cable, and power connection

8. Remove the 3.5-inch floppy drive from your lab workstation.
9. Stand clear of the case, and plug in the power cord.
10. Power on your lab workstation, and enter the CMOS Setup program.
11. Remove the 3.5-inch floppy drive from the Setup program.
12. Save your changes and reboot your lab workstation.

Removing the 3.5-inch floppy drive from Windows

1. Allow your lab workstation to boot into Windows 9x.
2. Double-click the **My Computer** icon.
3. Verify that Windows 9x does not recognize any floppy drives.
4. If there still is an icon for the 3.5-inch floppy drive, complete the following steps:
   a. Click the **Start** button.
   b. Point to **Settings** and click **Control Panel**.
   c. Double-click the **System** icon.
   d. Click the **Device Manager** tab.
   e. Double-click the **Floppy disk controllers** icon.
   f. Click the **3.5 floppy drive** icon to highlight it.
   g. Press **Delete**.
   h. Click the **Yes** button on the confirmation message.
   i. Reboot your lab workstation, then double-click the **My Computer** icon to verify that Windows doesn't recognize any floppy drives.

Installing a 5.25-inch floppy drive

1. Power off your PC.
2. Verify that you are properly grounded.
3. Unplug the power cord from the system unit.
4. Remove the top of the case.

5. Locate an available 5.25-inch drive bay.
6. Remove any blanks that may be in place.
7. Slide the 5.25-inch floppy drive into the bay.
8. Plug in the data cable.
9. Plug in the power connector.
10. Stand clear of the case and plug in the power cord.
11. Power on your lab workstation.
12. Enter the CMOS Setup program.
13. Configure the Setup program to recognize the 5.25-inch floppy drive.
14. Save the CMOS settings and reboot your lab workstation.

Testing the 5.25-inch floppy drive

1. Allow your lab workstation to boot into Windows 9x.
2. Double-click the **My Computer** icon.
3. Verify that Windows 9x recognizes the 5.25-inch floppy drive.
4. Note the information in Table 5-1, and then insert the 5.25-inch floppy disk into the 5.25-inch floppy drive.

Table 5-1 Floppy disk types

Type	Storage Capacity	Number of Tracks per Side	Number of Sectors per Side	Cluster Type
3½-inch extra-high-density	2.88 MB	80	36	2 sectors
3½-inch high-density	1.44 MB	80	18	1 sector
3½-inch double-density	720K	80	9	2 sectors
5¼-inch high-density	1.2 MB	80	15	1 sector
5¼-inch double-density	360K	40	9	2 sectors

5. Right-click the **5.25 floppy drive** icon, and select **Format**.
6. Click the **Start** button in the Format dialog box.
7. When the formatting is completed, click the **Close** button.
8. In the Format dialog box, click the **Close** button.
9. Close the My Computer window.

If Windows 9x does not detect the floppy drive

1. Click the **Start** button.
2. Point to **Settings** and click **Control Panel**.
3. Double-click the **Add New Hardware** icon.
4. Click the **Next** button three times to allow Windows to detect new hardware.
5. When the process is completed, allow Windows to install the proper device driver.
6. Reboot your lab workstation, and follow the steps in the section, "Testing the 5.25-inch floppy drive."

Lab Notes

How do I know which way to connect a data cable?—Most PC data cables have a red stripe along one side of the cable. This stripe always should be aligned with the number one pin on the attached device. The stripe is sometimes blue.

What is BOOT PRIORITY?—Boot priority is a value assigned to a bootable device that communicates to a computer the order in which it should attempt to boot from a bootable device. For example, if a floppy drive is assigned a boot priority of 1, and a hard drive in the same computer is assigned a boot priority of 2, the computer will attempt to boot from the floppy drive before the hard drive. Note that the boot priority is also known as the boot sequence and can normally be customized by using the CMOS Setup program.

Why does my computer boot from the CD-ROM?—Because CD-ROMs are becoming more common, some CD-ROM drives are now boot capable. This means that a boot-capable CD-ROM drive can be assigned a boot priority just like a floppy drive or a hard drive.

5

Review Questions

Circle True or False.

1. The standard PC floppy drive subsystem includes a floppy drive, data cable, and a power connection. True / False
2. There is no capacity difference between a 3.5-inch floppy disk and a 5.25-inch floppy disk. True / False
3. High density floppy disks typically have a higher storage capacity than do double-density floppy disks. True / False
4. If Windows 98 does not detect a new floppy drive, you can use Device Manager to install the correct driver. True / False
5. John's computer always attempts to boot from his CD-ROM drive before the floppy drive. What parameter can John modify in his computer's setup program to change that behavior?

   ____

   ____

   ____

   ____

   ____

6. Stacey just installed a floppy drive into her PC, but the floppy drive icon does not show up when she boots into Windows. Assuming that she installed the drive correctly, what would you recommend Stacey do to make Windows recognize her new floppy drive?

   ____

   ____

   ____

   ____

   ____

Lab 5.2 Configuring a Dual Floppy Drive

Objective

The objective of this lab is to provide you with the hands-on skills necessary to configure dual floppy drives on a personal computer. After completing this lab exercise, you will be able to:

- Install dual floppy disk drives in a personal computer.
- Properly configure a personal computer to use two floppy disk drives.

Materials Required

- Operating system: Windows 9x
- Lab workgroup size: 2–4 students
- Configuration type: simple

Simple Configuration

- 90 Mhz or better Pentium-compatible computer
- 16 MB of RAM
- 540 MB hard drive
- 1 NIC (Network Interface Card)

Additional Devices

- Necessary data cables and controllers to allow for a 5.25-inch and a 3.5-inch floppy drive installation
- One 3.5-inch floppy drive for each lab workstation
- One 5.25-inch floppy disk
- One 3.5-inch floppy disk
- Necessary tools to remove the case and to mount/dismount floppy drives

Lab Setup & Safety Tips

- Each lab workstation should have one 5.25-inch floppy drive installed and functioning properly.
- Each lab workstation should have one available 3.5-inch bay.
- Each group of students should be given one 3.5-inch floppy drive.
- Always unplug the power cord and properly ground yourself before touching any component inside a computer.

Activity

Installing a 3.5-inch floppy drive as drive A

1. Power off your PC.
2. Verify that you are properly grounded.
3. Unplug the power cord from the system unit.
4. Remove the top of the case.
5. Locate an available 3.5-inch drive bay.

6. Remove any blanks that may be in place.
7. Slide the 3.5-inch floppy drive into the bay.
8. Screw the floppy drive into place.
9. Plug in the data cable.
10. Plug in the power connector.
11. Stand clear of the case, and plug in the power cord.
12. Power on your lab workstation.
13. Enter the CMOS Setup program.
14. Configure the Setup program to recognize the 3.5-inch floppy drive.
15. Save the CMOS settings and reboot your lab workstation.

Testing the 3.5-inch floppy drive

1. Allow your lab workstation to boot into Windows 9x.
2. Double-click the **My Computer** icon.
3. Verify that Windows 9x recognizes the 3.5-inch floppy drive.
4. Insert the 3.5-inch floppy disk into the 3.5-inch floppy drive.
5. Right-click the **3.5 floppy drive** icon and select **Format**, as shown in Figure 5-2.

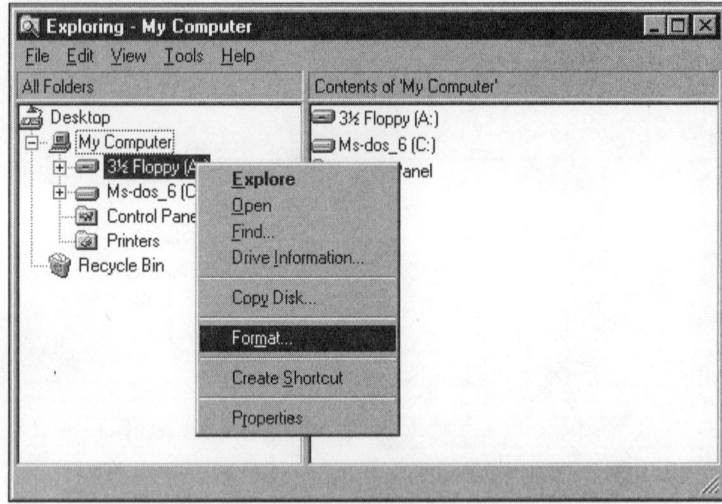

Figure 5-2 Menu to manage a floppy disk

6. Click the **Start** button in the Format dialog box.
7. When the formatting is completed, click the **Close** button.
8. In the Format dialog box, click the **Close** button.
9. Close the My Computer window.

Testing the 5.25-inch floppy drive

1. Allow your lab workstation to boot into Windows 9x.
2. Double-click the **My Computer** icon.
3. Verify that Windows 9x recognizes the 5.25-inch floppy drive.

4. Insert the 5.25-inch floppy disk into the 5.25-inch floppy drive.
5. Right-click the **5.25 floppy drive** icon, and select **Format**.
6. Click the **Start** button in the Format dialog box.
7. When the formatting is completed, click the **Close** button.
8. In the Format dialog box, click the **Close** button.
9. Close the My Computer window.

If Windows 9x does not detect the floppy drive

1. Click the **Start** button.
2. Point to **Settings** and click **Control Panel**.
3. Double-click the **Add New Hardware** icon.
4. Click the **Next** button three times to allow Windows to detect the new hardware.
5. When the process is completed, allow Windows to install the proper device driver.
6. Reboot your lab workstation, and follow the steps in the section, "Testing the 3.5-inch floppy drive."

Lab Notes

How do I configure two floppy drives using the same data cable?— Figure 5-3 shows an example of a typical floppy drive cable that could be used to configure multiple drives. Note that the twist in the data cable helps the computer differentiate between floppy drives A and B.

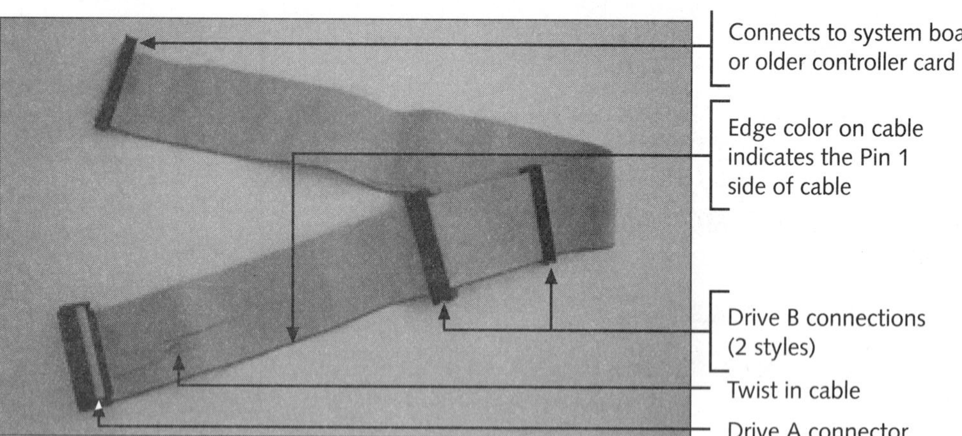

Figure 5-3 Twist in cable determines which drive will be drive A

Review Questions

Circle True or False.

1. PCs always boot to drive B first. True / False
2. Your drive A is always a hard drive. True / False
3. The twist in the data cable lets the computer differentiate between floppy drives A and B. True / False
4. The power connector of a 3.5-inch floppy drive is smaller than the power connector of a typical hard disk drive. True / False
5. Alice, who uses Windows 98, wants to know how to format a 3.5-inch floppy disk. List the steps below.

____
____
____
____
____

6. Amanda wants to run the Windows 95 Add New Hardware wizard to detect her floppy drive. Describe how to detect a new floppy drive using the Add New Hardware wizard.

____
____
____
____
____

CHAPTER

6

INTRODUCTION TO HARD DRIVES

LABS INCLUDED IN THIS CHAPTER

Lab 6.1 Understanding FDISK

Objective

The FDISK utility allows you to add, remove, and view your hard drive's partition configuration. After completing this lab exercise, you will be able to:

- Use the FDISK utility to view drive configuration information.
- Add and remove partitions using the FDISK utility.
- Use the FDISK utility to set an active partition.
- Describe the relationship between a logical drive and an extended partition.

Materials Required

- Operating system: Windows 9x
- Lab workgroup size: 2–4 students
- Configuration type: simple

Simple Configuration

- 90 Mhz or better Pentium-compatible computer
- 16 MB of RAM
- 540 MB hard drive
- 1 NIC (Network Interface Card)

Additional Devices

- A DOS system boot disk with the FDISK utility

Lab Setup & Safety Tips

- Each workstation's hard drive should contain at least one partition.
- *Warning*: The steps in the following activity will erase all data currently stored on your lab workstation. Back up any stored data before you proceed with this lab exercise.
- Any changes made using the FDISK utility will affect the data stored on the partition or partitions that were modified. *Be careful*!

Activity

Viewing the current hard drive configuration

1. Power off your lab workstation.
2. Insert the boot disk into drive A.
3. Power on your lab workstation and allow it to boot from the floppy disk.
4. At the A prompt, type **FDISK**. Your screen should resemble Figure 6-1.

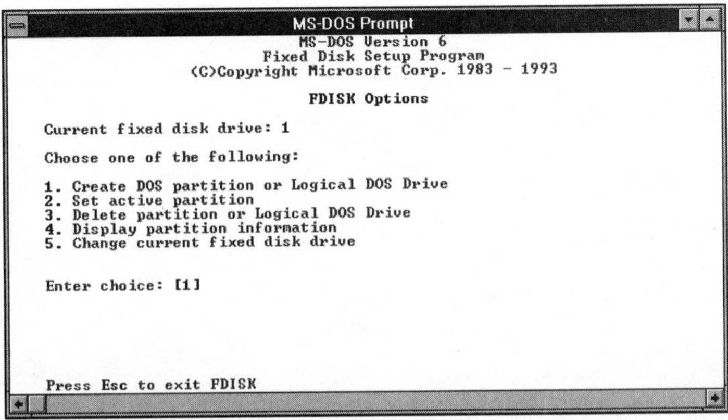

Figure 6-1 Fixed disk setup program (FDISK) menu

5. From the FDISK menu, select option 4 by typing **4** and then pressing **Enter**.
6. Observe your current hard drive configuration. In particular, note the volume label.

Deleting a partition

1. Press the **Esc** key to return to the Main Menu.
2. From the FDISK Main Menu, select option 3 by typing **3** and then pressing **Enter**.
3. Select the primary partition on your hard drive by typing **1** and pressing **Enter**.
4. Type **1** and press **Enter**.
5. Type the volume label of the primary partition.
6. Confirm the deletion by typing **Y** and pressing **Enter**.
7. Press the **Esc** key to return to the Main Menu.
8. Press **Esc** again to exit the FDISK utility.
9. Press the **spacebar** to restart the computer and the workstation.

Creating a partition

1. Boot the workstation using the floppy disk.
2. At the A prompt, type **FDISK**.
3. At the FDISK Main Menu, select option **1** and press **Enter**.
4. Type **1** and press **Enter**.
5. When the FDISK utility asks if you want to use all the available space for the primary partition and set it as active, select No by typing **N** and pressing **Enter**.
6. When FDISK prompts you to enter the amount of drive space you want to use, type **500** and press **Enter**.
7. If prompted for a volume label, type **DRIVE 1** and press **Enter**.
8. Press **Esc** to return to the FDISK Main Menu.

Setting an active partition

1. Select option **2** from the FDISK Main Menu.
2. Choose the primary partition that you created by typing **1** and pressing **Enter**.
3. Press **Esc** to return to the main menu.
4. Press **Esc** to exit FDISK and press any key. Your workstation will restart.

Lab Notes

Extended partition—An extended partition is a section of the hard drive that allows the partitioning of logical drives. Note that there can be only one extended partition per hard drive.

Logical drive—A logical drive is a partition that holds a drive letter and behaves as a separate physical drive. Note that logical drives can be created only within extended partitions.

Active partition—If a partition is set as active, the system will attempt to boot from that partition.

FDISK/MBR—This command is used to refresh the master boot record without causing any data loss.

Review Questions

Circle True or False.

1. When a partition's size is changed using the FDISK utility, the data contained on the partition is lost. True / False
2. The FDISK utility is used to partition and format hard drives. True / False
3. Extended partitions are always placed within logical drives. True / False
4. List three functions of the FDISK utility.

____

____

____

____

____

5. You are the desktop PC support technician for the Good Job Corporation. John, one of your customers, suspects that his hard drive is not partitioned to use its full capacity. Describe how you would use the FDISK utility to show John his current hard drive configuration.

____

____

____

____

____

6. Describe the relationship between a logical drive and an extended partition.

____

____

____

____

____

7. What is the difference between a physical drive and a logical drive?

____

____

____

____

____

Lab 6.2 Formatting and Disk Utilities

Objective

You must format a hard drive to install a file system. In this lab exercise you will learn how to properly install and optimize the FAT file system. After completing this lab exercise, you will be able to:

- Format a partition.
- Use the SCANDISK utility to optimize performance.
- Use the DEFRAG utility to optimize performance.

Materials Required

- Operating system: Windows 9x
- Lab workgroup size: 1 student
- Configuration type: simple

Simple Configuration

- 90 Mhz or better Pentium-compatible computer
- 16 MB of RAM
- 540 MB hard drive
- 1 NIC (Network Interface Card)

Additional Devices

- One DOS boot disk that includes the Format and SYS commands
- One DOS disk that contains both the SCANDISK and DEFRAG utilities

Lab Setup & Safety Tips

- Each workstation's hard drive should contain one unformatted primary partition that has been set as active.
- Be sure that the data stored on your lab workstation has been backed up before you proceed with this lab exercise.

Activity

Formatting the C drive

1. Power off your lab workstation.
2. Insert the boot disk into drive A.
3. Power on your lab workstation and allow it to boot from your DOS boot disk.
4. At the A prompt, type **FORMAT C:**.
5. When asked to confirm before proceeding, type **Y** and press **Enter**. The format command begins to format drive C.
6. When formatting is completed, type a volume label of **DRIVE 1**.

Making drive C bootable

You can use many different commands to make a drive bootable. Following are two examples of command sequences:

Example 1

1. Power off your lab workstation.
2. Insert the boot disk into drive A.
3. Power on your lab workstation and allow it to boot from your DOS boot disk.
4. At the A prompt, type **SYS A: C:** and press **Enter**.

Example 2

The /S switch tells DOS to add system information to the drive after it has been formatted. Use the /? option to view other FORMAT switches.

1. Power off your lab workstation.
2. Insert the boot disk into drive A.
3. Power on your lab workstation and allow it to boot from your DOS boot disk.
4. At the A prompt, type **FORMAT C: /S**.
5. When asked to confirm before proceeding, type **Y** and press **Enter**.
6. When formatting is completed, type a volume label of **DRIVE 1**.

Using the SCANDISK utility

1. Insert the disk that contains the SCANDISK utility.
2. At the A prompt, type **SCANDISK** and press **Enter**.
3. Allow SCANDISK to verify your file and directory structure, and to complete a surface scan.
4. When SCANDISK has completed, use the **View Log** option to view any errors that SCANDISK might have encountered.
5. After examining the view log, exit the SCANDISK utility.

Using the DEFRAG utility

1. Insert the disk that contains the DEFRAG utility.
2. At the A prompt, type **DEFRAG** and press **Enter**.
3. Allow DEFRAG to reorganize the hard drive (this should happen quickly if the drive was formatted recently).
4. When the defragmentation is completed, exit the DEFRAG utility.

Lab Notes

What is a switch?—A switch is a parameter or variable that can be added to the end of a DOS command and that will change or enhance the meaning of the command.

DEFRAG—This utility is designed to optimize file access by moving file clusters into a continuous chain, thus increasing the speed of data retrieval. This utility should be used at least once a month to maintain optimum system performance.

SCANDISK—This utility is designed to search a hard drive for lost or cross-linked clusters and attempt to repair them. SCANDISK should be used at least once a month to maintain optimum system performance.

Review Questions

Circle True or False.

1. Using the SCANDISK utility will delete all files less than 512 K in size. True / False
2. The DEFRAG utility places file clusters in consecutive order. True / False
3. You should run the SCANDISK utility only once every three months. True / False
4. Describe the functionality of the DEFRAG utility.

____

____

____

____

____

5. You are currently employed as a PC desktop support technician at My World. One of your customers, Jamie, calls to tell you that her computer is running more slowly than it did last month. List two utilities that Jamie might use to improve the performance of her computer.

____

____

____

____

____

6. John is currently running DEFRAG, and it is taking a long time. John called you to ask what the DEFRAG program does, and why it seems to be so slow. Over the last year John has never run the DEFRAG utility. Describe to John both the purpose of the DEFRAG utility and explain why it is taking so long to run.

____

____

____

____

____

Lab 6.3 File System Organization

Objective

The objective of this lab exercise is to provide you with hands-on experience manipulating files and directories in the DOS environment. After completing this lab exercise, you will be able to:

- Navigate the DOS directory.
- Copy files and directories.
- Rename files and directories.
- Move files and directories.
- Manipulate file attributes
- Identify DOS system files.
- Explain DOS filenaming conventions, and rename both files and directories.

Materials Required

- Operating system: DOS 5.0 or higher
- Lab workgroup size: 2–4 students
- Configuration type: simple

Simple Configuration

- 90 Mhz or better Pentium-compatible computer
- 16 MB of RAM
- 540 MB hard drive
- 1 NIC (Network Interface Card)

Additional Devices: None

Lab Setup & Safety Tips

- Each lab workstation should have DOS 5.0, or later, installed and functioning properly.

Activity

Navigating the DOS environment

1. Observe the sample subdirectory trees in Figure 6-2, noting the logic behind each. Then to briefly observe the DOS directory structure of your workstation, type **TREE C:** at the C prompt and press **Enter**. The result is a diagram of the current directory structure of your hard drive. (*Note:* The TREE command isn't available in some recent versions of DOS.)
2. Boot your lab workstation to the C prompt.
3. To create a directory named Student, type **MD STUDENT** and press **Enter**.
4. Observe where the Student directory is now located in the DOS directory structure. Type **TREE c:** and press **Enter**.
5. To change to the Student directory, type **CD STUDENT** and press **Enter**.
6. To copy the Config.sys file to the Student directory, type **COPY C:\CONFIG.SYS C:\STUDENT** and press **Enter**.

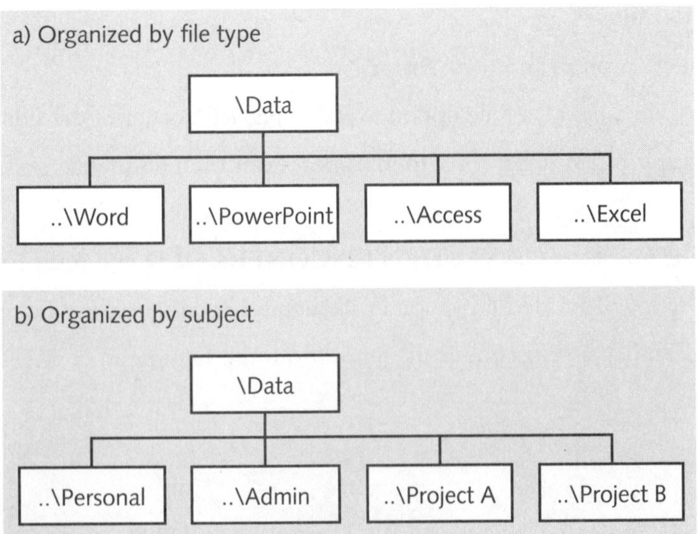

Figure 6-2 Two subdirectory trees to hold data on a hard drive

7. To view the contents of the Student directory, type **DIR** and press **Enter**.
8. Observe that the Config.sys file is now in the Student directory.

Renaming a file

1. To rename the Config.sys file in the Student directory, type **REN C:\STUDENT\CONFIG.SYS CONFIG.OLD**.
2. To observe the results, type **DIR** and press **Enter**.

Renaming (moving) a directory

1. Type **CD ** and press **Enter** ("\\" in DOS represents the root directory).
2. To rename the Student directory to Student2, type **MOVE C:\STUDENT C:\STUDENT2** and press **Enter**.
3. To observe the results, type **DIR** and press **Enter**.

Moving files

1. Move the CONFIG.SYS file to the root directory by typing the following: **MOVE C:\STUDENT2\CONFIG.OLD C:**. (Do not type the period.)
2. To observe the results, type **DIR** and press **Enter**.
3. Now move the CONFIG.SYS file back to the STUDENT2 directory by typing the following: **MOVE C:\CONFIG.OLD C:\STUDENT2**. (Do not type the period.)
4. To observe the results, type **DIR** and press **Enter**.

Viewing and changing file attributes

1. To change to the Student2 directory, type **CD STUDENT2** and press **Enter**.
2. To view the attributes of the config.old, type **ATTRIB C:\STUDENT2\CONFIG.OLD** and press **Enter**.
3. To make the config.old file a hidden file, type **ATTRIB +H C:\STUDENT2\CONFIG.OLD** and press **Enter**.
4. To observe the results, type **DIR** and press **Enter**.
5. To remove the hidden attribute from the config.old file, type **ATTRIB -H C:\STUDENT2\CONFIG.OLD** and press **Enter**.

Editing DOS configuration files

1. Type **EDIT** at the C prompt and press **Enter**.
2. Press the **Alt** key to highlight the File option in the upper-left corner of the Edit program.
3. Press the down arrow [↓] to select the **Open** option from the File menu.
4. Press **Enter**.
5. In the Open dialog box, type **C:\STUDENT2\CONFIG.OLD** and press **Enter**.
6. Press the **Alt** key to highlight the File option in the upper-left corner of the Edit program.
7. Use the down arrow [↓] to select the **Exit** option from the File menu.
8. Press **Enter**.

Lab Notes

ATTRIB +/- H—These commands set the Hidden file attribute.

ATTRIB +/- A—These commands set the Archive file attribute.

ATTRIB +/- R—These commands set the Read file attribute.

ATTRIB +/- S—These commands set the System file attribute.

The following is a list of the files used to initialize the DOS operating system.

- MSDOS.SYS
- COMMAND.COM
- IO.SYS

The following are text files stored in the root directory, and also are used to customize the DOS environment.

- AUTOEXEC.BAT
- CONFIG.SYS

DOS error messages

Incorrect DOS version—This error most commonly occurs when you try to execute a newer DOS command from an older version of DOS.

Error in CONFIG.SYS line xx—You see this error message during the boot process if there is an error in the CONFIG.SYS file. The xx is the line number starting from the top of the file and counting down.

Bad or missing COMMAND.COM—This error message appears when COMMAND.COM is not present, is corrupt, or is the wrong version.

Remember that the DOS filenaming convention includes an eight-character filename and a three-character file extension that is separated by a period.

Review Questions

Circle True or False.

1. The **TREE** command is not always available in recent versions of DOS. True / False
2. When you receive the error message "Bad or missing command.com," it means that the entire operating system is corrupt and must be reinstalled. True / False
3. What does the CD command stand for?

4. What is the ATTRIB command used for?

5. Name one required DOS system file.

6. Patrick, one of your customers, is trying to find a file located in the MyData directory on his computer. What command would you suggest that Patrick use to view the contents of the MyData directory?

7. John has attempted to rename a directory using the following command:

   REN C:\MYDATA C:\MYSTUFF

   Explain why this command might not work, and recommend a different command for John to use.

Lab 6.4 Installing Removable-Media Drives

Objective

The objective of this lab exercise is to install a removable drive. After completing this lab exercise, you will be able to:

- Install an external removable drive.
- Name several types of removable drive technology.

Materials Required

- Operating system: Windows 9x
- Lab workgroup size: 2–4 students
- Configuration type: simple

Simple Configuration

- 90 Mhz or better Pentium-compatible computer
- 16 MB of RAM
- 540 MB hard drive
- 1 NIC (Network Interface Card)

Additional Devices

- One removable-media disk or tape drive for each group of four students

Lab Setup & Safety Tips

- To ensure complete data safety, *never* install or remove a removable drive while the PC is powered on.
- The parallel port should be configured for use.
- Note that depending on the type of removable drive on your workstation, the driver installation steps will vary.

Activity

Installing and Configuring a Zip drive

1. Power off your lab workstation.
2. Connect the lab workstation's external drive to the parallel port.
3. Verify that the external drive is plugged in.
4. Power on the lab workstation and allow it to boot into Windows 9x.
5. Insert the driver disk for the external drive.
6. Follow the instructions for installing the drivers, or ask your instructor for details.
7. After the drivers are installed, reboot the lab workstation.
8. Test the drive installation by double-clicking **My Computer**.
9. If the drive installation was successful, you will see a removable drive icon in the **My Computer** window.

Lab Notes

Although Zip drives can be connected via the parallel port, many removable-media drives require a SCSI or IDE interface and must be attached internally (this applies to some Zip drives). Depending on the type of removable-media drive, the hardware and software installation requirements vary. Always read the manufacturer's instructions before proceeding with an installation.

The following is a list of some external removable-media drives:

- Iomega Zip drives
- Iomega Jaz drives
- Tape backup drives
- SyJet drives
- Magneto-optical drives
- Phase-dual (PD) optical drives
- CD-R (writeable CD-ROM drive)
- CD-RW (rewriteable CD-ROM drive)

Review Questions

Circle True or False.

1. A hard drive can be an example of a removable-media drive. True / False
2. Zip drives are always attached by way of a parallel port. True / False
3. Windows 9x always automatically detects an external drive. True / False
4. You are employed at the COMP Computer Outlet as a service technician. Bobby, one of your favorite customers, has just bought a new Zip drive and is trying to configure it. He explains to you that he is using Windows 98 and has attached his Zip drive to his computer. Briefly describe the remaining steps Bobby must take before his Zip drive will function properly.

____

____

____

____

____

Lab Notes

Although Zip drives can be connected via the parallel port, many removable-media drives require a SCSI or IDE interface and must be attached internally (this applies to some Zip drives). Depending on the type of removable-media drive, the hardware and software installation requirements vary. Always read the manufacturer's instructions before proceeding with an installation.

The following is a list of some external removable-media drives:

- Iomega Zip drives
- Iomega Jaz drives
- Tape backup drives
- SyJet drives
- Magneto-optical drives
- Phase-dual (PD) optical drives
- CD-R (writeable CD-ROM drive)
- CD-RW (rewriteable CD-ROM drive)

Review Questions

Circle True or False.

1. A hard drive can be an example of a removable-media drive. True / False
2. Zip drives are always attached by way of a parallel port. True / False
3. Windows 9x always automatically detects an external drive. True / False
4. You are employed at the COMP Computer Outlet as a service technician. Bobby, one of your favorite customers, has just bought a new Zip drive and is trying to configure it. He explains to you that he is using Windows 98 and has attached his Zip drive to his computer. Briefly describe the remaining steps Bobby must take before his Zip drive will function properly.

____

____

____

____

____

CHAPTER

7

HARD DRIVE INSTALLATION AND SUPPORT

LABS INCLUDED IN THIS CHAPTER

LAB 7.1 INSTALLING AN IDE HARD DRIVE

Objective

The objective of this lab exercise is to configure one IDE hard drive when a slave drive is not present. After completing this lab exercise, you will be able to:

- Install and remove an IDE hard drive.

Materials Required

- Operating system: Windows 9x
- Lab workgroup size: 2 students
- Configuration type: simple

Simple Configuration

- 90 Mhz or better Pentium-compatible computer
- 16 MB of RAM
- 540 MB hard drive
- 1 NIC (Network Interface Card)

Additional Devices: None

Lab Setup & Safety Tips

- Always unplug the power cord and properly ground yourself before touching any component inside a computer.

ACTIVITY

Removing an IDE hard drive

Student 1

1. Power off the lab workstation and unplug the power cord (it is not necessary to unplug all other cords).
2. Remove the case from the lab workstation.
3. Note the IDE hard drive in Figure 7-1, and then locate the IDE hard drive on your workstation.
4. Unplug the IDE cable and the power connector from the hard drive. Note the position of the data and power connector.
5. Read Table 7-1 for reference and then record the jumper configuration for your hard drive. (*Note:* Refer to the hard drive documentation for a description of jumper settings.)

   ____

6. Physically remove the hard drive from the system. If it is mounted with rails, remove them from the drive as well. Be sure to retain all mounting hardware (screws, washers, etc.) for use by the next student.
7. For safety, stand clear of the workstation and plug in the power cord.

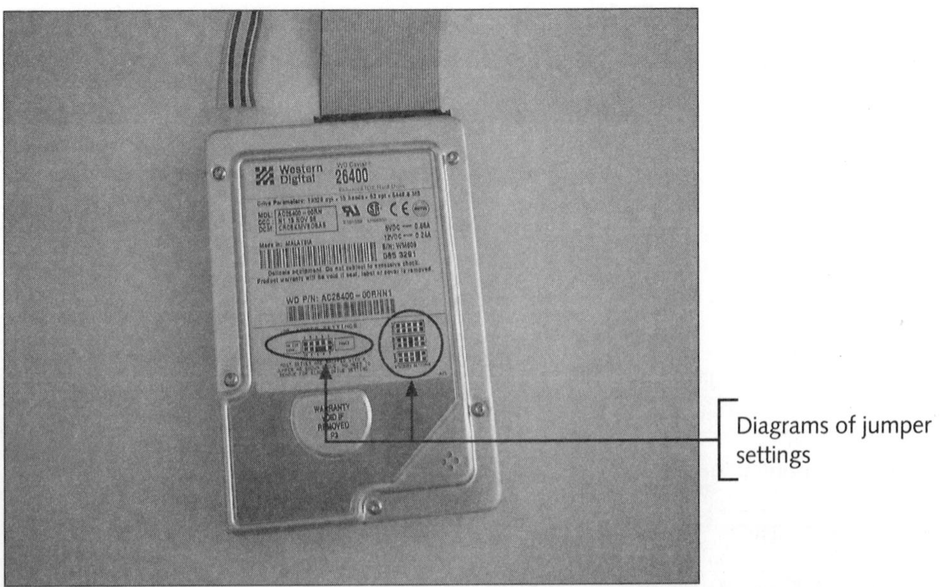

Figure 7-1 An IDE drive most likely will have diagrams of jumper settings for master and slave options printed on the drive housing

Table 7-1 Jumper settings on an IDE hard drive

Configuration	Description
Single-drive configuration	This is the only hard drive on this IDE channel. (This is the standard setting.)
Master-drive configuration	This is the first of two drives; it most likely is the boot device.
Slave-drive configuration	This is the second drive using this channel or data cable.
Cable-select configuration	The cable select data cable determines which drive is the master and which is the slave.

8. With the hard drive removed, power on the lab workstation and wait for the BIOS error message.
9. Enter the Setup program, if necessary, and follow the menu instructions for the workstation's BIOS to validate the removal of the hard drive.
10. When prompted, save the changes and then reboot the workstation.

Installing an IDE hard drive

Student 2

1. Power off the lab workstation and unplug the power cord.
2. Using the hard drive removed by Student 1, mount the hard drive into its original position.
3. Note the potential jumper settings in Figure 7-2. Then, using Student 1's recorded information, verify that the IDE hard drive jumpers are configured correctly. (*Note:* Refer to the hard drive documentation for a description of the jumper settings.)
4. Connect the IDE data cable and the power connector. (Be sure that you connect the cables in the same manner they previously were connected. The red stripe on the data cable should be aligned with the pin 1 setting on the hard drive.)
5. For safety, stand clear of the workstation and plug in the power cord.
6. When the workstation boots, enter the Setup program.
7. Verify that the BIOS automatically detected the hard drive.

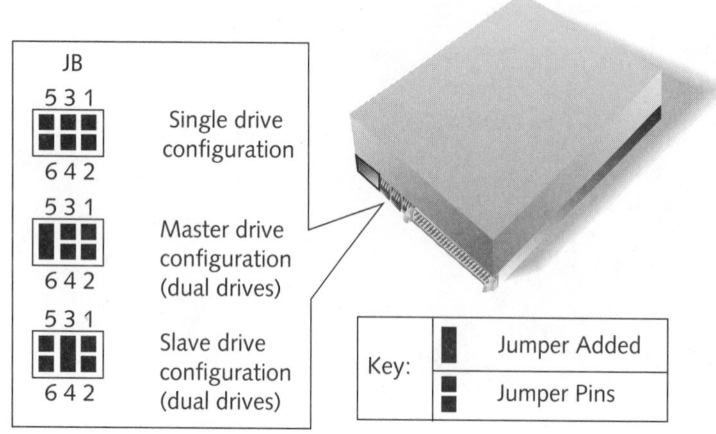

Figure 7-2 Potential jumper settings for a hard drive and their meanings

8. Save the BIOS changes and exit the Setup program.
9. Reboot the workstation and test the installation by booting into the operating system.
10. Shut down the workstation and power it off.
11. Unplug the power cable and secure the case.
12. Plug the workstation back in and power it on.

Lab Notes

IDE Controllers—Most system boards manufactured today have two integrated IDE controllers, although this practice is relatively new. There was a time when IDE controllers were typically purchased separately and installed into expansion slots. Then, your hard drive data cable would be plugged into the expansion card. System boards have evolved since then, but sometimes when you are servicing older computers, you might have to install an expansion card to provide an additional IDE controller.

Pin 1—Remember that the red stripe on an IDE data cable always should be aligned with the pin 1 on the device to which it is being connected. (*Note:* When you are connecting an IDE hard drive to an IDE data cable, the red stripe or pin on one side should be attached to the same side of the hard drive as the power connector.)

Review Questions

Circle True or False.

1. You can identify the location of pin 1 for an IDE ribbon cable by the red wire.
   True / False
2. Typically, the BIOS must be modified when the hard drive configuration has been changed.
   True / False
3. You always should unplug the hard drive cables while the PC is powered on. True / False
4. It is a good practice to write down the jumper configuration of a hard drive before you remove it from a computer. True / False
5. Are all IDE hard drive controllers integrated on a system board? Explain your answer.

   ____

   ____

   ____

   ____

   ____

6. Donna wants to install a second hard drive in her PC. She currently has only one IDE controller, which has both a hard drive and CD-ROM drive attached to it. Without upgrading the system board, describe how Donna can add a second hard drive to her system. Also list the hardware she needs to complete the upgrade.

   ____

   ____

   ____

   ____

   ____

Lab 7.2 Installing a Second IDE Hard Drive

Objective

The objective of this lab exercise is to configure one lab workstation to use two IDE hard drives at the same time. After completing this lab exercise, you will be able to:

- Install, remove, and configure a PC to use one or more IDE hard drives at the same time.
- Understand and describe the differences between the Cable Select and the Master/Slave configurations.

Materials Required

- Operating system: Windows 9x
- Lab workgroup size: 2 students
- Configuration type: simple

Simple Configuration

- 90 Mhz or better Pentium-compatible computer
- 16 MB of RAM
- 540 MB hard drive
- 1 NIC (Network Interface Card)

Additional Devices

- Two IDE hard drives (one should already be installed in the lab workstation)
- Two hard drive jumpers (normally already are on the hard drives)
- One Cable Select IDE data cable
- One standard IDE data cable (Master/Slave)
- Hard drive mounting brackets (if necessary, and as determined by your instructor)
- 1 mounting bay for the second hard drive

Lab Setup & Safety Tips

- The lab workstation should be previously configured with a standard IDE data cable and one IDE hard drive set to single drive configuration.
- Always unplug the power cord and properly ground yourself before touching any component inside a computer.

Activity

Installing a Slave drive using the Master/Slave configuration

Student 1

1. Power off the lab workstation and unplug the power cord (it is not necessary to unplug all other cords).
2. Remove the case from the lab workstation.
3. Locate the hard drive.
4. Unplug the IDE cable and the power connector from the hard drive.

5. View the hard drive jumper configuration (if necessary, physically remove the hard drive).
6. Verify that the installed hard drive is set to Master. (*Note:* Refer to the hard drive documentation for a description of the jumper settings.)
7. Set the jumper on the second hard drive to the Slave position.
8. Locate an available bay to mount the second hard drive.
9. Mount the second hard drive.
10. Plug in the power connectors to each hard drive.
11. Plug in the IDE data cable to each hard drive.
12. For safety, stand clear of the case and plug in the power cord.
13. With both hard drives plugged in, power on the lab workstation and wait for the BIOS error message.
14. Enter the Setup program, and follow the menu instructions for the workstation's BIOS to validate the hard drive changes. (*Note:* The BIOS should now recognize two hard drives.)
15. Save the changes and reboot the workstation.
16. Boot into the operating system to verify that it recognizes the additional drive.

Installing a Slave drive using Cable Select

Student 2

1. Power off the lab workstation and unplug the power cord.
2. Unplug the power connectors and the data cables of both IDE hard drives.
3. Unplug the IDE data cable from the system board.
4. Connect the Cable Select data cable to the system board in the same manner that the standard IDE data cable was connected. (*Note:* The difference between a Cable Select and a standard data cable is that the Cable Select data cable is marked by a notch or hole.)
5. Change the jumper settings on both hard drives to the Cable Select position.
6. Plug in the power connectors to each of the IDE hard drives.
7. Remember that the first hard drive on a Cable Select data cable will be the Master, and the second drive will be the Slave, plug in the IDE data cables, and set the original drive as Master.
8. With both hard drives plugged in, power on the lab workstation and wait for the BIOS error message.
9. Enter the Setup program and follow the menu instructions for the workstation's BIOS to validate the hard drive changes. (*Note:* The BIOS should now recognize two hard drives.)
10. Save the changes and reboot the workstation.
11. Boot into the operating system to verify that it recognizes the drives correctly.
12. Shut down the workstation and power it off.
13. Unplug the power cable and secure the case.
14. Plug the workstation back in and power it on.

Lab Notes

The following is a brief description of the most commonly used jumper settings:

Master—When a drive is set to Master, it normally is the first hard drive from which the PC attempts to boot.

Slave—When a drive is set to Slave, it is the secondary hard drive. This drive is normally referred to as D.

Cable Select—When a drive is configured to use Cable Select, the Master/Slave designation is determined by the drive's cable position rather than its jumper settings. Using a standard Cable Select data cable, the hard drive connected closest to the system board becomes the Master, and the drive farthest from the system board becomes the Slave.

How is a Cable Select data cable different from other cables?—All Cable Select data cables can easily be recognized as such by a small hole punched somewhere in the data cable. If you cannot locate a small hole somewhere in the data cable, then it is not Cable Select-compliant and you must use the Master/Slave configuration.

How does the Master/Slave configuration work?—When two IDE drives are jumpered to use the Master/Slave configuration, the drives begin sharing one onboard hard drive controller. This means that when a drive is configured as a slave, the electronics for its onboard controller are disabled. The electronics located on the master hard drive then begin to communicate with the IDE controller for both the master and the slave hard drive.

Review Questions

Circle True or False.

1. When using Cable Select, the location of a hard drive on the data cable determines whether it will be the Master or Slave. True / False
2. You can add as many as three devices to an IDE channel. True / False
3. When two hard drives are present, the Master drive is drive D. True / False
4. How can you easily identify a Cable Select data cable?

____

____

____

____

____

5. What are the three standard jumper options available with an IDE hard drive?

____

____

____

____

____

6. How many devices can be attached to an IDE cable?

____

____

____

____

____

Lab 7.3 Installing a SCSI Hard Drive

Objective

The objective of this lab exercise is to configure your lab workstation to utilize a SCSI hard drive. After completing this lab exercise, you will be able to:

- Install, remove, and configure a PC to use a SCSI hard drive.
- Describe the relationship between a SCSI host adapter and other SCSI devices.
- Compare SCSI adapter types.

Materials Required

- Operating system: Windows 9x
- Lab workgroup size: 2–4 students
- Configuration type: simple SCSI

Simple SCSI Configuration

- 90 Mhz or better Pentium-compatible computer
- 16 MB of RAM
- 540 MB SCSI hard drive
- 1 NIC (Network Interface Card)

Additional Devices: None

Lab Setup & Safety Tips

- The lab workstation should have both IDE channels disabled for this activity. (If the IDE channels can't be disabled, unplug the IDE data cables and power connectors for each IDE device.)
- Always unplug the power cord and properly ground yourself before touching any component inside a computer.

Activity

Removing a SCSI hard drive

Student 1

1. Power off the lab workstation and unplug the power cord (it is not necessary to unplug all other cords).
2. Remove the case from the lab workstation.
3. Locate the SCSI hard drive.
4. Unplug the SCSI cable and the power connector from the hard drive.
5. Physically remove the hard drive from the system. If it is mounted with rails, remove them from the drive as well. Be sure to retain all mounting hardware (screws, washers, etc.) for use by the next student.
6. Record the jumper configuration. (*Note:* Refer to the hard drive documentation for a description of jumper settings.) ______________________________

____

7. For safety, stand clear of the workstation and plug in the power cord.
8. With the hard drive removed, power on the lab workstation and wait for the BIOS error message.
9. Enter the SCSI Setup program, if necessary, and follow the menu instructions for the workstation's SCSI BIOS to validate the hard drive changes.
10. Save the changes and reboot the workstation.

Installing a SCSI hard drive

Student 2

1. Power off the lab workstation and unplug the power cord.
2. Using the hard drive removed by Student 1, mount the hard drive in its original position.
3. Using the recorded information from Student 1, verify that the SCSI hard drive jumpers are configured correctly. (*Note:* Refer to the hard drive documentation for a description of jumper settings.)
4. Connect the SCSI data cable and the power connector. (Be sure that you connect the cables the same way they were previously connected. The red stripe on the data cable should be aligned with the pin 1 setting on the hard drive.)
5. For safety, stand clear of the workstation and plug in the power cord.
6. When the workstation boots, enter the SCSI Setup program.
7. Verify that the SCSI BIOS detected the hard drive automatically and correctly.
8. Save the SCSI BIOS changes and exit the Setup program.
9. Reboot the workstation, and test the installation by booting into the operating system.
10. Shut down the workstation and power it off.
11. Unplug the power cable and secure the case.
12. Plug the workstation back in and power it on.

Lab Notes

Understanding SCSI—SCSI devices communicate directly with the SCSI host adapter rather than with the CPU. You can think of the SCSI bus as a separate little world for SCSI devices, as illustrated in Figure 7-3. Most SCSI host adapters do not need any configuration changes if you are simply adding or removing a device to or from the SCSI bus. However, specific devices might require that unit-ID specific changes be made in the host adapter's configuration. These changes might include (but might not be limited to) transfer speed, synchronous negotiation, or the host adapter sending a command to start a disk drive's spindle motor. Check your system or SCSI host adapter documentation for more information.

Lab Notes (continued)

SCSI ID—In the "SCSI world," rather than using the Master/Slave designation scheme, SCSI IDs are used. Typically, SCSI ID 7 is occupied by the SCSI host adapter and if a SCSI hard drive is present, it is normally given SCSI ID 0. If the SCSI host adapter being used can support Wide (16-bit data path) SCSI devices, additional IDs of 8–14 or 7–15 (depending on whether the host adapter has claimed address 7 or 15) may also be available. Note that the device(s) being attached also must be Wide-capable in order to use IDs above 7.

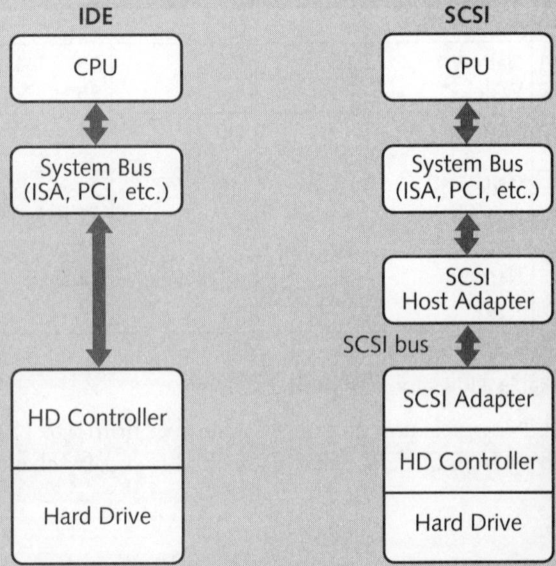

Figure 7-3 SCSI hard drives communicate with the CPU through the SCSI host adapter, but IDE drives communicate directly on the system bus

Different types of SCSI—Like IDE/ATA standards, SCSI standards have improved over the years. There are two general categories for all SCSI standards, 8-bit and 16-bit. These category names refer to the number of bits that can travel on the SCSI bus. Often, modern SCSI host adapters are backward-compatible and allow different SCSI standards to coexist on the same SCSI bus. Figure 7-4 illustrates an example of backward-compatibility using three different SCSI standards on the same SCSI bus. Table 7-2 summarizes modern SCSI standards.

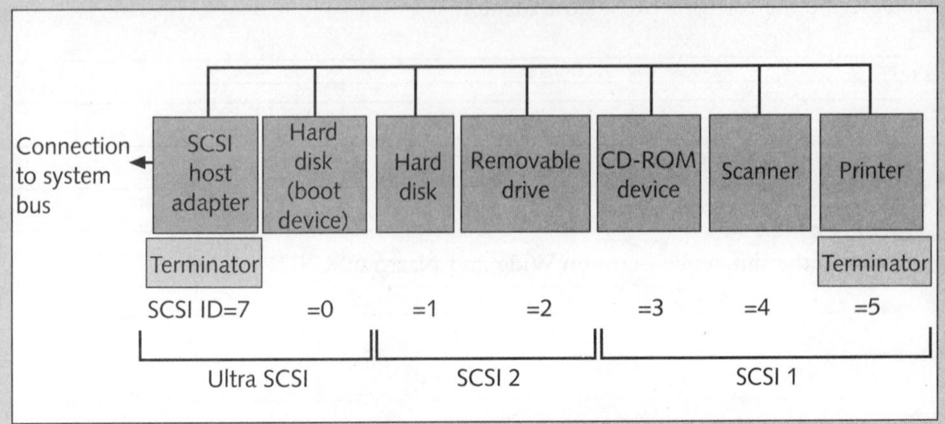

Figure 7-4 Sample SCSI subsystem configuration

Lab Notes (continued)

Table 7-2 Summary of SCSI standards

Names for the SCSI Interface Standard	Bus width Narrow = 8 bits Wide = 16 bits	Transfer ZRate (MB/sec)	Maximum Length of Single-ended Cable (meters)	Maximum Length of Differential Cable (meters)	Maximum Number of Devices
SCSI-1 (Regular SCSI)[1]	Narrow	5	6	25	8
SCSI-2 (**Fast SCSI** or Fast Narrow)	Narrow	10	3	25	8
Fast Wide SCSI (Wide SCSI)	Wide	20	3	25	16
SCSI-3 (**Ultra SCSI** or Ultra Narrow or Fast-20 SCSI)	Narrow	20	1.5	25	8
Wide Ultra SCSI (Fast Wide 20)	Wide	40	1.5	25	16
Ultra2 SCSI	Narrow	40		12 LVD[2]	8
Wide Ultra2 SCSI	Wide	80		12 LVD[2]	16
Ultra3 SCSI	Narrow	80		12 LVD[2]	8
Wide Ultra3 SCSI (Ultra 160 SCSI)	Wide	160		12 LVD[2]	16

[1]Bold indicates most common name
[2]LVD: Low voltage differential cable allows for lengths up to 12 meters

What is a LUN?—A LUN (logical unit number) is a number from 0 to 15 (also called the SCSI ID) assigned to each SCSI device that is attached to a daisy chain.

Review Questions

Circle True or False.

1. When using SCSI, the location of the hard drive on the data cable determines the SCSI ID. True / False
2. LUN and SCSI ID are two terms for the same thing. True / False
3. All devices connected to a SCSI bus must communicate with the SCSI host adapter to function properly. True / False
4. Some SCSI host adapters allow SCSI 2 and Ultra SCSI devices to utilize the same SCSI bus. True / False
5. Describe the role of a SCSI host adapter.

____

____

____

____

____

6. What is the difference between Wide and Narrow SCSI?

____

____

____

____

____

Lab 7.4 Using SCSI and IDE Together (Understanding Boot Priority)

Objective

The objective of this lab exercise is to configure your lab workstation to utilize both a SCSI and an IDE hard drive together. After completing this lab exercise, you will be able to:

- Configure a PC to operate SCSI and IDE hard drives together.
- Describe and resolve the unique problems that occur when SCSI and IDE technologies are used together.

Materials Required

- Operating system: any or none
- Lab workgroup size: 2–4 students
- Configuration type: simple SCSI

Simple SCSI Configuration

- 90 Mhz or better Pentium-compatible computer
- 16 MB of RAM
- 540 MB SCSI hard drive
- 1 NIC (Network Interface Card)

Additional Devices

- An IDE hard drive (any size)
- A DOS boot disk with the FDISK utility

Lab Setup & Safety Tips

- Always unplug the power cord and properly ground yourself before touching any component inside a computer.

Activity

Determine the CMOS type

1. Power on your lab workstation and enter the CMOS setup program.
2. Move through the menus and search for a **Boot Priority** option. Some computers don't have a boot priority menu. If your lab workstation doesn't have a Boot Priority menu, skip the following step sequence, "Configuring the Boot Priority Menu."

Configuring the Boot Priority Menu (if available)

1. While in the CMOS Setup program, configure the Boot Priority to the following:
   a. Network or remote boot
   b. Removable drives
   c. SCSI host adapter
   d. Integrated IDE
2. Although the exact phrase and options might not match the Boot Priority option in Step 1, it is important for this lab exercise that the SCSI bus has a higher Boot Priority than the IDE channel.
3. Save the changes and exit the CMOS Setup program.

Installing the IDE hard drive

1. Power off the lab workstation and unplug the power cord.
2. Remove the case from the lab workstation.
3. Configure the IDE hard drive to **Master**.
4. Install the IDE hard drive on the Primary IDE channel (Channel 0).
5. Plug in the power connector.
6. Replace the case.
7. Power on the lab workstation and enter the CMOS Setup program.
8. Verify that the Primary IDE channel is enabled (Channel 0) and that the hard drive has been detected properly.
9. Save and exit, and then power off the lab workstation.

Viewing the new configuration

1. Insert the DOS boot disk and power on the lab workstation.
2. At the **A:\>** prompt, type **FDISK** and press **Return**.
3. Press **5** to select the Change current fixed disk option.
4. Record the size of each fixed drive and circle the type (that is, SCSI or IDE):

   Drive 0 [SCSI] or [IDE] ______________________________

   Drive 1 [SCSI] or [IDE] ______________________________

Lab Notes

Boot Priority—The term Boot Priority refers to the order in which the computer attempts to start from attached bootable devices. For example, a typical PC configuration is to grant the removable drives (floppy disks and CD-ROMs) the highest boot priority. When the computer starts, it first attempts to boot from the floppy disk drive and other removable drives before it attempts to boot from the hard drive. In many modern computers, the Boot Priority can be configured through the CMOS Setup program. This is not always the case with older computers.

Does IDE always start before SCSI?—If the computer doesn't have a boot priority option in its CMOS setup screens to allow booting of SCSI devices before IDE, you cannot boot from a SCSI device at all unless all IDE hardware is removed or disabled. Why? Because most PC BIOS code is written so that it looks for boot devices from the system CMOS settings before it even initializes any expansion slot-based adapters. Not all systems are like this. Some do have menu settings in CMOS that allow you to configure booting from SCSI before the IDE drive(s) are initialized. However, some system board manufacturers might require that you use their own SCSI host adapter to accomplish this. Check the system board's documentation, or ask the manufacturer for more information. Another thing to keep in mind is that any SCSI host adapter must have its own BIOS on-board, or have direct support from the system board's BIOS, if you expect to be able to boot the system from a SCSI device. Some inexpensive SCSI adapters, such as those that are sometimes included with CD-ROM drives or scanners, might not have their own BIOS. A SCSI BIOS is not required if you do not intend to boot the system from a SCSI device.

Lab Notes (continued)

IDE/SCSI workarounds?—If your computer boots to a SCSI drive and your OS resides on an IDE drive, you can use boot management software to allow the computer to properly start the OS on the IDE drive.

Review Questions

Circle True or False.

1. The Boot Priority menu is accessible via the CMOS Setup program. True / False
2. If you configure a SCSI drive to 0, only one other SCSI drive can be attached to the computer. True / False
3. IDE must always boot first if the computer doesn't have a Boot Priority menu. True / False
4. You cannot configure a SCSI drive to 0 when you are using both Primary and Secondary IDE channels. True / False
5. Describe the purpose of the Boot Priority menu.

____
____
____
____
____

6. Jacob's C:\ drive is a 4-GIG SCSI hard drive. He is attempting to add capacity to his computer by installing a new 8.2-GIG IDE hard drive. After installing the new IDE hard drive, the computer will no longer boot into Windows 98. Assuming that Jacob has a Boot Priority menu, describe what the problem is, and how Jacob can resolve it.

____
____
____
____
____

7

CHAPTER

8

TROUBLESHOOTING FUNDAMENTALS

LABS INCLUDED IN THIS CHAPTER

- ♦ LAB 8.1 TROUBLESHOOTING IRQ CONFLICTS
- ♦ LAB 8.2 TROUBLESHOOTING I/O ADDRESSES AND DMA
- ♦ LAB 8.3 HARD DRIVE AND FLOPPY DRIVE TROUBLESHOOTING
- ♦ LAB 8.4 TROUBLESHOOTING THE BOOT PROCESS
- ♦ LAB 8.5 BENCHMARKING YOUR PC USING THE NUTS & BOLTS SOFTWARE
- ♦ LAB 8.6 DATA RECOVERY

Lab 8.1 Troubleshooting IRQ Conflicts

Objective

The objective of this lab exercise is to familiarize you with some of the problems that arise during the installation of an input/output device. After completing this lab exercise, you will be able to:

- Install and configure an I/O expansion card.
- Explore the installation of an I/O expansion card.
- Explore IRQ conflicts.

Materials Required

- Operating system: Windows 9x
- Lab workgroup size: 2 students
- Configuration type: simple

Simple Configuration

- 90 Mhz or better Pentium-compatible computer
- 16 MB of RAM
- 540 MB hard drive
- 1 NIC (Network Interface Card)

Additional Devices

- Lab workstation must have one available ISA slot
- One ISA I/O expansion card for each lab workstation (expansion card should be jumper-configurable rather than jumperless)

Lab Setup & Safety Tips

- Always unplug the power cord and properly ground yourself before touching any component inside a computer.
- If students are working in pairs, identify one as Student 1 and the other as Student 2.
- Configure the I/O expansion card, by way of jumpers, to use COM3 and COM4.

Activity

Installing the expansion card

Student 1

1. Power off the lab workstation and unplug the power cord (it is not necessary to unplug all other cords).
2. Remove the case from the lab workstation.
3. Locate an available ISA slot.
4. Remove the end-of-slot blank.
5. Gently slide the ISA expansion card into the ISA slot; move the card from end to end until it is completely seated. *Warning:* Do not bend the card from side to side.
6. For safety, stand clear of the case, and plug in the power cord.

7. Power on the lab workstation and enter the Setup program.
8. Within the BIOS Setup program, verify that the I/O expansion is recognized by your lab workstation.
9. Exit the BIOS Setup program and reboot the computer.

Creating and observing an IRQ conflict

Student 2

1. Power off the lab workstation and remove the I/O expansion card.
2. Unplug the power cord.
3. Gently ease the I/O card out of the ISA slot.
4. Change the COM port selection jumper to COM1.
5. Gently reseat the ISA card; remember to move the card from end to end, and not side to side.
6. For safety, stand clear of the case, and plug in the power cord.
7. Power on the lab workstation and observe the results.

Lab Notes

Legacy cards—The type of I/O card used in this lab exercise is sometimes referred to as a legacy expansion card. The most commonly used I/O cards are the Plug-and-Play jumperless I/O cards.

COM Confusion—Manufacturers typically adhere to the following standard:

COM1 and COM3: IRQ 4

COM2 and COM4: IRQ 3

However, most COM ports can't share an IRQ. This usually isn't a problem because manufacturers typically don't include more than two integrated COM ports (COM 1 and COM2) with a system board or computer. To use additional COM ports, an I/O expansion can be installed.

Fundamental Rules of Troubleshooting

Approach the problem systematically—Start at the beginning and walk through the situation in a thorough, careful way. This one rule is worth its weight in gold. Remember it and apply it every time.

Divide and Conquer—This rule is the most powerful. Isolate the problem. In the overall system, remove one hardware or software component after another, until the problem is isolated to a small part of the whole system. In this book you will learn many methods of applying this rule. A few ways you can apply this rule are:

1. Remove any memory-resident programs (TSRs) to eliminate them as the problem.
2. Boot from a disk to eliminate the OS and startup files on the hard drive as the problem.
3. Remove any unnecessary hardware devices, such as a scanner card, internal modem, and even the hard drive.

Once down to the essentials, start exchanging components you know are good for those you suspect are bad, until the problem goes away.

Don't overlook the obvious—Ask simple questions. Is the computer plugged in? Is it turned on? Is the monitor plugged in? Most problem solutions are so simple that you might overlook them because you expect the problem to be difficult to solve.

Lab Notes (continued)

Check the simple things first—It is more effective to first check the components that are easiest to replace. For example, if the video does not work, the problem might be with the monitor or the video card. When faced with the decision of which one to exchange first, choose the easy route: exchange the monitor before the video card.

Make no assumptions—This rule is the hardest one to follow, because there is a tendency to trust anything in writing and assume that people are telling you exactly what happened.

Become a researcher—Following this rule can be the most fun. When a computer problem arises that you can't easily solve, be as tenacious as a bulldog. Read, make phone calls, ask questions, and then read, make more calls, and ask more questions.

Write things down—Keep good notes as you're working. They'll help you think more clearly.

Reboot and start over—This is an important rule. Fresh starts are good for people and computers and can help uncover events or steps that you might have overlooked.

Establish your priorities—This rule can help make for a satisfied customer. Decide what your first priority is. For example, it might be to recover lost data, or to get the PC back up and running as soon as possible.

Don't assume the worst—When it's an emergency and your only copy of data is on a hard drive that is not working, don't assume that the data is lost.

Know your starting point—Before trying to solve a computer problem, know for certain that the problem is what the user says it is.

Review Questions

Circle True or False.

1. COM port settings are always modified using the CMOS Setup program. True / False
2. A COM port won't work properly when it is sharing an IRQ with another COM port. True / False
3. COM4 always uses IRQ 7. True / False
4. COM2 defaults to IRQ 3. True / False
5. If more than two COM ports are required, an expansion card can be installed to provide additional functionality. True / False
6. Describe how an IRQ conflict occurs.

____

____

____

____

____

7. What is an I/O expansion card?

____

____

____

____

____

8. Briefly describe, in your own words, each fundamental rule of PC troubleshooting.

LAB 8.2 TROUBLESHOOTING I/O ADDRESSES AND DMA

Objective

The objective of this lab is to provide you with experience troubleshooting I/O and DMA conflicts. After completing this lab exercise, you will be able to:

- Explain the importance of unique addresses.
- Identify and resolve any I/O address conflicts.
- Identify and resolve any DMA conflicts.
- Install a network interface card.

Materials Required

- Operating system: Windows 9x
- Lab workgroup size: 2–4 students
- Configuration type: simple

Simple Configuration

- 90 Mhz or better Pentium-compatible computer
- 16 MB of RAM
- 540 MB hard drive
- 1 NIC (Network Interface Card)

Additional Devices

- Documentation for the network interface card, including jumper settings

Lab Setup & Safety Tips

- This lab assumes that the NIC is not installed in the computer.
- Always unplug the power cord and properly ground yourself before touching any component inside a computer.

ACTIVITY

Creating the I/O address conflict

Your instructor will tell you at which I/O address you will be creating a conflict.

1. Start your lab workstation, and allow it to boot into Windows 9x.
2. Click the **Start** button.
3. Point to **Settings**.
4. Click **Control Panel**.
5. Double-click the **System** icon.
6. Click the **Device Manager** tab.
7. Click the **Properties** button.
8. Click the **Input/output (I/O)** option button.
9. Observe the current device configurations of the predetermined I/O address.

10. Record the name and I/O address of the device for which you have been instructed to create a resource conflict. ____
11. Click the **Cancel** button.
12. Close **Device Manager** and shut down Windows. Power off the lab workstation.
13. Verify that you are properly grounded.
14. Unplug the power cord from the system unit.
15. Remove the top of the case.
16. Locate the available slot where you plan to install the network interface card.
17. Using the provided documentation, verify that the network interface card is configured to use the predetermined I/O address and an available IRQ.
18. Gently install the network interface card into the slot. *Warning:* Don't bend the card from side to side; move the card only back and forth from end to end.
19. Screw the mounting screw into place.
20. Replace the top of the case.
21. Plug in the system unit.
22. Power on the lab workstation, and allow it to boot into Windows 9x.

(Only if the workstation fails to boot)

1. Power off the computer.
2. Wait five seconds and power the computer back on.
3. When prompted, choose the **Safe Mode** menu option using the arrow keys and press **Enter**.

Observing the I/O conflict

1. Click the **Start** button.
2. Point to **Settings**.
3. Click **Control Panel**.
4. Double-click the **System** icon.
5. Click the **Device Manager** tab.
6. Double-click the icon of the installed network card.
7. Click the **Resources** tab.
8. Observe the conflicting device list.
9. Click the **Cancel** button.
10. Close **Device Manager** and shut down Windows.

Resolving the I/O conflict

Your instructor will provide you with an available I/O address.

1. Unplug the power cord from the system unit.
2. Remove the top of the case.
3. Locate the network interface card.
4. Using the provided documentation, configure the network interface card to use the I/O address specified by your instructor.

5. Replace the top of the case.
6. Plug in the system unit.
7. Power on the lab workstation, and allow it to boot into Windows 9x.
8. If the workstation fails to boot properly, power cycle the PC, and, when prompted, choose **Safe Mode**.

Creating the DMA conflict

Your instructor will tell you at which DMA channel you will be creating a conflict.

1. Click the **Start** button.
2. Point to **Settings**.
3. Click **Control Panel**.
4. Double-click the **System** icon.
5. Click the **Device Manager** tab.
6. Click the **Properties** button.
7. Click the **Direct memory access (DMA)** option button.
8. Record the name and DMA channel of the device for which you have been instructed to create a resource conflict: ______________________________
9. Click the **Cancel** button.
10. Close **Device Manager** and shut down Windows.
11. Verify that you are properly grounded.
12. Unplug the power cord from the system unit.
13. Remove the top of the case.
14. Locate the NIC (Network Interface Card) from the last activity.
15. Using the provided documentation, configure the network interface card to use a DMA channel that will conflict with a device specified by your instructor.
16. Replace the top of the case.
17. Plug in the system unit.
18. Power on the lab workstation, and allow it to boot into Windows 9x.
19. If the workstation fails to boot properly, power cycle the PC, and, when prompted, choose **Safe Mode**.

Observing the DMA conflict

1. Click the **Start** button.
2. Point to **Settings**.
3. Click **Control Panel**.
4. Double-click the **System** icon.
5. Click the **Device Manager** tab.
6. Double-click the icon of the installed network card.
7. Click the **Resources** tab.
8. Observe the conflicting device list.

9. Click the **Cancel** button.
10. Close **Device Manager** and shut down Windows.

Resolving the DMA conflict

Your instructor will provide you with an available DMA channel.

1. Unplug the power cord from the system unit.
2. Remove the top of the case.
3. Locate the network interface card.
4. Using the provided documentation, configure the network interface card to use the DMA channel specified by your instructor.
5. Replace the top of the case.
6. Plug in the system unit.
7. Power on the lab workstation, and allow it to boot into Windows 9x.
8. If the workstation fails to boot properly, power cycle the PC, and, when prompted, choose **Safe Mode**.

Lab Notes

Resource Conflicts—As you have seen, symptoms of resource conflicts, such as those that you created in the previous activities, will vary. However, the key to troubleshooting conflicts is to follow The Fundamental Rules of Troubleshooting and use tools such as Device Manager to identify and resolve problems.

Review Questions

Circle True or False.

1. Only two devices at a time can use an I/O address. True / False
2. Every device attached to a computer requires a DMA address. True / False
3. An I/O address "resource conflict" occurs when two devices attempt to use the same I/O address. True / False
4. An I/O address is a physical location on the hard drive where the CPU stores data. True / False
5. All PCs have 3 DMA channels. True / False
6. Describe the difference between an I/O address and a DMA channel.

____

____

____

____

____

Lab 8.3 Hard Drive and Floppy Drive Troubleshooting

Objective

The objective of this lab exercise is to develop hard drive and floppy drive troubleshooting skills. After completing this lab exercise, you will be able to:

- Troubleshoot a PC floppy drive configuration.
- Troubleshoot a PC hard drive configuration.
- Describe and implement the troubleshooting process.

Materials Required

- Operating system: Windows 9x
- Lab workgroup size: 2–4 students
- Configuration type: simple

Simple Configuration

- 90 Mhz or better Pentium-compatible computer
- 16 MB of RAM
- 540 MB hard drive
- 1 NIC (Network Interface Card)

Additional Devices: None

Lab Setup & Safety Tips

- Always unplug the power cord and properly ground yourself before touching any component inside a computer.
- If students are working in pairs, identify one as Student 1 and the other as Student 2.

Activity

Creating problem 1

Student 1

While Student 2 is away from the lab workstation, proceed with the following steps:

1. Power off the lab workstation and unplug the power cord (it is not necessary to unplug all other cords).
2. Remove the case from the lab workstation.
3. Locate the hard drive.
4. Unplug the IDE cable and the power connector from the hard drive.
5. Replace the case.
6. Plug in the power cord.

Troubleshooting and resolving problem 1

Student 2

After Student 1 has reconfigured the lab workstation, power on the workstation, answer the following questions, and then repair the lab workstation.

Are there any error messages? If so, write them down.

What is the problem? Be specific.

List several possible solutions.

Test your theory (solution) and record the results.

How did you discover the problem?

What could you do differently in the future to improve your troubleshooting process?

Creating problem 2

Student 2

While Student 1 is away from the lab workstation, proceed with the following steps:

1. Power off the lab workstation and unplug the power cord (it is not necessary to unplug all other cords).
2. Remove the case from the lab workstation.
3. Locate the floppy drive.
4. Unplug the floppy drive data cable from the system board.
5. Reverse the floppy drive data cable and plug it back into the system board.
6. Replace the case.
7. Plug in the power cord.

Troubleshooting and resolving problem 2

Student 1

After Student 2 has reconfigured the lab workstation, power on the workstation, answer the following questions, and then repair the lab workstation.

Are there any error messages? If so, write them down.

____

____

____

____

____

What is the problem? Be specific.

____

____

____

____

____

List several possible solutions.

____

____

____

____

____

Test your theory (solution) and record the results.

____

____

____

____

____

How did you discover the problem?

____
____
____
____
____

What could you do differently in the future to improve your troubleshooting process?

____
____
____
____
____

TIP

Lab Notes

The six steps of the troubleshooting process are:

1. Let the customer explain the problem.
2. Search for answers.
3. Develop a hypothesis.
4. Test your theory.
5. Resolve the problem and explain your changes to the customer.
6. Complete proper documentation.

What is troubleshooting documentation?—Troubleshooting documentation includes any documentation required by your employer and/or your own collection of notes and files.

The "No Operating System Found" error message—The PC cannot find the hard disk or the hard disk is not formatted. For more information about other error messages, refer to Appendix A of this lab book.

Review Questions

Circle True or False.

1. Hardware configuration changes can cause CMOS errors because the setup information doesn't agree with the actual hardware configuration. True / False
2. While you are troubleshooting a problem, it is best to make only one change at a time. True / False
3. The error message "No Operating System found" normally indicates that the computer's hard drive isn't formatted or could not be found. True / False
4. List three of the six troubleshooting steps below.

____
____
____
____
____

5. Describe how a floppy drive will behave if it is not plugged in correctly.

6. Write a hardware troubleshooting question (use any hardware component). There must be only one correct answer.

LAB 8.4 TROUBLESHOOTING THE BOOT PROCESS

Objective

The objective of this lab exercise is to develop your troubleshooting skills and master the PC boot process. After completing this lab exercise, you will be able to:

- Successfully troubleshoot the boot process for a PC configuration.
- Describe and implement the troubleshooting process, and explain how it pertains to the PC boot process.

Materials Required

- Operating system: Windows 9x
- Lab workgroup size: 2–4 students
- Configuration type: typical

Typical Configuration

- 166 Mhz or better Pentium-compatible computer
- 24 MB of RAM
- 800 MB hard drive
- CD-ROM Drive
- 1 NIC (Network Interface Card)

Additional Devices: None

Lab Setup & Safety Tips

- If students are working in pairs, identify one as Student 1 and the other as Student 2.
- Always unplug the power cord and properly ground yourself before touching any component inside a computer.

ACTIVITY

Creating problem 1

Student 1

While Student 2 is away from the lab workstation, proceed with the following steps:

1. Power off the lab workstation and unplug the power cord (it is not necessary to unplug all other cords).
2. Remove the case from the lab workstation.
3. Unplug the P8 and P9 connectors from the system board.
4. Replace the case.
5. Plug in the power cord.

Troubleshooting and resolving problem 1

Student 2

After Student 1 has reconfigured the lab workstation, power on the workstation, answer the following questions, and then repair the lab workstation.

Are there any error messages? If so, write them down.

What is the problem? Be specific.

List several possible solutions.

Test your theory (solution) and record the results.

How did you discover the problem?

What could you do differently in the future to improve your troubleshooting process?

Creating problem 2

Student 2

While Student 1 is away from the lab workstation, proceed with the following steps:

1. Power off the lab workstation and unplug the power cord (it is not necessary to unplug all other cords).
2. Remove the case from the lab workstation.
3. Locate the hard drive.
4. Move the jumper of the hard drive to the Slave position.
5. Replace the case.
6. Plug in the power cord.

Troubleshooting and resolving problem 2

Student 1

After Student 2 has reconfigured the lab workstation, power on the workstation, answer the following questions, and then repair the lab workstation.

Are there any error messages? If so, write them down.

____

____

____

____

____

What is the problem? Be specific.

____

____

____

____

____

List several possible solutions.

____

____

____

____

____

Test your theory (solution) and record the results.

____

____

____

____

____

How did you discover the problem?

____

____

____

____

____

What could you do differently in the future to improve your troubleshooting process?

____

____

____

____

____

TIP

Lab Notes

Which way should the P8 and P9 connectors be attached?—When connecting the P8 and P9 power connectors, remember that the ground, or the black, wires should always face each other.

How do I improve my troubleshooting skills?—Troubleshooting is a skill that takes time and experience to develop. Exercises such as the one in this lab will help you improve your troubleshooting skills by providing you experience without the pressure of a customer's expectations. When you see a new error message, rather than avoiding the problem, become a relentless investigator and search for the answer. Your troubleshooting skills and experience will grow exponentially from the process of your investigations.

What does POST stand for?—POST is an acronym for Power On Self Test. This is the time during the boot process when the BIOS tests all essential hardware.

Review Questions

Circle True or False.

1. Although PC problems vary, the methodology to troubleshooting tends to stay the same. True / False
2. If a problem is detected during POST, the BIOS normally returns an error message. True / False
3. If a problem is detected during POST, it most likely is software related. True / False
4. POST stands for ____________ ____________ ____________ ____________.
5. Describe the symptoms of an unplugged hard drive.

____

____

____

____

____

BENCHMARKING YOUR PC USING THE NUTS & BOLTS SOFTWARE

Objective

The objective of this lab exercise is to benchmark your lab workstation. After completing this lab exercise, you will be able to:

- Benchmark a personal computer's hardware components.
- Use the Nuts & Bolts software package to run hardware diagnostics.

Materials Required

- Operating system: Windows 9x
- Lab workgroup size: 2 students
- Configuration type: typical

Typical Configuration

- 166 Mhz or better Pentium-compatible computer
- 24 MB of RAM
- 800 MB hard drive
- CD-ROM Drive
- 1 NIC (Network Interface Card)

Additional Devices

- A copy of the Nuts & Bolts software, which is included with the textbook, for each group of students

Lab Setup & Safety Tips

- Each lab workstation should have the Nuts & Bolts software installed and functioning properly.

ACTIVITY

Benchmarking your CPU

1. Power on your lab workstation and allow it to boot into Windows 9x.
2. Click the **Start** button.
3. Click the **Nuts & Bolts** icon.
4. Click the **Discover Pro** icon.
5. Select the **System** tab.
6. Record the following information about your CPU:

   Model ______________________________

   Stepping ______________________________

   L1 cache ______________________________

   L2 cache ______________________________

   Speed in Mhz ______________________________

LAB 8.

6. Write a scenario question using the following information:

   Allan the PC technician

   Linda the customer

   Amanda the senior technician

   Problem: Linda's CMOS battery has failed.

   Your scenario question must involve all three characters, describe th problem, and have only one correct answer.

   ____

   ____

   ____

   ____

   ____

   ____

   ____

   ____

   ____

   ____

   ____

   ____

   ____

   ____

   ____

La
Activ

Benchmarking your hard drive

1. Click the **Start** button.
2. Click the **Nuts & Bolts** icon.
3. Click the **Discover Pro** icon.
4. Select the **Benchmarks** tab.
5. Record the following:

   Transfer rates in MB/Second ______________________________

   Average seek time in Msec ______________________________

Running diagnostics

1. Click the **Start** button.
2. Click the **Nuts & Bolts** icon.
3. Click the **Discover Pro** icon.
4. Select the **Diagnostic** tab.
5. Observe the results.

Lab Notes

What is Nuts & Bolts?—The Nuts & Bolts software included with your textbook is a third-party software package designed to help you troubleshoot and benchmark your PC.

Review Questions

Circle True or False.

1. L1 cache and L2 cache are both housed within the CPU. True / False
2. L2 cache is housed inside the processor. True / False
3. CPU speed is measured in megahertz. True / False
4. The Nuts & Bolts software always uses a diagnostic card to test a PC's components. True / False
5. The hard drive seek time is the amount of time it takes your hard drive to locate a particular data cluster, and is normally measured in milliseconds. True / False
6. Write a scenario question that utilizes the Nuts & Bolts software to identify a computer's hardware problem. Answer the question with a description of how to use the diagnostic mode of the Nuts & Bolts software.

LAB 8.6 DATA RECOVERY

Objective

The objective of this lab exercise is to provide hands-on experience recovering files in the Windows 9x environment. After completing this lab exercise, you will be able to:

- Describe how Windows 9x deletes files.
- Describe how the FAT file system deletes files.
- Use the undelete command to recover files from the FAT file system.

Materials Required

- Operating system: Windows 9x
- Lab workgroup size: 2–4 students
- Configuration type: simple

Simple Configuration

- 90 Mhz or better Pentium-compatible computer
- 16 MB of RAM
- 540 MB hard drive
- 1 NIC (Network Interface Card)

Additional Devices

- A DOS boot disk with the UNDELETE command

Lab Setup & Safety Tips

- The UNDELETE.EXE file can be found in any full installation of DOS 6.2. (UNDELETE.EXE is not included in Windows 9x.)
- *Warning:* The following Activity requires an empty Recycle Bin.
- This lab exercise has been designed for use with the FAT file system. FAT32 and other file systems are not compatible with the following Activity.

ACTIVITY

Empty the Recycle Bin

1. Power on the lab workstation and allow it to boot into the Windows environment.
2. Right-click the **Recycle Bin** icon.
3. Click **Empty Recycle Bin** from the menu.
4. Click **Yes** if you are prompted to confirm a file deletion.

Create a text file on the Desktop

1. Right-click the **Desktop**.
2. Point to **New**, and then click **Text Document**.
3. Type **MyFile** and press **Enter**.

4. Double-click the **MyFile** icon.
5. In the Notepad window, type **This is the MyFile text file text**.
6. Click the **File** menu, and then click **Save**.
7. Click the **File** menu, and then click **Exit**.

Delete MyFile

1. Right-click the **MyFile** icon.
2. Click **Delete** on the menu.
3. Click **Yes** when prompted to confirm the file deletion.

Restore MyFile from the Recycle Bin

1. Double-click the **Recycle Bin** icon.
2. In the Recycle Bin window, single-click **MyFile** to highlight it.
3. While MyFile is highlighted, click the **File** menu.
4. Click **Restore**.
5. Click the **File** menu, and click **Close**.

Delete MyFile

1. Right-click the **MyFile** icon.
2. Click **Delete** on the menu.
3. Click **Yes** when prompted to confirm the file deletion.

Empty the Recycle Bin

1. Right-click the **Recycle Bin** icon.
2. Click **Empty Recycle Bin** from the menu.
3. Click **Yes** if you are prompted to confirm a file deletion.

Recover MyFile from the emptied Recycle Bin

1. Insert the DOS boot disk and reboot your lab workstation.
2. Allow your lab workstation to boot from the DOS boot disk.
3. Type **C:** and press the **Enter** key.
4. Type **CD RECYCLED** and press the **Enter** key.
5. Type **LOCK** and press the **Enter** key.
6. Press the **Y** key and and press **Enter** when prompted by the lock command.
7. Type **A:\UNDELETE C:\RECYCLED*.txt** and press **Enter**.
8. Press the **Y** key to confirm restoration when prompted by the undelete command.
9. Type **M** when prompted to provide a first letter for the restored file.
10. Type **N** if you are prompted to restore additional text files.

8

Verify MyFile data

1. Type **DIR** and press **Enter**.
2. In the directory listing you will see one file that begins with the letter "M." Although it might not be named MyFile.txt, this file that begins with the letter "M" is actually the correct file. It will have a different name because when it was deleted, Windows renamed the file.
3. Type **TYPE C:\RECYCLED*NEWNAME.TXT***, where *NEWNAME.TXT* is the filename from the directory listing, and then press **Enter**.

Lab Notes

The UNDELETE Command—The UNDELETE command attempts to recover files that have been deleted. Following are some variations of the UNDELETE command:

To list the files that can be undeleted, without actually undeleting them, use the following command: A:\>UNDELETE /list

To recover deleted files without prompting for confirmation on each file, use the following command: A:\>UNDELETE /all

Where is the Recycle Bin directory?—When a file or directory is moved to the Recycle Bin, Windows moves the data to a hidden directory named RECYCLED. There is a RECYCLED directory located at the root of every logical drive.

What happens when a file is deleted in Windows?—In the Windows environment, when a file is deleted, it is simply moved to the Recycle Bin and stored there for actual deletion at a later time. To actually delete the file(s), one must use the Empty Recycle Bin option. Note that this does not hold true if the Recycle Bin has been configured to delete incoming files. If that is the case, the act of deleting one or more files will indeed delete them immediately.

What happens when a file is deleted from the FAT?—When a file is deleted from the FAT, the operating system simply renames the first character of the file and updates the file allocation table.

How does UNDELETE work?—The DOS Undelete command restores files by locating a recently deleted file and its associated starting cluster, and then renaming the first character of the file and updating the file allocation table. *Warning:* The Undelete command is successful only when the deleted file has not been overwritten by new data; therefore, data recovery is typically more successful when attempted immediately after a file has been deleted.

Third-party applications—Although Undelete can be used to recover files from the FAT file system, it isn't compatible with other file systems (FAT32 and NTFS). However, there are some third-party utilities available that can accomplish data recovery from various file systems.

Review Questions

Circle True or False.

1. All Windows 9x computer have only one Recycled directory. True / False
2. Using the Recycle Bin restore feature will return a file or directory to its original location. True / False
3. Undelete is included with the Windows 9x operating system. True / False
4. Undelete can restore only text files. True / False
5. Why is it important to attempt file recovery immediately after a file is deleted?

   ____

   ____

   ____

   ____

   ____

6. From the operating system's perspective, briefly summarize the life cycle of MyFile.txt.

   ____

   ____

   ____

   ____

   ____

CHAPTER

9

SUPPORTING I/O DEVICES

LABS INCLUDED IN THIS CHAPTER

- ♦ LAB 9.1 SERIAL PORT CONFLICT RESOLUTION
- ♦ LAB 9.2 PARALLEL PORT CONFLICT RESOLUTION
- ♦ LAB 9.3 SCSI ADAPTER INSTALLATION
- ♦ LAB 9.4 SCSI CHAIN CONFLICT RESOLUTION

Lab 9.1 Serial Port Conflict Resolution

Objective

Serial port conflicts commonly occur when an internal modem is installed in a PC. You can approach troubleshooting these conflicts in several ways, depending on the environment. This lab exercise shows you how to properly troubleshoot a serial port conflict in the Windows 9x environment. After completing this lab exercise, you will be able to:

- Define a serial port conflict.
- Describe the symptoms of a serial port conflict.
- Use the Device Manager to discover which device is conflicting with the serial port.
- Resolve serial port conflicts.

Materials Required

- Operating system: Windows 9x
- Lab workgroup size: 2–4 students
- Configuration type: typical

Typical Configuration

- 166 Mhz or better Pentium-compatible computer
- 24 MB of RAM
- 800 MB hard drive
- CD-ROM Drive
- 1 NIC (Network Interface Card)

Additional Devices

- One jumper-configurable internal modem, including documentation for the internal modem's jumper settings (a phone line is not necessary)
- At least one COM port must be configured and functioning properly

Lab Setup & Safety Tips

- Each lab workstation should have an internal modem installed and functioning properly.
- Each lab workstation's modem should be configured to use COM2.
- Each lab workstation should be configured to use COM1.
- Always unplug the power cord and properly ground yourself before touching any component inside a computer.

Activity

Creating and observing the conflict

1. Power off the lab workstation.
2. Unplug the power cord.
3. Remove the case from the lab workstation.
4. Locate the modem.

5. Using the documentation provided, change the modem jumper settings from COM2 to COM1.
6. Replace the case and plug in the power cord.
7. Power on your lab workstation and allow it to boot into Windows 9x. Note that depending on the type of system, you might receive an error message during the POST. Observe any error messages and continue booting the system by following the instructions on the screen.
8. Click the **Start** button, point to **Settings**, then click **Control Panel**.
9. Double-click the **System** icon.
10. Click the **Device Manager** tab.
11. Look for yellow exclamation points located on top of COM1 and the modem icon. If you see the yellow exclamation points, you have successfully created a resource conflict between the two devices.

Resolving the conflict

You can resolve this conflict in several ways. The needs of the user will determine the best method. For example, you already know that you can easily resolve this conflict simply by changing the modem jumper settings back to the original settings. Another solution would be to disable or reassign the COM port's resources.

Reassigning or disabling the COM port's resources

1. Reboot your lab workstation.
2. Enter the BIOS Setup program.
3. Locate the serial configuration section.
4. Change your serial port configuration from COM2 to Disabled.
5. Save the changes and reboot the lab workstation.

Note the default port assignments in Table 9-1 and remember that not all serial ports are configurable through the BIOS. If the COM port configuration is not available through the BIOS Setup program of your lab workstation, ask your instructor for the I/O card configuration.

Table 9-1 Default port assignments on many computers

Port	IRQ	I/O Address (in Hex)	Type
COM1	IRQ 4	03F8 – 3FF	Serial
COM2	IRQ 3	02F8 – 2FF	Serial
COM3	IRQ 4	03E8 – 3EF	Serial
COM4	IRQ 3	02E8 – 2EF	Serial
LPT1	IRQ 7	0378 – 37F	Parallel
LPT2	IRQ 5	0278 – 27F	Parallel

Lab Notes

Note that in some of the more severe cases, a PC completely freezes when a serial port conflict occurs.

Viewing device resources—You can use the Device Manager to view resource settings by double-clicking the device icon.

Are there yellow exclamation points in the Device Manager?—When the Device Manager displays a yellow exclamation point over a device, it means that the device is conflicting with another device.

Review Questions

Circle True or False.

1. The Device Manager can be found by opening the Control Panel and then double-clicking the Network icon. True / False
2. All serial ports can be configured using the BIOS Setup program. True / False
3. Serial ports can conflict only with modems. True / False
4. To what IRQ does COM4 default?

   ____

5. Describe how to view the IRQ of a device using the Device Manager.

   ____

   ____

   ____

   ____

   ____

6. You are the desktop PC support technician for the Good Job Corporation. Janet, one of your customers, suspects that she has a resource conflict between her newly installed modem and one of the serial ports on her laptop. Describe how you would use the Device Manager to confirm or eliminate her suspicions.

   ____

   ____

   ____

   ____

   ____

Lab 9.2 Parallel Port Conflict Resolution

Objective

Parallel port conflicts commonly occur when a sound card is installed into a PC. In this lab exercise, you examine the process of locating and resolving a parallel port conflict. After completing this lab exercise, you will be able to:

- Define a parallel port conflict.
- Describe the symptoms of a parallel port conflict.
- Use the Device Manager to discover which device is causing the parallel port conflict.
- Resolve parallel port conflicts.

Materials Required

- Operating system: Windows 9x
- Lab workgroup size: 2–4 students
- Configuration type: simple

Simple Configuration

- 90 Mhz or better Pentium-compatible computer
- 16 MB of RAM
- 540 MB hard drive
- 1 NIC (Network Interface Card)

Additional Devices

- One 8- or 16-bit sound card
- At least one LPT port
- Documentation containing your sound card's jumper settings

Lab Setup & Safety Tips

- Each lab workstation should have a sound card installed and functioning properly.
- Each lab workstation's sound card should be configured to use IRQ 5.
- LPT1 should be configured to use default settings.
- Always unplug the power cord and properly ground yourself before touching any component inside a computer.

Activity

Creating and observing the conflict

1. Power off the lab workstation.
2. Unplug the power cord.
3. Remove the case from the lab workstation.
4. Locate the sound card.
5. Using the documentation provided, change the sound card jumper settings from IRQ 5 to IRQ 7.

9

6. Replace the case and plug in the power cord.
7. Power on your lab workstation and allow it to boot to Windows 9x. Note that depending on the type of system, you might receive an error message during the POST. Observe any error messages and continue to boot the system by following the instructions on the screen.
8. Click the **Start** button, point to **Settings**, and then click **Control Panel**.
9. Double-click the **System** icon.
10. Click the **Device Manager** tab.
11. Look for yellow exclamation points located on top of LPT1 and the sound card icon. If you see the yellow exclamation points, you have successfully created a resource conflict between the two devices.

Resolving the conflict

You can resolve a parallel port conflict in several ways. Like serial conflicts, you also can resolve a parallel conflict simply by disabling the parallel port. Under most circumstances, however, you cannot disable the parallel port because the user needs it for the printer. This leaves you with two options. One is to reassign the resources of the conflicting device, and the other is to reassign the resources of the parallel port.

Reassigning or disabling the parallel port's resources

1. Reboot your lab workstation.
2. Enter the BIOS Setup program, as shown in Figure 9-1.

ROM PCI/ISA BIOS (<<P2B>>)
CHIPSET FEATURES SETUP
AWARD SOFTWARE, INC.

SDRAM CONFIGURATION	: By SPD	Onboard FDC Controller	: Enabled
SDRAM CAS Latency	: 2T	Onboard FDC Swap A & B	: No Swap
SDRAM RAS to CAS Delay	: 3T	Onboard Serial Port 1	: 3F8H/IRQ4
SDRAM RAS Precharge Time	: 3T	Onboard Serial Port 2	: 2F8H/IRQ3
DRAM Idle Timer	: 16T	Onboard Parallel Port	: 378H/IRQ7
SDRAM MA Wait State	: Normal	Parallel Port Mode	: ECP-EPP
Snoop Ahead	: Enabled	ECP DMA Select	: 3
Host Bus Fast Data Ready	: Enabled	VART2 Use Infrared	: Disabled
16-bit I/O Recovery Time	: 1 BUSCLK	Onboard PCI IDE Enable	: Both
8-bit I/O Recovery Time	: 1 BUSCLK	IDE Ultra DMA Mode	: Auto
Graphics Aperture Size	: 64MB	IDE0 Master PIO/DMA Mode	: Auto
Video Memory Cache Mode	: UC	IDE0 Slave PIO/DMA Mode	: Auto
PCI 2.1 Support	: Enabled	IDE1 Master PIO/DMA Mode	: Auto
Memory Hole At 15W-16W	: Disabled	IDE1 Slave PIO/DMA Mode	: Auto
DRAM are 64 (Not 72) bits wide			
Data Integrity Mode	: Non-ECC		

ESC	: Quit	↑↓→←:	Select Item
F1	: Help	PU/PD/-/- :	Modify
F5	: Old Values	(Shift)F2 :	Color
F6	: Load BIOS Defaults		
F7	: Load Setup Defaults		

Figure 9-1 CMOS setup screen for chipset features

3. Locate the parallel configuration section.
4. Change your parallel port resources settings to IRQ 5, and be sure to use a different I/O address.
5. Save the changes and reboot the lab workstation.

Verifying the resource conflict has been resolved

1. Power on your lab workstation and allow it to boot into Windows 9x.
2. Click the **Start** button, point to **Settings**, and then click **Control Panel**.
3. Double-click the **System** icon.
4. Click the **Device Manager** tab.
5. Double-click **Ports**.
6. Double-click **LPT1**.
7. Click the **Resources** tab.

Note that the IRQ and I/O settings now read what you previously chose in the BIOS Setup program.

8. Click the **Cancel** button.
9. Double-click **Sound**, **video**, and **game controllers**.
10. Double-click the **sound card** icon.
11. Click the **Resources** tab.
12. Observe the IRQ and I/O settings of the sound card.

Note: Not all parallel ports can be configured through the BIOS. If the parallel port configuration is not available through the BIOS Setup program of your lab workstation, ask your instructor for the proper configuration.

Lab Notes

COM port assignment vs. LPT assignment—Unlike COM ports, parallel ports do not allow you to simply change the LPT number from LPT1 to LPT2 and maintain the same system resources. You can assign a COM port number (1, 2, 3, 4) to any I/O address and IRQ that are reserved for COM use. However, the BIOS assigns a parallel port its LPT number (1, 2, 3) in the order of highest I/O address first.

Do parallel ports work only on printers?—Parallel communication was originally intended for use with printers only. However, because parallel port communication is faster than serial communication, it is commonly used for fast data transfers over short distances. To accomplish this sort of data transfer, a bidirectional parallel port is used.

EPP (enhanced parallel port)—An EPP is parallel port that allows data to flow in both directions (bi-directional port) and is faster than original parallel ports on PCs that allow communication in only one direction.

Review Questions

Circle True or False.

1. Parallel ports are assigned an LPT number (LPT 1) by the BIOS. True / False
2. Parallel ports do not need an IRQ. True / False
3. You can have only one parallel port per computer. True / False
4. Serial ports commonly conflict with parallel ports. True / False
5. Briefly describe how parallel ports are assigned LPT numbers.

____

____

____

____

____

6. You are working on a PC that has the parallel port built into the system board. You are about to install a new sound card that will use IRQ 7. Describe the steps you need to take to avoid an IRQ conflict with the sound card.

____

____

____

____

____

Lab 9.3 SCSI Adapter Installation

Objective

The objective of this lab exercise is to properly install and configure a SCSI host adapter. After completing this lab exercise, you will be able to:

- Properly install a SCSI host adapter.
- Describe several ways to use SCSI host adapters.
- Use the Device Manager to view a SCSI host adapter's resources.
- Describe the difference between the SCSI BIOS Setup program and the system CMOS Setup program.

Materials Required

- Operating system: Windows 9x
- Lab workgroup size: 2–4 students
- Configuration type: simple

Simple Configuration

- 90 Mhz or better Pentium-compatible computer
- 16 MB of RAM
- 540 MB hard drive
- 1 NIC (Network Interface Card)

Additional Devices

- One SCSI host adapter for each lab workstation
- Several disks containing the necessary Windows 9x drivers for each SCSI card
- Documentation containing your SCSI card's jumper settings

Lab Setup & Safety Tips

- The instructor will provide the students with the proper resource settings for their lab workstations.
- Always unplug the power cord and properly ground yourself before touching any component inside a computer.

Activity

Installing the SCSI host adapter

1. Power off the lab workstation.
2. Unplug the power cord.
3. Remove the case from the lab workstation.
4. Examine Figure 9-2 and then locate an available expansion slot for your SCSI host adapter.
5. Using the documentation provided, verify that your SCSI card is configured to your instructor's resource specifications.
6. Insert the SCSI card and then secure the card using a screw.

7. Replace the case and plug in the power cord.
8. Power on your lab workstation and allow it to boot to Windows 9x.
9. While Windows 9x is booting, note whether it automatically detects the new SCSI card.

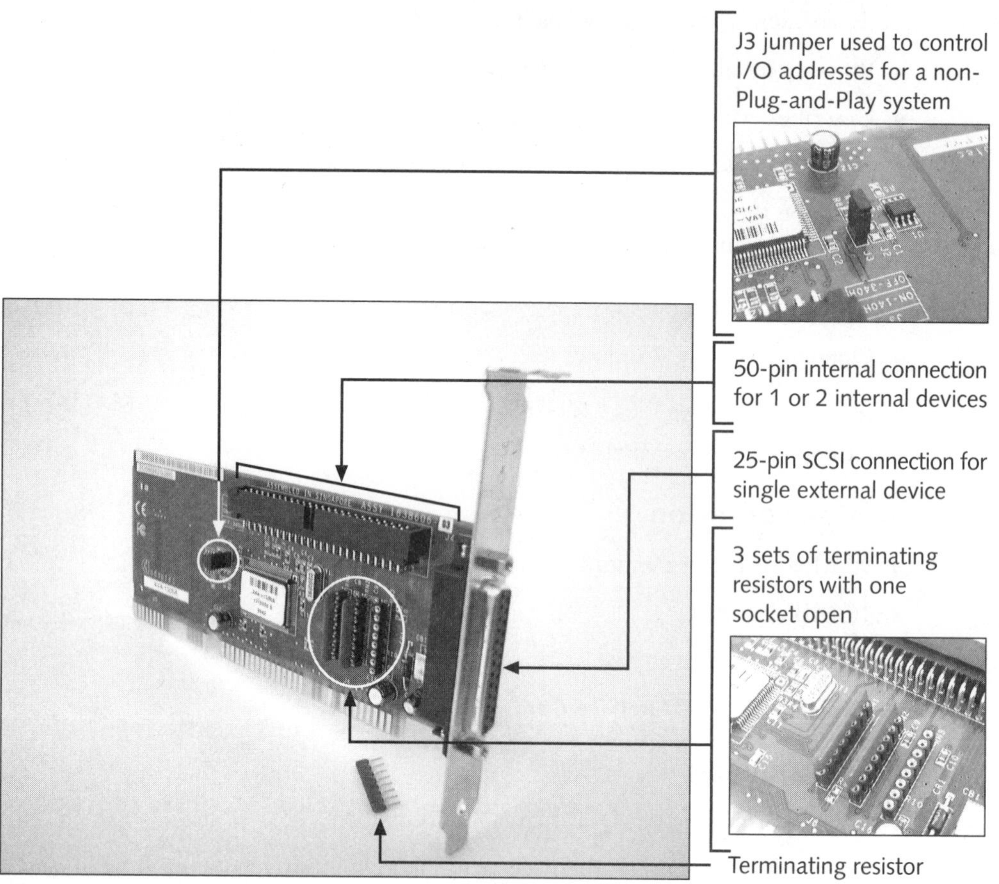

Figure 9-2 SCSI host adapter for a single external and multiple internal devices

If Windows 9x detects the SCSI card and prompts you for the drivers

1. Insert the driver disk.
2. Click the **Drivers provided by the hardware manufacturer** option button.
3. Click the **OK** button.
4. Click the **Browse** button to locate the drivers on the disk.
5. Click **OK**.
6. Select the driver for the SCSI card that you installed.
7. Click **OK**.
8. If you are prompted for the Windows 9x cab files, click the **Browse** button to locate them.

If Windows 9x does not detect the SCSI card

1. Click the **Start** button, point to **Settings**, and then click **Control Panel**.
2. Double-click the **Add New Hardware** icon.
3. Click the **Next** button three times to allow Windows 9x to detect the SCSI card.
4. Install the driver from the disk when prompted.

Verifying the SCSI host adapter driver installation

1. Click the **Start** button, point to **Settings**, and then click **Control Panel**.
2. Double-click the **System** icon.
3. Click the **Device Manager** tab.
4. Double-click the **SCSI Controllers** icon, as shown in Figure 9-3.
5. Verify that the SCSI host adapter driver is properly installed without any errors (there shouldn't be any yellow exclamation points).

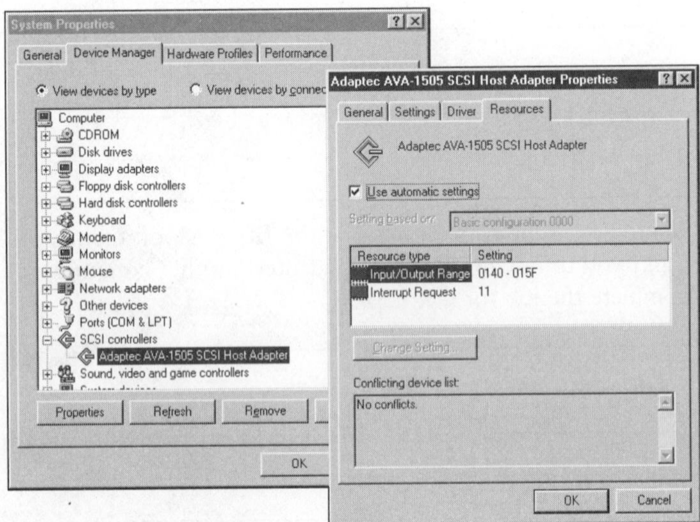

Figure 9-3 Device Manager displays the newly installed host adapter

Viewing the SCSI Setup program

1. Reboot your lab workstation. After the standard system POST is complete, you should see a SCSI BIOS screen.
2. Follow the directions on the SCSI BIOS screen and enter the SCSI CMOS Setup program.
3. Follow the directions for the SCSI BIOS and observe the options.

Lab Notes

Is SCSI an acronym?—Yes, SCSI (pronounced "scuzzy") is a acronym for Small Computer System Interface.

Different types of SCSI host adapters—There are several types of SCSI host adapters, ranging from single proprietary host adapters to large-scale host adapters that support many SCSI devices. Many of the single proprietary SCSI host adapters don't have a built-in SCSI BIOS, while the large-scale adapters typically do.

What is the difference between SCSI and IDE?— One of the most significant differences between SCSI and IDE is that SCSI uses substantially less system resources in terms of CPU time. This makes it considerably faster than IDE when it comes to supporting (on the same bus) multiple peripheral devices and multiple types of peripheral devices. This difference is especially noticeable under high-end operating systems, such as Unix and Windows NT, that are written to take full advantage of SCSI's hardware multitasking features.

Review Questions

Circle True or False.

1. SCSI is faster than IDE. True / False
2. To install a SCSI host adapter on a PC, there must be one available IRQ. True / False
3. Not all SCSI host adapters have a built-in SCSI BIOS. True / False
4. You can modify the SCSI BIOS by way of the computer's CMOS Setup program. True / False
5. SCSI is an acronym for what?

   ____
   ____
   ____
   ____
   ____

6. You are working as a desktop PC support technician at the Black Moon Company. Carol, one of your customers, asks you to install a SCSI host adapter into her computer. Describe the steps necessary to complete the job for Carol.

   ____
   ____
   ____
   ____
   ____

Lab 9.4 SCSI Chain Conflict Resolution

Objective

The objective of this lab exercise is to troubleshoot and resolve a SCSI chain conflict. After completing this lab exercise, you will be able to:

- Describe how a SCSI chain conflict occurs.
- Install and configure a SCSI hard drive.
- Properly identify a SCSI chain conflict.
- Resolve a SCSI chain conflict.

Materials Required

- Operating system: Windows 9x
- Lab workgroup size: 2–4 students
- Configuration type: simple

Simple Configuration

- 90 Mhz or better Pentium-compatible computer
- 16 MB of RAM
- 540 MB hard drive
- 1 NIC (Network Interface Card)

Additional Devices

- One SCSI host adapter installed
- Two SCSI hard drives for each lab workstation
- Documentation for each SCSI hard drive jumper configuration

Lab Setup & Safety Tips

- Always unplug the power cord and properly ground yourself before touching any component inside a computer.
- One SCSI hard drive should be properly installed and configured prior to starting the lab exercise.
- The previously installed IDE hard drive should be configured as drive C and contain the operating system.

Activity

Creating the SCSI chain conflict

For the purpose of this lab exercise, the installed SCSI hard drive will be referred to as the SCSI drive. The second SCSI hard drive, used to create the conflict, will be referred to as SCSI drive 2.

1. Power off the lab workstation.
2. Unplug the power cord.
3. Remove the case from the lab workstation.
4. Using the jumper documentation provided, set both SCSI hard drives to the same SCSI ID.

5. Mount SCSI drive 2.
6. Plug in the power and data cables to SCSI drive 2.
7. For safety, stand clear of the case and plug in the power cord.
8. Power on your lab workstation and allow it to boot into Windows 9x.
9. Observe the error messages during the boot process.

Resolving the SCSI chain conflict

1. Power off the lab workstation.
2. Unplug the power cord.
3. Locate SCSI drive 2.
4. Dismount SCSI drive 2.
5. Unplug the power and data cables.
6. Using the jumper documentation provided, set SCSI drive 2 to an available SCSI ID.
7. Mount SCSI drive 2.
8. Plug in the power and data cables to SCSI drive 2.
9. Replace the case and plug in the power cord.
10. Power on the lab workstation and enter the SCSI BIOS Setup program.
11. Verify that the SCSI BIOS correctly recognizes both SCSI drives.
12. Exit the Setup program and reboot the lab workstation.
13. Allow your lab workstation to boot into Windows 9x.
14. Double-click the **My Computer** icon.
15. Verify that Windows 9x recognizes both SCSI hard drives.

Lab Notes

What is SCAM?—SCAM stands for SCSI configuration automatically. It is a method by which SCSI devices and the host adapter are Plug-and-Play-compliant, so the user does not need to manually set the ID on the device.

What is termination?—Any SCSI bus requires proper termination to prevent signal degradation. There are many different types of terminators and termination schemes. However, in general, a properly configured SCSI bus requires that the two devices at each extreme end of the physical bus cable have termination installed, while all devices between those two remain unterminated. Consult your SCSI host adapter's documentation for proper termination specifications.

Unusual behavior—One symptom of two devices on a SCSI bus with the same SCSI ID is a repeated occurrence (as many as seven or eight times) of the same device in Device Manager.

Review Questions

Circle True or False.

1. A SCSI chain conflict occurs when a SCSI device is not plugged into the SCSI cable. True / False
2. A SCSI chain conflict occurs when two or more SCSI drives are set to Master. True / False
3. All SCSI device chains require some sort of termination. True / False
4. SCAM stands for SCSI configuration automatically. True / False
5. How is SCAM used?

____
____
____
____
____

6. You are working as a desktop PC support technician at the Black Moon Company. Bob, one of your customers, wants you to give him written directions for installing and configuring a SCSI hard drive. Write the instructions you would give to Bob.

____
____
____
____
____

CHAPTER

10

MULTIMEDIA TECHNOLOGY

LABS INCLUDED IN THIS CHAPTER

LAB 10.1 MULTIMEDIA VIDEO

Objective

The objective of this lab exercise is to install and configure a video adapter card. After completing this lab exercise, you will be able to:

- Install a video adapter card.
- Install drivers for a video adapter card.
- Configure a video adapter card.

Materials Required

- Operating system: Windows 9x
- Lab workgroup size: 2-4 students
- Configuration type: simple

Simple Configuration

- 90 Mhz or better Pentium-compatible computer
- 16 MB of RAM
- 540 MB hard drive
- 1 NIC (Network Interface Card)

Additional Devices

- One video adapter for each lab workstation
- Necessary drivers for each video adapter card

Lab Setup & Safety Tips

- Always unplug the power cord and properly ground yourself before touching any component inside a computer.

ACTIVITY

Installing the video adapter card

1. Power off the lab workstation and unplug the power cord.
2. Remove the case from the lab workstation.
3. Observe the video card functions listed in Figure 10-1, and then locate an available PCI slot. (*Note*: Video adapters normally use the AGP or PCI bus because it is faster than the ISA bus.)
4. Remove the end-of-slot blank.
5. Gently slide the PCI expansion card into the PCI slot, moving the card from end to end until it is completely seated. *Warning*: Do not bend the card from side to side.
6. Attach the video cable from the back of the monitor to the video card.
7. Plug in the power cord.
8. For safety, stand clear of the case and power on the lab workstation. If you can view the POST screen, then the adapter has been properly installed.
9. Power off the lab workstation and unplug the power cord.

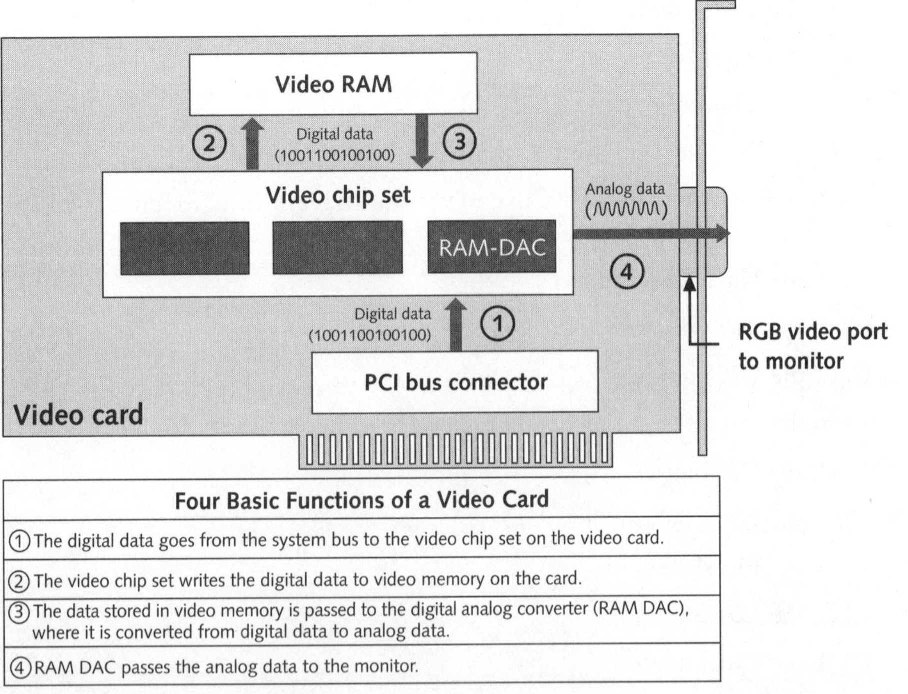

Four Basic Functions of a Video Card
① The digital data goes from the system bus to the video chip set on the video card.
② The video chip set writes the digital data to video memory on the card.
③ The data stored in video memory is passed to the digital analog converter (RAM DAC), where it is converted from digital data to analog data.
④ RAM DAC passes the analog data to the monitor.

Figure 10-1 Four basic functions of a video card

10. Replace the case.
11. Plug in the power cord.
12. Power on the lab workstation and allow it to boot into Windows 9x.

Installing the video driver (Windows 95)

1. Right-click the desktop, and select **Properties** from the shortcut menu.
2. Click the **Settings** tab.
3. Click the **Advanced** button.
4. Click the **Change** button next to the Adapter Type heading.
5. In the Update Device Driver Wizard, click **Next**.
6. Click to select the **Display a list of all the drivers in a specific location** option, and then click **Next**.
7. Click the **Have Disk** button.
8. Insert the disk with the video drivers.
9. Click the **OK** button.
10. From the menu, select the video adapter driver that you want to use.
11. Click the **OK** button.
12. Click the **Close** button.
13. Click the **Close** button.
14. Click the **Yes** button when prompted to restart your computer.

Installing the video driver (Windows 98)

1. Right-click the **Desktop**, and select **Properties** from the shortcut menu.
2. Click the **Settings** tab.

3. Click the **Advanced** button.
4. Click the **Adapter** tab.
5. Click the **Change** button.
6. In the Update Device Driver Wizard, click **Next**.
7. Click to select the **Display a list of all the drivers in a specific location** option, and then click **Next**.
8. Click the **Have Disk** button.
9. Insert the disk with the video drivers.
10. Click the **OK** button.
11. From the menu, select the video adapter driver that you want to use.
12. Click the **OK** button.
13. Click the **Next** button.
14. Click the **Finish** button.
15. Click the **Close** button.
16. Click the **Close** button.
17. Click the **Yes** button when prompted to restart your computer.

Configuring the video adapter

1. Right-click the **Desktop**, and select **Properties** from the shortcut menu.
2. Click the **Settings** tab.
3. Change the color palette to **256 colors**.
4. Change your screen area to **1024 × 768**.
5. Click the **OK** button.
6. Click the **Yes** button when prompted to restart your computer.

Lab Notes

Table 10-1 Some features of a monitor

Monitor Characteristic	Description
Screen size	Diagonal length of the screen surface
Refresh rate	The number of times an electronic beam fills a video screen with lines from top to bottom in one second
Interlaced	The electronic beam draws every other line with each pass, which lessens the overall effect of a lower refresh rate.
Dot pitch	The distance between adjacent dots on the screen
Resolution	The number of spots, or pixels, on a screen that can be addressed by software
Multiscan	Monitors that offer a variety of refresh rates so they can support several video cards
Green monitor	A monitor that saves electricity and supports the EPA Energy Star program

Lab Notes (continued)

What is display resolution and dot pitch?—Note the monitor features in Table 10-1. In particular, you should note that display resolution is the measure of pixels on the screen that are addressable by software. Dot pitch is the distance between each adjacent pixel. The smaller the dot pitch, the closer together each pixel, and the more clearly your image appears.

AGP (Accelerated graphics port)—An AGP port is a slot on a system board for a video card that provides the transfer of video data from the CPU. The video data transfer is synchronized with the memory bus.

Video RAM (VRAM)—VRAM is the RAM on video cards and holds the data being passed from the computer to the monitor. VRAM can be accessed by two devices simultaneously. Higher resolutions often require more video memory.

Monitors and Video cards—Just as video cards have different levels of performance, so do monitors. In fact, it is not uncommon for a computer's video card to be able to provide a better quality of picture than the monitor to which it is attached! However, if the video card is configured to provide a higher quality of picture than the monitor can produce, the image will become scrambled and no longer viewable.

Review Questions

Circle True or False.

1. The more memory your video card has, the better picture quality it will be able to produce. True / False
2. VRAM is rarely found on a video card. True / False
3. It is not uncommon for a video card to be able to display a higher resolution than the monitor to which it is connected. True / False
4. If Windows 9x doesn't have the video driver for your video adapter, you can install the correct video driver by using the Have Disk button and loading the driver from another location. True / False
5. Describe the relationship between VRAM, display resolution, and color quality.

____

____

____

____

____

6. Jimmy recently installed a new video adapter. Now each time that Jimmy turns on his computer, the screen is displayed in "large mode." All of Jimmy's icons are twice the size they were before he installed his new adapter. Assuming that Jimmy has already installed the correct video drivers, what can he do to return his screen and icon size to normal?

____

____

____

____

____

Lab 10.2 Installing and Configuring CD-ROM Drives (CD-R, CD-RW, DVD)

Objective

The objective of this lab exercise is to install and configure a CD-ROM drive. After completing this lab exercise, you will be able to:

- Install an IDE CD-ROM drive.
- Describe how to load a device driver for an IDE CD-ROM drive.

Materials Required

- Operating system: Windows 9x
- Lab workgroup size: 2-4 students
- Configuration type: typical

Typical Configuration

- 166 Mhz or better Pentium-compatible computer
- 24 MB of RAM
- 800 MB hard drive
- CD-ROM Drive
- 1 NIC (Network Interface Card)

Additional Devices: None

Lab Setup & Safety Tips

- The installation files for Windows 9x should be copied to the hard drive of each lab workstation.
- Always unplug the power cord and properly ground yourself before touching any component inside a computer.
- The CD-ROM drive should not be installed prior to beginning this lab.

Activity

Installing an IDE CD-ROM drive

1. Note the rear view of the IDE CD-ROM drive in Figure 10-2, and then power off the lab workstation and unplug the power cord.
2. Remove the case from the lab workstation.
3. Locate an available 5¼-inch drive bay.
4. Remove from the front of the case any blanks that might be present.
5. Verify that the hard drive is set to Master.
6. Change the CD-ROM jumper to Slave.
7. Slide the CD-ROM drive into the drive bay and use the screw to mount it to the inside of the case.
8. Connect the IDE data cable and be sure that the red stripe is aligned with pin one. (*Note*: Sometimes the stripe is blue.)
9. Plug in the power connector.

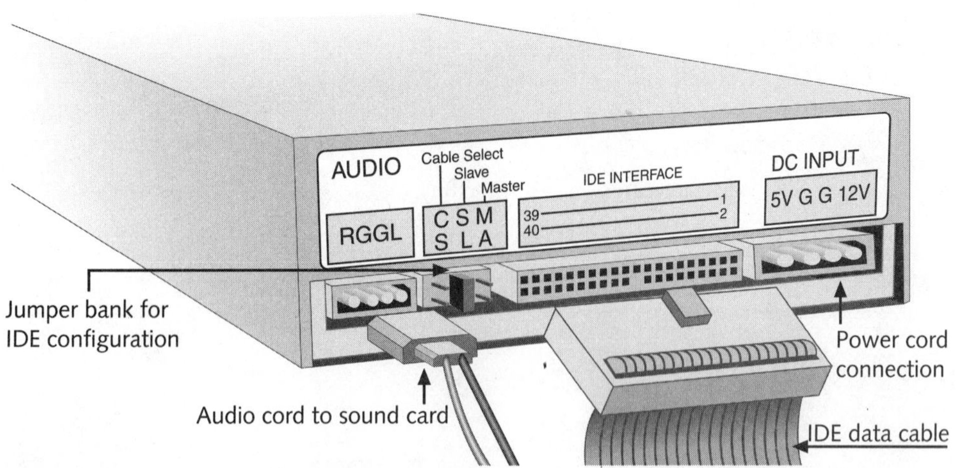

Figure 10-2 Rear view of an IDE CD-ROM drive

10. If there is a sound card present, connect the audio cable to the back of the CD-ROM drive.

Verify that the workstation boots properly

1. Stand back from the case and plug in the power cord.
2. Turn on the workstation and verify that the system boots properly. If the workstation doesn't boot properly, the jumpers might be set incorrectly.
3. Power off the workstation.
4. Remove the power cord.
5. Replace the case.
6. Plug in the power cord.

Testing an IDE CD-ROM installation

1. Allow your lab workstation to boot into Windows 9x.
2. Double-click the **My Computer** icon.
3. Verify that Windows 9x recognizes the CD-ROM drive.
4. Insert a CD-ROM into the drive.
5. Double-click the **CD-ROM drive** icon and verify that you can view the contents of the disc. If a CD-ROM icon doesn't appear in the My Computer window, follow the steps in "Installing an IDE CD-ROM driver in Windows 9x" below.

Installing an IDE CD-ROM driver in Windows 9x

Windows 9x normally detects a CD-ROM drive installation the first time it is booted with one installed. In the event that Windows 9x doesn't detect a CD-ROM drive, follow the steps below.

1. Click the **Start** button.
2. Point to **Settings** and click **Control Panel**.
3. Double-click the **Add New Hardware** icon.
4. Click the **Next** button three times to allow Windows to detect new hardware.
5. When the process is completed, allow Windows to install the proper device driver.
6. Reboot your lab workstation, and follow the steps in the section, "Testing an IDE CD-ROM installation."

10

Lab Notes

Ejecting a stuck CD—Most CD-ROM drives have an emergency eject hole, as shown in Figure 10-3, that can be used to eject a CD-ROM from the drive in the event of a mechanical failure.

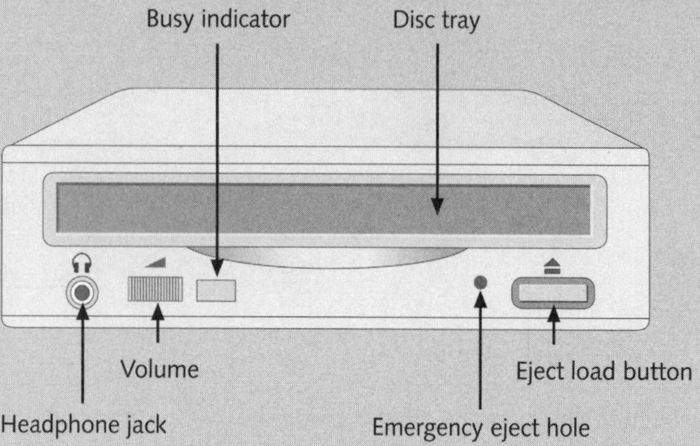

Figure 10-3 Front view of a typical CD-ROM drive

Multisession—Multisession is a feature that allows data to be read (or written) on a CD during more than one session. This is important if the disc was only partially filled during the first write.

CD-R (recordable CD)—A CD-R is a type of CD-ROM drive that can record or write data to a CD. The drive may or may not be multisession, but the data cannot be erased once it is written. A CD-R is often referred to as a "burner" because it can write or "burn" data to the CD only once.

CD-RW (rewritable CD)—A CD-RW is a type of CD-ROM drive that can record or write data to a CD. Later, the data can be erased and overwritten. CD-RW drives may or may not be multisession. It also is referred to as a burner.

Digital video disc (DVD)—A faster, larger CD-ROM format that can read older CDs, store over 8 gigabytes of data, and hold full-length motion picture videos.

Installing other types of CD-ROM drives—Although technology has progressed and there are now many different types and speeds of CD-ROM drives, generally speaking, all of them are installed the same way. Typically the exceptions are CD-R, CD-RW, and DVD, all of which require additional software to be installed so that the operating system can take full advantage of the drives' extended capabilities.

Review Questions

Circle True or False.

1. All CD-ROM drives are installed into 3½-inch bays. True / False
2. A CD-RW drive has the ability to read, write, and rewrite data to a disc. True / False
3. DVDs can hold up to 10 gigabytes of data. True / False
4. A computer can have only one CD-ROM drive installed at a time. True / False
5. The term burner is used to refer to what type of CD-ROM drives?

____

____

____

____

____

6. Amanda has installed a CD-ROM drive into her computer. Now when she powers on the Windows 95 system, it doesn't recognize the CD-ROM drive. Describe how Amanda could use the Add/Remove hardware wizard to resolve her CD-ROM issue.

____

____

____

____

____

Lab 10.3 Multimedia Sound (Sound Cards)

Objective

This lab exercise is designed to allow you to install and configure a sound card. After completing this lab exercise, you will be able to:

- Install a sound card.

Materials Required

- Operating system: Windows 9x
- Lab workgroup size: 2-4 students
- Configuration type: simple

Simple Configuration

- 90 Mhz or better Pentium-compatible computer
- 16 MB of RAM
- 540 MB hard drive
- 1 NIC (Network Interface Card)

Additional Devices

- One 8- or 16-bit sound card
- Documentation containing each sound card's jumper settings

Lab Setup & Safety Tips

- Verify that IRQ 5 and DMA 0 are available for use on all lab workstations.
- Always unplug the power cord and properly ground yourself before touching any component inside a computer.

Activity

Installing a sound card

1. Power off the lab workstation.
2. Unplug the power cord.
3. Remove the case from the lab workstation.
4. Locate an available ISA slot for the sound card.
5. Remove the end-of-slot blank.
6. Using the provided documentation, verify that the sound card jumpers are configured to use IRQ 5 and DMA 0.
7. Gently slide the PCI expansion card into the PCI slot, moving the card from end to end until it is completely seated. *Warning*: Do not bend the card from side to side.
8. Mount the sound card.
9. If a CD-ROM drive is present, attach the audio cable to the sound card and the back of the CD-ROM drive (refer to the sound card documentation).
10. Replace the case.

11. Plug in the power cord.
12. Click the **Start** button, point to **Settings**, and then click **Control Panel**.
13. Double-click the **Add New Hardware** icon.
14. Click the **Next** button three times and allow Windows 9x to detect your sound card.
15. When the process is completed, allow Windows to install the proper device driver.
16. Restart Windows when prompted.

Windows does not have a compatible driver for the sound card (Windows 95)

1. Click the **Start** button, point to **Settings**, and then click **Control Panel**.
2. Double-click the **System** icon.
3. Click the **Device Manager** tab.
4. Double-click **Other Devices**.
5. Double-click the sound card that you installed.
6. Click the **Driver** tab.
7. Click the **Update Driver** button.
8. Click the **No** option button when you are prompted to search for a Windows driver.
9. Click **Next**.
10. Click **Sound, video and game controller**, then click **Next**.
11. Click the **Have Disk** button, if available. If it is not available, manually make your manufacturer and model selections.
12. Insert the appropriate disk and use the **Browse** button to locate the driver.
13. Click the **OK** button.
14. Click **Next**.
15. Click **Finish**.
16. Click **Close** in the Device Manager window.
17. When prompted, click **Yes** to reboot your computer.

Windows does not have a compatible driver for the sound card (Windows 98)

1. Click the **Start** button, point to **Settings**, and then click **Control Panel**.
2. Double-click the **System** icon.
3. Click the **Device Manager** tab.
4. Double-click **Other Devices**.
5. Double-click the sound card that you installed.
6. Click the **Driver** tab.
7. Click the **Update Driver** button.
8. Click **Next**.
9. Click **Display a list of all the drivers in a specific location**, so you can select the one you want, and then click **Next**.
10. Click **Sound, video and game controller**, and then click **Next**.
11. Click the **Have Disk** button.

12. Insert the appropriate disk and use the **Browse** button to locate the driver.
13. Click the **OK** button.
14. Click **Next**.
15. Click **Finish**.
16. Click **Close** in the Device Manager window.
17. When prompted click **Yes** to reboot your computer.

Testing the sound card

1. Allow your lab workstation to boot into Windows 9x.
2. Verify that your speakers are properly plugged in and powered on.
3. Click the **Start** button and select **Run**.
4. Type **C:\WINDOWS\CHIMES.WAV** and press **Enter**.
5. If necessary, click the **play arrow**, which points to the right, to preview the sound. Your workstation should respond by playing the chimes.wav file.

Lab Notes

What is a WAV file?—A WAV file is a sound file that is most commonly used to store multimedia sounds.

What is a MID file?—A MID, or MIDI, is a sound file that is most commonly used to store music.

What is the difference between an 8-bit and 16-bit sound card?—An 8-bit sound card uses 8 bits to store a sample value, and has a 256 sample size range. A 16-bit sound card uses 16 bits to store a sample value and has a sample size of up to 65,536.

Review Questions

Circle True or False.

1. An 8-bit sound card produces a higher quality sound than does a 16-bit sound card. True / False
2. All sound cards use a PCI bus. True / False
3. You can install a sound card's device driver by using the Add/Remove Programs icon in the Control Panel. True / False
4. To use a sound card you must have a set of speakers or headphones. True / False
5. Most sound cards include a built-in microphone and speakers. True / False
6. Jacob just installed a new sound card into his Windows 95 PC. Windows did not detect the sound card when he used the Add New Hardware option in the Control Panel. Describe how Jacob can use Device Manger to install the correct device driver for his new sound card.

____

____

____

____

____

CHAPTER

11

ELECTRICITY AND POWER SUPPLIES

LABS INCLUDED IN THIS CHAPTER

- ♦ LAB 11.1 BASIC ELECTRICAL CIRCUITS
- ♦ LAB 11.2 DC ELECTRICITY
- ♦ LAB 11.3 POWER PROTECTION
- ♦ LAB 11.4 POWER CHAIN TROUBLESHOOTING

Lab 11.1 Basic Electrical Circuits

Objective

The objective of this lab exercise is to demonstrate and define basic concepts and terminology related to the study and use of electricity. After completing this lab exercise, you will be able to:

- Create a simple switched circuit.
- Describe the relationship between voltage, amperage, ohms, and wattage.
- Use a multimeter to measure voltage and amperage.

Materials Required

- Operating system: none
- Lab workgroup size: 4 students
- Configuration type: N/A

Additional Devices

- One 9-volt battery (AA is an acceptable substitute)
- One multimeter (capable of measuring amps)
- One incandescent light bulb rated at 12 volts
- One switch
- Three pieces of standard-grade electrical wire
- Electrical tape to attach wires to the battery, if necessary

Lab Setup & Safety Tips

- Each group will require a clean desktop area for building their switched circuit.
- The instructor must demonstrate for each student group how to configure the multimeter to measure volts and amps.

Activity

Creating a circuit

1. Attach one piece of wire to each lead on the light bulb.
2. Attach one of the wires to the battery's lead.
3. Attach the second wire to the other battery lead.
4. Observe the results.

5. In the space provided below, draw a diagram demonstrating the flow of electricity in the circuit you have created. Be sure to note the direction of the current's flow.

Adding a switch

1. Disconnect the wire from the negative side of the battery.
2. Attach the wire to an available lead on the switch.
3. Attach the third wire to the other switch lead and then attach it to the battery.
4. Observe how the switch manages the circuit.

Measuring voltage

1. Configure your multimeter to measure the voltage of your circuit.
2. Attach the +/- leads from your multimeter to the respective +/- sides of the light bulb.
3. Be sure that the switch is turned to the ON position.
4. Record the voltage of your circuit: ______________________________________

Measuring amps

1. Configure your multimeter to measure the amps of your circuit.
2. Disconnect the wire that is not currently attached to the switch.
3. Attach the respective +/- side of the multimeter to the battery lead that is not attached to any wires.
4. Attach the respective +/- side of the multimeter to the light bulb that is not attached to any wires.
5. Turn the switch to the ON position.
6. Record the amps found in your circuit: ___________________________________

Lab Notes

What does AC mean?—Alternating current (AC) is current that cycles back and forth rather than traveling in only one direction. Normally between 110 and 125 AC volts are supplied from a standard wall outlet.

What are amps?—Amps are units of measurement for electrical current. One volt across a resistance of one ohm will produce a flow of one amp.

What are volts?—A volt is a measure of electrical pressure differential. A computer power supply usually provides four separate voltages: +12 V, -12 V, +5 V, and -5 V.

What is wattage?—Wattage is a measure of the total amount of power that is needed to operate an electrical device.

What are ohms?— An ohm is the standard unit of measurement for electrical resistance. Resistors are rated in ohms.

Review Questions

Circle True or False.

1. Resistance is measured in ohms. True / False
2. A switch can act as a break in a circuit. True / False
3. AC is the acronym for ampere. True / False
4. A multimeter can measure only voltage. True / False
5. In a circuit, amps and volts are always the same amount when measured. True / False
6. Describe the difference in multimeter placement for measuring volts and amps.

____

____

____

____

____

Lab 11.2 DC Electricity

Objective

The objective of this lab exercise is to familiarize you with the different functions of a PC's power supply. After completing this lab exercise, you will be able to:

- Describe the function of a PC power supply.
- Use a multimeter to test and measure the power supply output of a PC.
- Successfully troubleshoot power supply issues.

Materials Required

- Operating system: Windows 9x
- Lab workgroup size: 2–4 students
- Configuration type: simple

Simple Configuration

- 90 Mhz or better Pentium-compatible computer
- 16 MB of RAM
- 540 MB hard drive
- 1 NIC (Network Interface Card)

Additional Devices

- One multimeter
- Tools necessary to remove the lab workstation's case and power supply

Lab Setup & Safety Tips

- Always unplug the power cord and properly ground yourself before touching any component inside a computer.
- For the purpose of this lab exercise, the system board power connectors will be referred to as the P8 and P9 connectors.
- If students are working in pairs, identify one as Student 1 and the other as Student 2.
- If an AT-style system board isn't available, your instructor will provide additional instructional materials.

Activity

Measuring the +12V DC wire of a PC's power supply

1. Unplug your lab workstation.
2. Configure your multimeter to measure voltages within the following range: -5V DC/+15V DC
3. Remove the case.
4. Using Figure 11-1 for reference, attach the respective multimeter leads to the ground and +12V wires. (Connect the multimeter to the power supply connector outside the case; work on a flat surface that can be easily seen and controlled.)

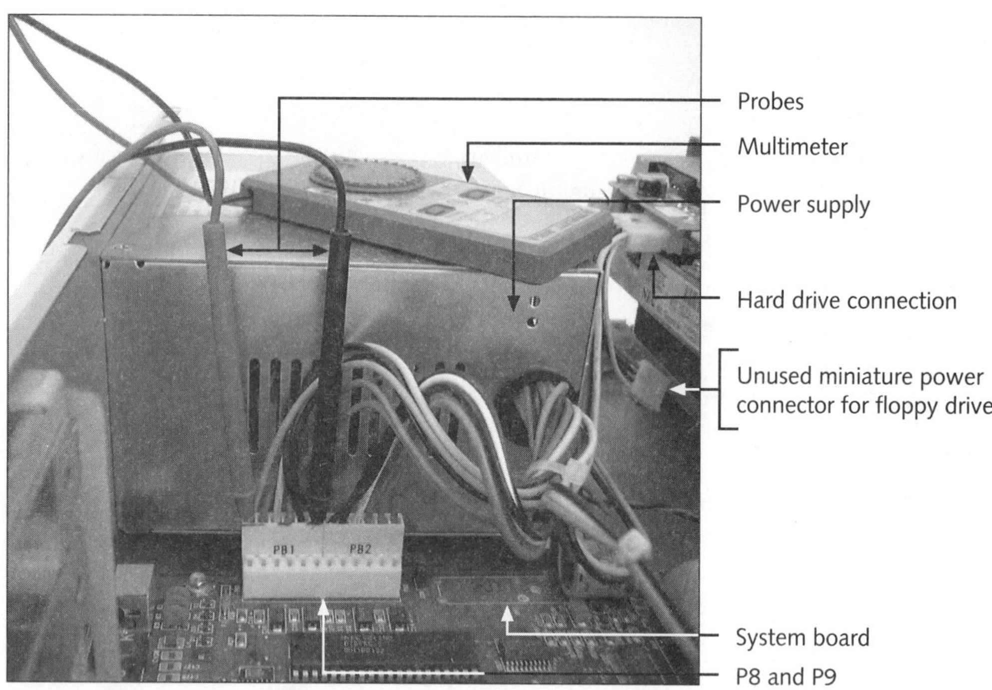

Figure 11-1 Multimeter measuring voltage on an AT system board

5. Before plugging in the PC, verify that no other metal pieces are touching the system board or power supply, which could cause a short.
6. Plug in the power cord.
7. Stand clear of the lab workstation and power it on.
8. Record the results that appear on the multimeter: ______________________
9. Refer to Table 11-1 to verify that the recorded voltage falls within the acceptable range.
10. Power off your lab workstation.

Table 11-1 Twelve leads to the AT system board from the AT power supply

Connection	Lead	Description	Acceptable Range
P8	1	"Power Good"	
	2	Not used or +5 volts	+4.5 to +5.5 volts
	3	+12 volts	+10.8 to +13.2 volts
	4	-12 volts	-10.8 to -13.2 volts
	5	Black ground	
	6	Black ground	
P9	7	Black ground	
	8	Black ground	
	9	-5 volts	-4.5 to -5.5 volts
	10	+5 volts	+4.5 to +5.5 volts
	11	+5 volts	+4.5 to +5.5 volts
	12	+5 volts	+4.5 to +5.5 volts

Measuring the +5V DC wire of the P9 system board power connector

1. Unplug your lab workstation.
2. Configure your multimeter to measure voltages within the following range: -5V DC/+15V DC.
3. Using Figure 11–1, attach the respective multimeter leads to the ground and +5V DC wires. (Connect the multimeter to the power supply connector outside the case; work on a flat surface that can be easily seen and controlled.)
4. Before plugging in the PC, verify that no other metal pieces or objects are touching the system board or power supply, which could cause a short.
5. Plug in the power cord.
6. Stand clear of the lab workstation and power it on.
7. Record the results that appear on the multimeter: ______________________________
8. Refer to the table from the first exercise to verify that the recorded voltage falls within the acceptable range.
9. Power off the computer.

Measuring the +12V DC wire of the P8 system board power connector

1. Unplug your lab workstation.
2. Configure your multimeter to measure voltages within the following range: -5VDC/+15V DC
3. Using Figure 11-1, attach the respective multimeter leads to the ground and +12V DC wires. (Connect the multimeter to the power supply connector outside the case; work on a flat surface that can be easily seen and controlled.)
4. Before plugging in the PC, verify that no other metal pieces or objects are touching the system board or power supply, which could cause a short.
5. Plug in the power cord.
6. Stand clear of the lab workstation and power it on.
7. Record the results that appear on the multimeter: ______________________________
8. Refer to Table 11-1 to verify that the recorded voltage falls within the acceptable range.
9. Power off the computer.

Removing a power supply

Student 1

1. Unplug your lab workstation.
2. Unplug all of the power connectors.
3. Locate the mounting screws of the power supply.
4. Unscrew and dismount the power supply.
5. Give the power supply and mounting screws to Student 2.

Installing a power supply

Student 2

1. Place the power supply into the mounting position.
2. After verifying that the power supply is properly aligned, screw the screws into place.

3. Attach each of the power connectors to their respective devices.
4. Plug in the power cord.
5. Stand clear of the lab workstation and power it on. Verify that all of the devices are functioning properly.

Lab Notes

Are power connectors for SCSI devices different from those for IDE devices?—No, the power connectors generally used for SCSI devices provide the same functionality as they would for an IDE device.

Review Questions

Circle True or False.

1. A hard drive connector's red wire should have a voltage that falls within the range of –15V DC to +15V DC. True / False
2. The P8 and P9 connectors are used with SCSI devices. True / False
3. Removing a power supply is as simple as removing the power connectors and dismounting the power supply True / False
4. The ground wire should have a voltage reading that falls within the ranges of –5V DC to –15V DC. True / False
5. The power supply is normally mounted to the system board. True / False
6. Ginger's PC keeps rebooting by itself. She suspects that the power supply is faulty. In the space below, describe why Ginger's suspicion is or is not realistic.

____

____

____

____

____

7. John tested one of his power supply connectors by attaching his multimeter's leads to the two center wires of a hard drive connector with the system powered on. He received a reading of 0 volts. He believes that he will need to replace the power supply. In the space below, describe why John should or should not replace the power supply.

____

____

____

____

____

Lab 11.3 Power Protection

Objective

The objective of this lab exercise is for you to install and configure a surge protector and an uninterruptible power supply (UPS) device. After completing this lab exercise, you will be able to:

- Describe the functionality of a surge protector.
- Properly install and configure a surge protector.
- Describe the functionality of a UPS device.
- Properly install and configure a UPS device.
- Properly install and configure a power conditioner.

Materials Required

- Operating system: Windows 9x
- Lab workgroup size: 4 students
- Configuration type: simple

Simple Configuration

- 90 Mhz or better Pentium-compatible computer
- 16 MB of RAM
- 540 MB hard drive
- 1 NIC (Network Interface Card)

Additional Devices

- One surge protector
- One UPS device of any type
- One power conditioner

Lab Setup & Safety Tips

- Always unplug the power cord and properly ground yourself before touching any component inside a computer.

Activity

Installing a surge protector

1. Power off your lab workstation.
2. Power off your monitor and any other peripheral devices.
3. Plug the provided surge protector into the wall outlet.
4. Plug each of your peripheral devices into the surge protector (this includes the system unit and monitor).
5. Power on the surge protector.
6. Power on your lab workstation.
7. Power on your monitor and other peripheral devices (this includes the system unit and monitor).
8. Verify that your PC is functioning properly.

Installing a UPS device

1. Power off your system unit.
2. Power off any additional peripherals that you want to be protected by the UPS device.
3. Unplug the system unit and the peripheral devices.
4. Plug the UPS device into the wall outlet.
5. Plug the system unit into the UPS device.
6. Plug the additional peripheral devices into the UPS.
7. Power on the UPS device.
8. Power on the system unit and the additionally protected peripherals.
9. Verify that the system unit and each additionally protected device are functioning properly.

Observing the functionality of a UPS device

1. Power on your system unit and allow it to boot into Windows 9x.
2. Power on your additional peripheral devices.
3. Unplug the UPS device.
4. Record the results.

   ____

   ____

   ____

   ____

   ____

Installing a power conditioner

1. Power off your system unit.
2. Power off any additional peripherals you want to be protected by the power conditioner.
3. Unplug the system unit and the peripheral devices.
4. Plug the provided power conditioner into the wall outlet.
5. Plug the system unit into the power conditioner.
6. Plug the additional peripheral devices into the power conditioner.
7. Power on the system unit and the additionally protected peripherals.
8. Verify that the system unit and each additionally protected device are functioning properly.

Lab Notes

What is an in-line UPS?—An in-line UPS is a device that continuously provides power through a battery-powered circuit. Because it requires no switching, it ensures continuous power to the user.

What is a standby UPS?—A standby UPS is a device that quickly switches from an AC power source to a battery-powered source during a brownout or power outage.

What is an intelligent UPS?—An intelligent UPS is connected to a computer by way of a serial cable so that software on the computer can monitor and control the UPS.

What is a power conditioner?—A power conditioner is a device that regulates, or conditions, the power, providing continuous voltage during brownouts.

Review Questions

Circle True or False.

1. An in-line UPS can provide continuous power without downtime for switching from AC to battery. True / False
2. A power conditioner will provide battery power for only five minutes in the case of an outage. True / False
3. If a computer is protected by a standby UPS, the computer will most likely reboot if there is a power outage. True / False
4. An intelligent UPS can be controlled by software. True / False
5. Describe how a surge protector provides protection from power spikes.

   ____
   ____
   ____
   ____
   ____

6. You are employed as a network administrator at Pictures, Inc. Your employer has asked you to assess the need for UPS devices for each of their 10 servers. After talking with the staff, you learn that seven of the servers are used for e-mail and bulletin board communications. The other three servers are used to maintain the company's accounting inventory databases. Pictures, Inc. has asked that you provide two proposals for them: the first should outline the ideal protection plan, and the other should outline the minimum protection requirements.

   Power Protection Plan A (ideal)

   ____
   ____
   ____
   ____
   ____

   Power Protection Plan B (minimum requirements)

   ____
   ____
   ____
   ____
   ____

11

Lab 11.4 Power Chain Troubleshooting

Objective

The objective of this lab exercise is to develop your electrical troubleshooting skills. After completing this lab exercise, you will be able to:

- Identify a power issue.
- Repair an electrical problem.
- Describe some common symptoms of electrical problems.

Materials Required

- Operating system: Windows 9x
- Lab workgroup size: 4 students
- Configuration type: simple

Simple Configuration

- 90 Mhz or better Pentium-compatible computer
- 16 MB of RAM
- 540 MB hard drive
- 1 NIC (Network Interface Card)

Additional Devices: None

Lab Setup & Safety Tips

- Always unplug the power cord and properly ground yourself before touching any component inside a computer.
- If students are working in pairs, identify one as Student 1 and the other as Student 2.

Activity

Troubleshooting a power supply

Student 1

The following should be completed while Student 2 is away from the lab workstation.

1. Power off your lab workstation.
2. Unplug the power cord.
3. Remove the case.
4. Unplug the P8 connector from the system board.
5. Replace the case.
6. Plug in the power cord.
7. Power on the lab workstation.

Student 2

After Student 1 has reconfigured the lab workstation, answer the following questions, and then repair the lab workstation.

1. Are there any error messages? If so, write them down:

2. What is the problem? Be specific.

3. List several possible solutions:

4. Test your theory (solution) and record the results:

5. How did you discover the problem?

6. In the future, what would you do differently to improve your troubleshooting process?

Student 2

The following should be completed while Student 1 is away from the lab workstation.

1. Power off your lab workstation.
2. Unplug the power cord.
3. Remove the case.
4. Reverse the P8 and P9 power connectors.
5. Replace the case.
6. Plug in the power cord.
7. Power on the lab workstation.

Student 1

After Student 2 has reconfigured the lab workstation, answer the following questions and repair the lab workstation.

1. Are there any error messages? If so, write them down:

   ____
   ____
   ____
   ____
   ____

2. What is the problem? Be specific.

   ____
   ____
   ____
   ____
   ____

3. List several possible solutions:

   ____
   ____
   ____
   ____
   ____

4. Test your theory (solution) and record the results:

   ____
   ____
   ____
   ____
   ____

5. How did you discover the problem?

____
____
____
____
____

6. In the future, what would you do differently to improve your troubleshooting process?

____
____
____
____
____

Lab Notes

How should I repair a power supply that is shorting?—As a PC technician, you should *never* open or attempt to repair the internal working of a power supply. Your job is to diagnose the problem and replace the power supply, if necessary.

An electrical troubleshooting tip—When troubleshooting electricity, mentally follow the path the electricity follows, starting from the wall outlet and working your way through the entire PC. In this way, it quickly becomes obvious which part of a PC is having a power problem and, more importantly, which device is causing the electrical problem.

Review Questions

Circle True or False.

1. If a power supply's fan does not spin, one possibility is that the power supply has failed. True / False
2. The P8 and P9 power connectors can be attached to the system board in any order. True / False
3. Hard drive connectors and the system board connector use the same voltage. True / False
4. A common mistake is to attach the hard drive power connector to the system board. True / False
5. What should be the voltage of a power supply's ground wires?

____
____
____
____
____

6. Elliot has just replaced his system board, and now his computer won't boot. List three possible power-related problems that could be wrong with his system.

____
____
____
____
____

CHAPTER

12

SUPPORTING WINDOWS 9X

LABS INCLUDED IN THIS CHAPTER

Lab 12.1 Installing Windows 95

Objective

The objective of this lab exercise is for you to install the Windows 95 operating system. After completing this lab exercise, you will be able to:

- Install Windows 95.
- Accurately describe the Windows 95 installation process.
- Locate and describe the function of Windows 95 system files.

Materials Required

- Operating system: Windows 95
- Lab workgroup size: 4 students
- Configuration type: simple

Simple Configuration

- 90 Mhz or better Pentium-compatible computer
- 16 MB of RAM
- 540 MB hard drive
- 1 NIC (Network Interface Card)

Additional Devices

- Windows 95 installation files
- One DOS system disk
- One blank, formatted disk
- A valid Windows 95 product ID for each lab workstation

Lab Setup & Safety Tips

- Each lab workstation should be preloaded with the Windows 95 installation files, which should be placed in a directory named C:\WIN95.

Activity

Installing Windows 95

1. Insert the system disk into the A: drive.
2. Power on your lab workstation and allow it to boot from the DOS system disk.
3. At the C prompt, type **CD C:\WIN95** and press **Enter**.
4. Type **SETUP** and press **Enter**.
5. Press **Enter** to allow the Setup program to run the SCANDISK utility.
6. Click the **Continue** button.
7. Click the **Yes** button.
8. Click the **Next** button.
9. Select the **Other Directory** option and click the **Next** button.
10. Type **C:\WINDOWS.95** and click the **Next** button.

11. In the Setup Option window, click the **Typical** option and then click the **Next** button.
12. Type the product ID provided by your instructor.
13. Type your name.
14. Click the **Next** button.
15. Select the hardware components installed on your lab workstation, and click the **Next** button.
16. Click the **Next** button to accept the defaults on the next three windows.
17. Insert your blank floppy disk into drive A.
18. Click the **OK** button.
19. Remove the floppy disk and click the **OK** button.
20. Click the **Finish** button.
21. Select the proper time zone, and click the **OK** button.
22. Click the **Cancel** button when prompted to install a printer driver.
23. Click the **OK** button to restart the computer.

Identifying Windows 95 system files

1. Using your lab workstation and textbook for reference, write the path of the following system files and describe their functionality.

   a. IO.SYS

   ____

   ____

   ____

   ____

   ____

   b. MSDOS.SYS

   ____

   ____

   ____

   ____

   ____

   c. COMMAND.COM

   ____

   ____

   ____

   ____

   ____

d. WIN.INI

____

____

____

____

____

e. PROGMAN.INI

____

____

____

____

____

f. SYSTEM.DAT

____

____

____

____

____

g. USER.DAT

____

____

____

____

____

Lab Notes

What do I do if the Setup program stops?—If the Windows 95 Setup program stops during the installation, you restart it by simply rebooting the PC and running the Setup program again. Unlike Windows 3.x, however, Windows 95 has the ability to learn from its mistakes. For example, if Windows 95 crashes during the installation process, when you restart, the Setup program automatically skips the process that hung the system during the previous installation attempt.

Express Setup—Express Setup allows Windows 95 to automatically install a group of preselected operating system components.

Custom Setup—Custom Setup allows you to select the components that you want to install.

Reinstalling Windows—This option, sometimes referred to as upgrading Windows, allows you to install Windows 95 over the currently installed version. You can use this option to repair a damaged installation of Windows 95.

Review Questions

Circle True or False.

1. Windows 95 provides an upgrade path from Windows 3.x. True / False
2. During the Windows 95 installation, you are given the option to install MSN connectivity. True / False
3. The Windows 95 Setup program launches the SCANDISK utility before installing or upgrading the operating system. True / False
4. During the Windows 95 installation, you can create an emergency repair disk. True / False
5. What are the filenames of the SYSTEM.DAT and the USER.DAT backup files that are created automatically by Windows 95?

____

____

____

____

____

6. If you were installing Windows 95 on a laptop, which of the following component packages would be ideal, and why would or wouldn't they?

   Typical

   Custom

   Portable

____

____

____

____

____

Lab 12.2 Customizing Windows 95

Objective

This lab exercise allows you to configure some common settings in the Windows 95 environment. After completing this lab exercise, you will be able to:

- Properly configure Windows 95 to use a screen saver, desktop wallpaper, and customized shortcuts.
- Modify the Start menu.
- Install a printer driver in the Windows 95 environment.

Materials Required

- Operating system: Windows 95
- Lab workgroup size: 4 students
- Configuration type: simple

Simple Configuration

- 90 Mhz or better Pentium-compatible computer
- 16 MB of RAM
- 540 MB hard drive
- 1 NIC (Network Interface Card)

Additional Devices: None

Lab Setup & Safety Tips

- Each lab workstation should have Windows 95 installed and functioning properly.

Activity

Configuring your desktop wallpaper in Windows 95

1. Power on your lab workstation and allow it to boot into Windows 95.
2. Right-click the desktop, and then click **Properties** on the shortcut menu.
3. In the **Wallpaper** list box, click the **Clouds** wallpaper or the wallpaper of your choice.
4. Click the **Apply** button.
5. Click the **OK** button.

Configuring your screen saver in Windows 95

1. Power on your lab workstation and allow it to boot into Windows 95.
2. Right-click the desktop, and then click **Properties** on the shortcut menu.
4. Click the **Screen Saver** tab.
5. Click the **Screen Saver** list arrow.
6. Click **Mystify** or the screen saver of your choice.
7. Click the **Apply** button.
8. Click the **OK** button.

Creating personalized program shortcuts

1. Right-click the desktop, and then point to **New** on the shortcut menu.
2. Click **Shortcut**.
3. Type **C:\WINDOWS.95\WINFILE.EXE** and press **Enter**.
4. In the Select a name for the shortcut box, type **File Manager**.
5. Click the **Finish** button.

Customizing your Start menu

1. Right-click the taskbar.
2. Select **Properties** from the shortcut menu, as shown in Figure 12-1.

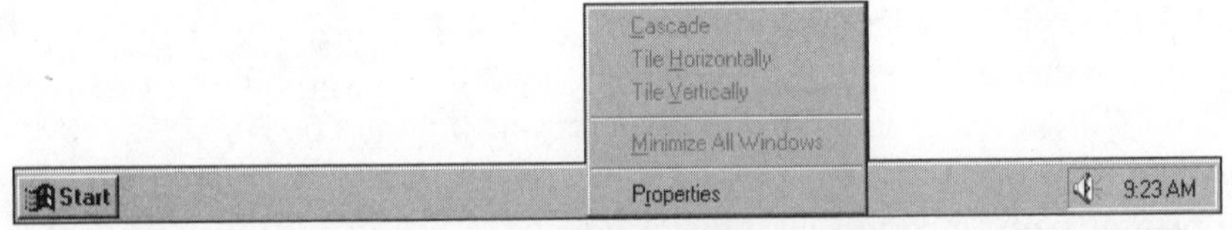

Figure 12-1 To customize the desktop, use the Properties sheet of the Windows 9x taskbar

3. Click the **Start Menu Programs** tab.
4. Click the **Add** button to see the Taskbar Properties dialog box.
5. Type **C:\WINDOWS.95\WINFILE.EXE**.
6. Click the **Next** button.
7. Double-click the **Accessories** folder.
8. In the Select a name for the shortcut text box, type **File Manager**.
9. Click the **Finish** button.
10. Click the **OK** button.
11. Verify that the shortcut was properly added to the Accessories group by clicking the **Start** button, pointing to **Programs**, and then pointing to **Accessories**.
12. Click the newly created **File Manager** shortcut.

Installing a printer driver

1. Power on your lab workstation and allow it to boot into Windows 95.
2. Double-click the **My Computer** icon.
3. Double-click the **Printers** folder.
4. Double-click **Add Printer**.
5. Click the **Next** button.
6. Choose the **My computer** option, and click the **Next** button.
7. Choose the correct printer driver by selecting the appropriate manufacturer and printer model, and then click the **Next** button.
8. Select the appropriate printer port, and click the **Next** button.
9. Click the **Next** button again to use the default printer name.
10. Click the **Finish** button to complete the printer driver installation.

12

Lab Notes

What is Safe Mode?—Safe mode is a way of starting Windows 95 with a minimum amount of Windows drivers. Note that Safe mode is designed to be used for troubleshooting only.

What is DOS Mode?—Like Windows 3.x, Windows 95 uses DOS as its underlying operating system. DOS 7.0 is the version used by Windows 95; therefore DOS mode is simply a DOS 7.0 command prompt.

How can I enable multiboot?—In the Windows 95 environment, you can edit the MSDOS.SYS file to create a multiboot environment.

How do I install applications?—Most Windows applications include a Setup program that is designed to automatically install the application after you answer a few simple questions.

What are the symptoms of a stalled Windows 95 print spooler?—When the Windows 95 print spooler stalls, the operating system at first appears to hang (stop responding). After the operating system has recovered, you will notice that when you access the Printer folder, none of your printer icons appear. The fastest way to resolve a spooler problem in Windows 95 is to simply reboot the PC.

The printer won't print at all. Now what?—When working with a printer in any environment, you should always do the following:

- Verify that the printer, CMOS, and operating system are all configured to use the same type of protocol (bidirectional, unidirectional, ECP, or EPP).
- Verify that the operating system has the correct printer driver installed.
- Check the spooler; be sure it has not stalled.
- Verify that the printer driver is configured to use the proper printer port (LPT1, COM1, or LPT2).

Where can I get more information about Windows 95?—You can purchase a Windows 95 user's manual, but it is easier and more cost-effective to use the built-in help features of Windows 95. To find Windows 95 Help, click the Start button and then click Help.

What is the Conflict troubleshooter?—The Conflict troubleshooter is an interactive help menu designed to resolve resource conflicts in the Windows 95 environment.

How do I get help?—All Microsoft operating systems are released with integrated Help. To quickly access the Help menu in Windows 95, press the F1 key.

What is REGEDIT and how do I execute it?—REGEDIT.EXE is a Windows-based utility that is used to manually modify the Windows registry. The REGEDIT utility can be found in the Windows directory and can be executed by double-clicking on it or by typing **REGEDIT** in the Run box. *Warning*: Using the REGEDIT utility can permanently damage an operating system.

Review Questions

Circle True or False.

1. You can configure your desktop wallpaper with the Control Panel Accessories option. True / False
2. In the Windows 95 environment, the desktop includes the wallpapered area of your screen. True / False
3. Shortcuts in Windows 95 are configured the same way as are shortcuts in Windows 3.x. True / False
4. The Start menu is a compilation of shortcuts. True / False
5. Describe how to create a new folder and add it to the Start menu.

____

____

____

____

____

6. Describe how to place a shortcut to My Computer in the Start menu.

____

____

____

____

____

Lab 12.3 Installing Windows 98

Objective

The objective of this lab exercise is to install the Windows 98 operating system. After completing this lab exercise, you will be able to:

- Install Windows 98.
- Accurately describe the Windows 98 installation process.
- Locate and describe the function of Windows 98 system files.

Materials Required

- Operating system: Windows 98
- Lab workgroup size: 4 students
- Configuration type: simple

Simple Configuration

- 90 Mhz or better Pentium-compatible computer
- 16 MB of RAM
- 540 MB hard drive
- 1 NIC (Network Interface Card)

Additional Devices

- One DOS system disk
- One blank formatted disk
- A valid Windows 98 product ID for each lab workstation

Lab Setup & Safety Tips

- Each lab workstation should be preloaded with the Windows 98 installation files, which should be placed in a directory named C:\WIN98.

Activity

Installing Windows 98

1. Insert the system disk into drive A.
2. Power on your lab workstation and allow it to boot from the DOS system disk.
3. At the C prompt, type **CD C:\WIN98** and press **Enter**.
4. Type **SETUP** and press **Enter**.
5. Press **Enter** to allow the Setup program to run the SCANDISK utility.
6. Click the **Continue** button.
7. Click the **I accept the agreement** option button.
8. Click the **Next** button.
9. Select the **Other Directory** option and click the **Next** button.
10. Type **C:\WINDOWS.98** and click the **Next** button.

11. Click the option button next to the **Typical** setup option, and then click the **Next** button.
12. Type your name and the name of the school you are attending.
13. Click the **Next** button.
14. Choose the Recommended Windows components by clicking the **Next** button.
15. Enter a computer name and workgroup name as indicated by your instructor.
16. Click the **Next** button.
17. Click the **Next** button to specify the United States as your country.
18. Click the **Next** button to begin creating an Emergency Startup Disk.
19. When prompted, insert a blank disk into the A drive and click the **OK** button.
20. Click the **OK** button when the operation has completed successfully.
21. Click the **Next** button, and the Setup program will begin copying the Windows 98 files to your hard drive.
22. Click the **OK** button and Setup will automatically restart your workstation.
23. You may be prompted to configure legacy devices that are attached to your workstation. (Note that the Setup program may need to be restarted before continuing to the next step.)
24. Click the **list** arrow to set the appropriate time zone, and then click the **Close** button.
25. Click the **Cancel** button when prompted to configure a printer.
26. Click the **Restart Now** button.

Converting a FAT16 file system to FAT32

1. Click the **Start** button.
2. Point to **Programs** and then point to **Accessories**.
3. Point to **System Tools** and then click **Drive Converter(FAT32)**.
4. Click the **Next** button.
5. Select the drive that you want to convert by clicking it, and then click the **Next** button.
6. When you see a message that FAT32 will not be compatible with DOS or certain versions of Windows, click **OK**.
7. The Drive Converter wizard may prompt you to turn off antivirus software or any other programs running in the background.
8. Click the **Next** button until you begin the conversion.

Lab Notes

What is the difference between Windows 95 and Windows 98?—There are very few differences between Windows 95 and Windows 98. The core of the operating systems is the same. However, Windows 98 added some utilities not available in Windows 95, and also has expanded on the compatibility of Windows 95. Many of the newer enhancements and utilities of Windows 98 are included in Table 12-1.

Table 12-1 Features new to Windows 98

Feature	Description
Troubleshooting utilities	Windows 95 had a few troubleshooting utilities, but the 15 utilities that come with Windows 98 are more interactive.
Update Wizard	The Update Wizard connects to the Microsoft Web site and automatically downloads any new drivers or fixes.
Maintenance Wizard	The Maintenance Wizard can be used to regularly schedule several maintenance tasks, including running Disk Defragmenter and ScanDisk, which were discussed in earlier chapters.
DriveSpace 3	An improved version of DriveSpace for Windows 95, it includes a third level of data compression, called UltraPack, which takes up less space per file than does regular compression, called HiPack.
Power management support	Windows 98 supports some power management features, if both hardware and software are present to use them.
Registry Checker	Backs up and restores the registry
Web tools and features	Several Windows 98 features take on an Internet look and feel. Windows 98 also supports viewing TV and interactive programs. You'll need a special TV interface card to do it.
FAT32	Recall that FAT32 is a file system that allows for a smaller cluster size on large drives than does the earlier FAT16.
New hardware support	With 1,200 device drivers, Windows 98 supports many more hardware devices than did Windows 95. Also, Windows 98 supports DMA channels for IDE CD-ROM drives, USB, DVD, and multiple video cards supporting multiple monitors.
Win32 Driver Model (WDM)	A new device driver model, also used by Windows NT, makes it possible for the same driver to be used by both the Windows 95 and Windows 98 operating systems.

USB and Windows 9x—Unlike the original version of Windows 95, Windows 98 can support USB technology. In fact, Windows 98 will typically detect and install the appropriate drivers automatically.

Review Questions

Circle True or False.

1. Windows 98 and Windows 95 have the same core operating system. True / False
2. FAT32 has a larger cluster size than FAT16. True / False
3. One of the features added to Windows 98 is USB compatibility. True / False
4. Windows 98 is compatible with drivers designed for Windows NT. True / False
5. List three utilities that are unique to Windows 98:

   ____

   ____

   ____

   ____

   ____

6. Nancy has just completed installing her new USB hub and USB scanner. She also recently purchased a copy of Windows 98. Nancy currently is using the Windows 95 operating system. Describe the steps Nancy has to complete before she can use her USB scanner.

   ____

   ____

   ____

   ____

   ____

LAB 12.4 WINDOWS 9X HARDWARE PROFILES

Objective

This lab exercise helps you create a new hardware profile in the Windows 9x environment. After completing this lab exercise, you will be able to:

- Add and delete hardware profiles.
- Describe when to use a hardware profile.
- Configure a Windows 9x hardware profile.

Materials Required

- Operating system: Windows 9x
- Lab workgroup size: 4 students
- Configuration type: simple

Simple Configuration

- 90 Mhz or better Pentium-compatible computer
- 16 MB of RAM
- 540 MB hard drive
- 1 NIC (Network Interface Card)

Additional Devices: None

Lab Setup & Safety Tips

- Each lab workstation should have Windows 9x installed and functioning properly.

ACTIVITY

Viewing hardware profiles

1. Right-click **My Computer** and click **Properties**.
2. Click the **Hardware Profiles** tab.
3. Every computer has a least one hardware profile named "Original Configuration." If additional hardware profiles have been created for your lab workstation, they will be listed under the Original Configuration profile on this tab.
4. Record each of the hardware profiles found on your lab workstation in the lines provided:

____

____

____

____

____

Creating a new hardware profile

1. Click **Original Configuration** to highlight it.
2. Click the **Copy** button, type **Lab Configuration**, and then click **OK**.

3. Click the **OK** button in the System Properties window.
4. Click the **Start** button and click **Shut Down**.
5. Click the **Restart the computer** option button, and then click **OK**.

Starting a Windows 9x computer with multiple hardware profiles

1. At the hardware profile menu, type the number next to the Lab Configuration profile and press **Enter**. (Windows may redetect some of your hardware).
2. Note that you have now booted your lab workstation into the Lab Configuration hardware profile.

Configuring the Lab Configuration hardware profile

1. Right-click **My Computer** and click **Properties**.
2. Click the **Device Manager** tab.
3. Double-click **Network Adapters**.
4. Double-click the icon for your NIC.
5. On the General tab, check the **Disable in this hardware profile** check box. Note that some versions of Windows 9x require you to deselect the hardware profile rather than checking the Disable in this hardware profile check box.
6. Click the **OK** button.
7. Notice that the NIC now has a red X over its icon.
8. Click the **OK** button in the System Properties window.
9. Click the **Start** button and click **Shut Down**.
10. Click the **Restart the computer** option button, and then click **OK**.

Viewing the Original Configuration

1. At the hardware profile menu, type the number next to the Original Configuration profile and press **Enter**.
2. Right-click **My Computer** and click **Properties**.
3. Click the **Device Manager** tab.
4. Double-click **Network Adapters**.
5. Record the state of the NIC (enabled, disabled or removed):

    ____

Deleting the Lab Configuration

1. Click the **Hardware Profiles** tab.
2. Click **Original Configuration** to highlight it.
3. Click the **Delete** button.
4. Click the **OK** button.
5. Click the **Start** button and click **Shut Down**.
6. Click the **Restart the computer** option button then click **OK**.

7. What changes have occurred in the boot process since the last time you rebooted? Why have they occured?

Lab Notes

So what exactly is a hardware profile?—A hardware profile creates an additional device driver configuration for the same computer. Hardware profiles are most often created for laptop computers because the hardware configuration on such a computer can change often. For example, if you used your laptop on a network at work and then took it home to continue working, ideally you would have two configurations—one with the NIC installed (Work Configuration) and one with the network card disabled (Home Configuration).

Review Questions

Circle True or False.

1. A hardware profile is a device driver configuration for a computer. True / False
2. When a device is disabled in a hardware profile, the CMOS will no longer initialize the device. True / False
3. A hardware profile selection menu will appear if you have only one hardware pofile configured. True / False
4. A hardware profile can be deleted only after all devices have been enabled using Device Manager. True / False
5. Write a scenario question containing only one correct answer that involves a laptop and two hardware configurations.

6. Ralph wants his Windows 9x computer to have three hardware profiles with the following names:
   - Original Configuration
   - Work Configuration
   - Home Configuration

   The Original Configuration must have all of the drivers enabled.

   The Work Configuration must have the modem disabled and all other drivers enabled.

   The Home Configuration must have the NIC disabled and all other drivers enabled.

   Describe the steps to configure Ralph's computer starting with only the Original Configuration hardware profile.

   ____

   ____

   ____

   ____

   ____

CHAPTER

13

UNDERSTANDING AND SUPPORTING WINDOWS NT WORKSTATION

LABS INCLUDED IN THIS CHAPTER

LAB 13.1 UPGRADING TO WINDOWS NT WORKSTATION

Objective

The objective of this lab exercise is to use the upgrade path from Windows 3.x to Windows NT 4.0. After completing this lab exercise, you will be able to:

- Upgrade from Window 3.x to Windows NT 4.0 Workstation.
- Describe the upgrade path from Windows 3.x to Windows NT 4.0.

Materials Required

- Operating system: Windows 3.x
- Lab workgroup size: 4 students
- Configuration type: simple

Simple Configuration

- 90 Mhz or better Pentium-compatible computer
- 16 MB of RAM
- 540 MB hard drive
- 1 NIC (Network Interface Card)

Additional Devices

- Installation files for Windows NT Workstation
- A blank, formatted floppy disk

Lab Setup & Safety Tips

- Each lab workstation should have the Window 3.x operating system installed and functioning properly. Prior to the beginning of class, Windows NT installation files should be copied into a directory named C:\i386.

ACTIVITY

Upgrading to Windows NT Workstation

1. Read the benefits of Windows NT in Table 13-1, and then power on your lab workstation and allow it to boot into Windows 3.x.

Table 13-1 Benefits of Windows NT

Feature	Benefits
Hardware requirements	High, requiring a Pentium with 16–32 MB RAM
Hardware compatibility	Supports most current devices, but does not claim backward compatibility with legacy devices
Software compatibility	Does not offer Plug and Play and offers less device-driver support
Power management	None
Performance	Offers preemptive multitasking for 32-bit applications and cooperative multitasking for 16-bit applications; performs better on systems with at least 32 MB of RAM
Reliability and stability	Offers high reliability and stability and all applications run in protected memory space
Security	Offers high security down to the file level

2. Open **Program Manager**.
3. Click the **File** menu.
4. Select **Run**.
5. Type **C:\I386\WINNT /B** and press **Enter**.
6. Press **Enter** when the copying is completed.
7. In the Program Manager, click **File** and select **Exit Windows**.
8. Click **OK** in the confirmation message box.
9. Power cycle your lab workstation.
10. Select the **NT Installation/Upgrade** option and press **Enter**.
11. Press the **Enter** key twice, until you see the license agreement.
12. Press the **Page Down** key several times through the license agreement.
13. Press the **F8** key to accept the license agreement.
14. Press **Enter** to accept the detected hardware defaults.
15. Press **Enter** three times until you restart your lab workstation.
16. Click the **Next** button to accept the defaults on the next few windows.
17. Type your name and press **Enter**.
18. Type the product ID provided by your instructor, and press **Enter**.
19. Type the lab workstation's name provided by your instructor, and press **Enter**.
20. Click the **Next** button four times to accept the defaults on the next four windows.
21. Click the **Select From List** option button.
22. Select **Msloopback adapter** and click the **OK** button.
23. Click the **Next** button.
24. Clear the **TCP/IP** check box and click the **NetBeui** check box.
25. Click the **Next** button four times to accept the defaults on the next four windows.
26. Click the **Finish** button.
27. Select the proper time zone and click the **Close** button.
28. Click the **OK** button.
29. Click the **Test** button in the video display window and then click **OK**.
30. Click the **Yes** button.
31. Click the **OK** button to close the video display window.
32. Click the **OK** button.
33. Insert the blank, formatted floppy disk, and click the **OK** button.
34. Click the **Restart** button when prompted.

Lab Notes

Express Setup—Express Setup allows Windows NT to automatically install a group of preselected operating system components.

Custom Setup—Custom Setup allows you to select the components that you want to install.

NT Hardware Qualifier (NTHQ)—A utility found on the NT installation CD-ROM that examines your system to determine if all hardware present is Windows NT compatible.

Review Questions

Circle True or False.

1. Windows NT does not include an upgrade path from Windows 3.x. True / False
2. Windows NT is Plug and Play compliant. True / False
3. Windows NT includes Express, Custom, and Portable options similar to the Windows 95 Setup program. True / False
4. Windows NT is a 16-bit operating system. True / False
5. When upgrading from Windows 3.x to Windows NT, the installation program automatically attempts to migrate the installed applications. True / False
6. Jim wants to install Windows NT on his PC. Jim has all of the necessary software, but doesn't have a NIC. Does Jim have to purchase a NIC before proceeding with the Windows NT installation? Explain your answer.

____

____

____

____

____

Lab 13.2 Installing Windows NT Workstation

Objective

The objective of this lab exercise is to install Windows NT Workstation. After completing this lab exercise, you will be able to:

- Install Windows NT Workstation.
- Create an emergency repair disk (ERD).

Materials Required

- Operating system: Windows NT 4.0 Workstation
- Lab workgroup size: 4 students
- Configuration type: typical

Typical Configuration

- 166 Mhz or better Pentium-compatible computer
- 24 MB of RAM
- 800 MB hard drive
- CD-ROM drive
- 1 NIC (Network Interface Card)

Additional Devices

- A set of Windows NT installation disks and an installation CD-ROM for each group of students

Lab Setup & Safety Tips

- The following activity will erase all data stored on drive C.

Activity

Installing Windows NT Workstation

1. Note the system requirements in Table 13-2, and then insert the Windows NT installation Disk 1 and allow your system to boot from drive A.
2. When prompted, insert Disk 2 and press **Enter**.
3. Press **Enter** on the next two windows.
4. Insert Disk 3 and press the **Enter** key.
5. Press the **Enter** key.
6. Press the **Page Down** button seven times.
7. Press the **F8** key.
8. Press the **Enter** key to accept the detected hardware defaults.
9. Select drive C and press the **Enter** key to install Windows NT.
10. Select the **Format the partition using the NTFS file system** option, and then press **Enter**.
11. Press the **F** key.

12. Press **Enter** to accept the default directory.
13. Press **Enter** to continue.
14. Remove the disk, and then press **Enter** to restart your computer.
15. Click the **Next** button to accept the defaults on the next two windows.
16. Type your name and click the **Next** button.
17. Enter the product ID and click the **Next** button.
18. Enter a computer name and click the **Next** button.
19. Enter a password and click the **Next** button.
20. Click the **Next** button to accept the defaults on the next three windows.
21. Select the **Do not connect this computer to a network at this time** option button.
22. Click the **Next** button.
23. Click the **Finish** button.
24. Select a time zone.
25. Click the **Close** button.
26. Click the **OK** button in the video display window.
27. Click the **Test** button in the video display window.
28. Click the **Yes** button to verify the display settings.
29. Click the **OK** button to close the video display window.
30. Click the **OK** button.
31. Insert a floppy disk, and then click the **OK** button.
32. Click the **Restart** button.

Table 13-2 Windows NT system requirements (Intel only)

Feature	System Requirements
Processor	486/66 or higher
Memory	16 MB
Hard disk space	110 MB
Video	VGA
Floppy disk drive	High-density 3.5-inch
CD-ROM drive	Required for installation not performed over a network
Mouse or pointing device	Required

Lab Notes

What is NTFS all about?—NTFS stands for New Technology File System. Unlike FAT or VFAT, NTFS includes security built right into the file system. Also, NTFS uses a reduced cluster size, which minimizes the space commonly wasted by large FAT volumes. (*Note*: Without special third-party software, an NTFS volume cannot be accessed from DOS.)

FAT vs. VFAT?—FAT stands for file allocation table and is the file system that was introduced with MS-DOS. Since then Microsoft has updated FAT to be used in the Windows 95 environment; this update is VFAT. The V stands for Virtual. VFAT is an additional area in FAT that is reserved to store long filename information. Note that VFAT and FAT32 are not the same type of file system.

What is an ERD?—ERD stands for emergency repair disk. An ERD contains a partial backup copy of your Windows NT registry. Each ERD is specific to the operating system and hardware setup on which it was created; ERDs are not interchangeable between hardware platforms or operating systems.

How do you make an ERD?—An ERD can be created during the Windows NT installation or at any time after Windows NT has been installed. To create an ERD after Windows NT has been installed, click the Start button, point to Programs, and click Command Prompt. Type RDISK /S. The RDISK utility is used to create an ERD and the /S tells Windows NT not only to back up the registry files, but also to include the Windows NT security file (SAM).

Review Questions

Circle True or False.

1. To install Windows NT, you must have a network interface card. True / False
2. The Windows NT installation gives you the option to create and delete partitions.
   True / False
3. Windows NT allows you to configure a network interface card during the installation process.
   True / False
4. The Windows NT operating system does not support PCs that use a 486 processor.
   True / False
5. What is the name of the directory that contains the Windows NT installation files for x86 computers?

   ____

   ____

   ____

   ____

   ____

6. List the four questions you have to answer during the installation of Windows NT.

   ____

   ____

   ____

   ____

   ____

Lab 13.3 Customizing and Repairing Windows NT Workstation

Objective

This lab exercise is designed to provide you the opportunity to configure some common settings in the Windows NT environment. After completing this lab exercise, you will be able to:

- Configure Windows NT to use customized shortcuts.
- Use an ERD (Emergency Repair Disk) to repair a Windows NT installation.
- View and modify the Boot.ini file.
- Install a printer driver in the Windows NT environment.

Materials Required

- Operating system: Windows NT 4.0 Workstation
- Lab workgroup size: 4 students
- Configuration type: typical

Typical Configuration

- 166 Mhz or better Pentium-compatible computer
- 24 MB of RAM
- 800 MB hard drive
- CD-ROM drive
- 1 NIC (Network Interface Card)

Additional Devices

- The Windows NT Workstation installation disks and CD-ROM
- An ERD for each lab workstation

Lab Setup & Safety Tips

- Each lab workstation should have Windows NT installed and functioning properly.

Activity

Using shortcuts to manage memory

1. Right-click the desktop, and then point to **New** on the shortcut menu.
2. Click **Shortcut**.
3. Type **C:\WINNT\SYSTEM32\WINFILE.EXE** and press **Enter**.
4. In the Select a name for the shortcut box, type **File Manager**.
5. Click the **Finish** button.
6. Right-click the newly created **File Manager** shortcut.
7. Select **Properties** from the shortcut menu to see the Properties dialog box.
8. Click the **Shortcut** tab.
9. Observe the location of the **Run in Separate Memory Space** check box.

10. How does Windows NT respond when the Run in Separate Memory Space check box is checked?

____

____

____

____

____

Repairing a Windows NT installation

1. Insert the Windows NT installation Disk 1 and allow your system to boot from drive A.
2. Insert Disk 2 and press **Enter**.
3. Press **Enter**.
4. Press the letter **R** key.
5. Press **Enter** on the next two windows.
6. Insert Disk 3 and press **Enter**.
7. Press the **Enter** key on the next three windows.
8. Insert the emergency repair disk.
9. Insert the Windows NT CD-ROM. If necessary, type **A** to repair all files.
10. Press **Enter** to restart the computer.

Installing a printer driver

1. Power on your lab workstation and allow it to boot into Windows NT.
2. Double-click the **My Computer** icon.
3. Double-click the **Printers** folder
4. Double-click **Add Printer**.
5. Click the **Next** button.
6. Click the **My computer** option and click the **Next** button.
7. Select the appropriate printer port and click the **Next** button.
8. Choose the correct printer driver by first selecting the appropriate manufacturer, and then selecting the printer model. Click the **Next** button when you are done.
9. Click the **Next** button again to use the default printer name.
10. If necessary, click the **Next** button to accept the default on the next window.
11. Click the **Finish** button to complete the driver installation.

Lab Notes

Repairing Windows NT—Windows NT includes a repair process as part of its Setup program. If a Windows NT installation becomes damaged or corrupt, you can use the Setup program to repair it.

Review Questions

Circle True or False.

1. The Windows NT repair process can be used to repair Windows if it becomes damaged. True / False
2. An ERD is always necessary when using the emergency repair process. True / False
3. A CD-ROM drive must be present to execute the emergency repair process. True / False
4. The Run in Separate Memory Space check box tells Windows NT to store that application in the swap file at all times. True / False
5. List two tasks that can be accomplished by using the Windows NT repair process.

   ____

   ____

   ____

   ____

   ____

6. Janet's Windows NT workstation has been rendered useless by a virus. You are Janet's PC support technician and have cleaned the virus but the system still won't boot properly. Janet does not have an ERD. Describe how you would attempt to restore Janet's PC without reinstalling Windows NT.

   ____

   ____

   ____

   ____

   ____

Lab 13.4 The Windows NT Registry

Objective

The objective of this lab exercise is to enable you to understand and modify the Windows NT registry. After completing this lab exercise, you will be able to:

- Name and describe some different values commonly used in the registry.
- Create and modify registry values.

Materials Required

- Operating system: Windows NT 4.0 Workstation
- Lab workgroup size: 4 students
- Configuration type: simple

Simple Configuration

- 90 Mhz or better Pentium-compatible computer
- 16 MB of RAM
- 540 MB hard drive
- 1 NIC (Network Interface Card)

Additional Devices: None

Lab Setup & Safety Tips

- Each lab workstation should have Windows NT installed and functioning properly.
- *Warning*: Modifying the Registry can cause the operating system to become corrupt.

Lab Activity

Activity

Viewing the registry

1. Allow your lab workstation to boot into Windows NT.
2. Log on to Windows NT.
3. Click the **Start** button.
4. Select **Run**.
5. Type **REGEDIT** and press **Enter**.
6. Using the registry editor, locate an example of a key, hive, and each type of value, listed below. Write the path to each example on the lines provided.

   Hive

   ____

   ____

   Key

   ____

   ____

Binary value

____

____

String value

____

____

DWord value

____

____

Modifying the right-click menu using the Registry Editor

1. Click the **Start** button.
2. Select **Run**.
3. Type **REGEDIT** and press **Enter**.
4. Double-click the **HKEY_LOCAL_MACHINE** hive.
5. Double-click the **Software** key.
6. Double-click the **Classes** key.
7. Double-click the **Directory** key.
8. Double-click the **Shell** key.
9. Click the **Edit** menu and point to **New**.
10. Click **Key**.
11. Type **File Manager** and press **Enter**.
12. Double-click the **File Manager** key, if necessary.
13. Click the **Edit** menu and point to **New**.
14. Click **Key**.
15. Type **Command** and press **Enter**.
16. Look at the right window in the Registry Editor, and locate the value **Default** (this is a string value).
17. Right-click the **Default** string value and select **Modify** from the menu.
18. Type **C:\WINNT\SYSTEM32\WINFILE.EXE**.
19. Click the **OK** button.
20. Click the **Close** button to close the Registry Editor.

Testing your work

1. Right-click the **Start** button.

   There should now be a File Manager option on this menu.
2. Click the **File Manager** option.

   If your registry entries are completed correctly, File Manager will start.

Lab Notes

Where is the Windows NT registry stored?—The Windows NT registry is stored in C:\%systemroot%\system32\config. The user registry is stored in the user's personal profile.

What is the difference between REGEDIT and REGEDT32?—The REGEDIT utility has the ability to perform complex registry searches but cannot modify permissions of registry keys. REGEDT32 has the ability to modify permissions, but cannot conduct any type of registry search functions.

Review Questions

Circle True or False.

1. Using the Registry Editor is an excellent way for beginning PC users to learn more about the operating system on their computer. True / False
2. REGEDIT can modify permissions. True / False
3. Windows NT stores its registry in one file named REG.DAT. True / False
4. One example of a key is HKEY_LOCAL_MACHINE. True / False
5. Windows NT stores each user's personal registry information in the user's profile directory. True / False
6. Jamie wants to use the Registry Editor to change her Netscape proxy configuration, but she is not familiar with the Registry Editor utility. In the space below describe how Jamie can use the REGEDIT utility to search for her current proxy settings.

____

____

____

____

____

13

Lab 13.5 Configuring a Dual Boot System

Objective

The objective of this lab exercise is for you to gain experience configuring a computer to dual boot to the Windows 95 and Windows NT operating systems. After completing this lab exercise, you will be able to:

- Configure a computer to dual boot between Windows 95 and Windows NT 4.0 Workstation operating systems.
- Describe the purpose and location of the boot.ini.
- State the file system limitation of a dual boot configuration.

Materials Required

- Operating system: Windows 95 and Windows NT 4.0 Workstation
- Lab workgroup size: 4 students
- Configuration type: simple

Simple Configuration

- 90 Mhz or better Pentium-compatible computer
- 16 MB of RAM
- 540 MB hard drive
- 1 NIC (Network Interface Card)

Additional Devices

- Windows 95 installation files
- One DOS system disk
- One blank, formatted disk
- A valid Windows 95 product ID for each lab workstation
- A set of Windows NT Workstation installation disks and an installation CD-ROM for each group of students

Lab Setup & Safety Tips

- Each lab workstation should be preloaded with the Windows 95 installation files that should be placed in a directory named C:\WIN95.

Activity

Installing Windows 95

1. Insert the system disk into drive A.
2. Power on your lab workstation and allow it to boot from the DOS system disk.
3. At the C prompt, type **CD C:\WIN95** and press **Enter**.
4. Type **SETUP** and press **Enter**.
5. Press **Enter** to allow the Setup program to run the SCANDISK utility.
6. Click the **Continue** button.
7. Click the **Yes** button.

8. Click the **Next** button.
9. Select the **Other Directory** option and click the **Next** button.
10. Type **C:\WINDOWS.95** and click the **Next** button.
11. In the Setup Option window, click the **Typical** option and then click the **Next** button.
12. Type the product ID provided by your instructor.
13. Type your name.
14. Click the **Next** button.
15. Select the hardware components installed on your lab workstation, and click the **Next** button.
16. Click the **Next** button three times to accept the defaults on the next three windows.
17. Insert your blank floppy disk into drive A.
18. Click the **OK** button.
19. Remove the floppy disk and click the **OK** button.
20. Click the **Finish** button.
21. Select the proper time zone, and click the **OK** button.
22. Click the **Cancel** button when prompted to install a printer driver.
23. Click the **OK** button to restart the computer.

Installing Windows NT 4.0 Workstation

1. Insert the Windows NT installation Disk 1 and allow your system to boot from drive A.
2. When prompted, insert Disk 2 and press **Enter**.
3. Press **Enter** on the next two windows.
4. Insert Disk 3 and press the **Enter** key.
5. Press the **Enter** key.
6. Insert the Windows NT Workstation CD-ROM, and then press Enter.
7. Press the **Page Down** button until you reach the end of the license agreement.
8. Press the **F8** key.
9. Press the **Enter** key to accept the detected hardware defaults.
10. Select drive **C** and press the **Enter** key to install Windows NT.
11. Select the **Use current file system** option, and then press **Enter**.
12. Press **Enter** to accept the default directory.
13. Press **Enter** to continue.
14. Remove the disk, and then press **Enter** to restart your computer.
15. Notice that when the computer reboots, there will be two options for Windows NT workstation, and one for MS-DOS (the MS-DOS option is Windows 95).
16. Click the **Next** button to accept the defaults on the next two windows.
17. Type your name and click the **Next** button.
18. Enter the product ID and click the **Next** button.
19. Enter a computer name and click the **Next** button.

20. Enter a password and click the **Next** button.
21. Click the **Next** button to accept the defaults on the next three windows.
22. Select the **Do not connect this computer to a network at this time** option button.
23. Click the **Next** button.
24. Click the **Finish** button.
25. Select a time zone.
26. Click the **Close** button.
27. Click the **OK** button in the video display window.
28. Click the **Test** button in the video display window.
29. Click the **Yes** button to verify the display settings.
30. Click the **OK** button to close the video display window.
31. Click the **OK** button.
32. Insert a floppy disk, and then click the **OK** button.
33. Click the **Restart** button.

Lab Notes

How do I boot into Windows 95?—When Windows NT is installed on a FAT16 partition that already contains an operating system, it will automatically create a menu option in the boot.ini file. This option allows you to boot into your previous environment. If Windows 95 was the previous operating system installed on the FAT16 partition, then by choosing the MS-DOS option from the boot menu, you are instructing Windows NT to pass control of the computer over to the Windows 95 operating system.

Why does the boot menu read MS-DOS?—Sometimes Windows NT doesn't recognize the existing operating system as Windows 95; in those cases, it will label the operating system as MS-DOS rather than Windows 95. This doesn't affect the functionality of either operating system; it is simply a label in the boot.ini.

The dual boot file system—Before configuring a computer to dual boot, you must first determine where each operating system will reside. If the operating systems are to share a partition, the partition must contain a file system that both operating systems can utilize. For example, in the previous activity, you configured a computer to dual boot using the Windows 95 and Windows NT operating systems. In this scenario, you had to choose the FAT16 file system because Windows 95 can't access an NTFS volume.

Review Questions

Circle True or False.

1. The term dual boot refers to two operating system functioning at the same time on the same computer. True / False
2. Windows 95 automatically generates a boot.ini file during installation so that if you decide to dual boot your computer at a later date, the file only has to be modified. True / False
3. The NTFS file system cannot be used when both Windows 95 and Windows NT must reside on the same logical drive. True / False
4. Configuring a computer to dual boot consumes more hard drive space than does a computer that isn't configured to dual boot. True / False
5. In which file is the boot menu data stored?

   ____

   ____

   ____

   ____

   ____

6. Explain why the boot menu may read MS-DOS even though the operating system is Windows 9x.

   ____

   ____

   ____

   ____

   ____

CHAPTER

14

SUPPORTING WINDOWS 2000 PROFESSIONAL

LABS INCLUDED IN THIS CHAPTER

Lab 14.1 Upgrading to Windows 2000

Objective

The objective of this lab exercise is to use the upgrade path to change your computer from Windows NT 4.0 Workstation to Windows 2000 Professional. After completing this lab exercise, you will be able to:

- Upgrade from Windows NT 4.0 Workstation to Windows 2000 Professional.
- Describe the upgrade path from Windows NT 4.0 Workstation to Windows 2000 Professional.

Materials Required

- Operating system: Windows NT 4.0 Workstation
- Lab workgroup size: 2–4 students
- Configuration type: modern

Modern Configuration

- 200 Mhz or better Pentium-compatible computer
- 64 MB of RAM
- 2 GB hard drive
- CD-ROM drive
- 1 NIC (Network Interface Card)
- 1 sound card

Additional Devices

- The Windows 2000 Professional installation CD-ROM

Lab Setup & Safety Tips

- Each group of students needs an NT account with administrative rights on their lab workstation.

Activity

Beginning the upgrade to Windows 2000 Professional

1. Power on your lab workstation and allow it to boot into Windows NT 4.0 Workstation.
2. Log on to Windows with the NT account provided by your instructor.
3. Insert the Widows 2000 Professional CD into the CD-ROM drive.
4. If you are not prompted to upgrade, click **Install Windows 2000**, as shown in Figure 14-1.

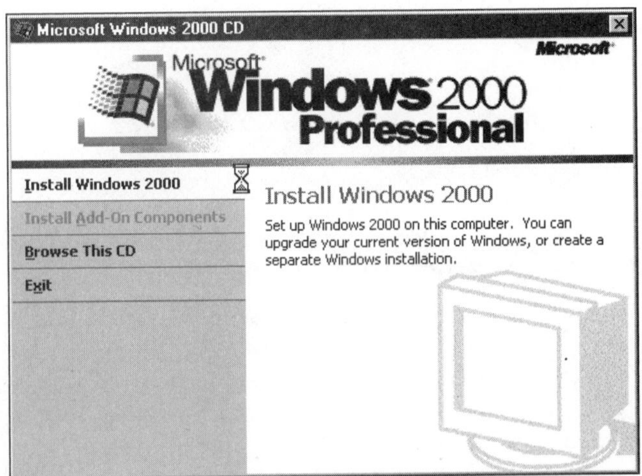

Figure 14-1 Windows 2000 setup screen

5. When you receive the Would you like to upgrade to Windows 2000? prompt, click the **Yes** button.

The Windows 2000 Setup Wizard

1. Click the **Upgrade to Windows 2000 (Recommended)** option button and click the **Next** button.
2. Click the **I accept this agreement** option button and click the **Next** button.
3. Type the product ID, and then click the **Next** button.
4. Click the **Finish** button, if necessary, to restart the computer.

Windows 2000 Setup (no action required)

1. After rebooting your computer, the Windows 2000 Setup program automatically starts.
2. The Windows 2000 Setup program begins by creating a list of files that must be copied to the hard drive for installation.
3. It then continues by copying the necessary files to the hard drive, and rebooting the computer.

Windows 2000 Setup continued (GUI Setup)

1. After rebooting your computer, the Windows 2000 Setup program automatically starts again.
2. The Windows 2000 Setup program attempts to detect the hardware devices that are attached to your computer.
3. It then continues by copying the necessary files to the hard drive and installing the appropriate drivers.
4. The Windows Setup program then completes the installation by installing and registering all necessary components, saving the configuration, and removing all unnecessary temporary files.

Finishing the Windows 2000 upgrade

1. After rebooting your computer, Windows 2000 boots for the first time.
2. When prompted, type your user name and password to log on to Windows 2000. The installation is now completed.

Lab Notes

Stop Messages—Stop messages typically fall into one of the following categories:

- Messages that occur during the use of Windows 2000.
- Messages that occur during the installation of Windows 2000
- Messages that occur because of a software condition
- Messages that occur only during the relatively short phase-4 period of the Windows 2000 Executive initialization sequence.

Stop messages that occur during the installation of Windows 2000—Typically, stop messages that occur during the installation of Windows 2000 are directly related to hardware components attached to the computer. The first step you should take to troubleshoot a Stop message that occurs during an installation is to verify that all of the computer's hardware components can be found on the HCL (Windows 2000 Hardware Compatibility List).

The Windows 2000 Hardware Compatibility List (HCL)—The Windows 2000 HCL is a list of hardware components that have been thoroughly tested for compatibility with Windows 2000. The Windows 2000 HCL can be found on the installation CD-ROM in the /Support directory or at *http://www.microsoft.com/hcl.*

Review Questions

Circle True or False.

1. The Windows 2000 HCL is accessible only via the Microsoft Web site. True / False
2. When using the Windows NT 4.0 Workstation upgrade path for Windows 2000, the user is required to manually configure many of the hardware components. True / False
3. The HCL is a list of hardware components that Microsoft has thoroughly tested for compatibility with Windows 2000. True / False
4. Stop messages that occur during an installation or upgrade to Windows 2000 most often occur because of hardware incompatibilities. True / False
5. Jacob has received a Stop message during a Windows 2000 upgrade. He suspects that he may have an incompatible hardware component. How can Jacob confirm or deny his suspicion?

____
____
____
____
____

6. What are the advantages of upgrading (versus installing a new operating system) to Windows 2000 Professional?

____
____
____
____
____

Lab 14.2 Installing Windows 2000 Professional

Objective

The objective of this lab exercise is to install Windows 2000 Professional. After completing this lab exercise, you will be able to:

- Install Windows 2000 Professional.

Materials Required

- Operating system: Windows 2000 Professional
- Lab workgroup size: 2–4 students
- Configuration type: modern

Modern Configuration

- 200 Mhz or better Pentium-compatible computer
- 64 MB of RAM
- 2 GB hard drive
- CD-ROM drive
- 1 NIC (Network Interface Card)
- 1 sound card

Additional Devices

- A set of Windows 2000 installation disks and an installation CD-ROM for each group of students

14

Lab Setup & Safety Tips

- The following activity will erase all data stored on drive C.
- The instructor must provide appropriate networking and domain logon information for each group of students.

Activity

Installing Windows 2000 Professional

1. Insert the Windows 2000 installation Disk 1, and allow your system to boot from drive A.
2. When prompted, insert Disk 2 and press **Enter**.
3. When prompted, insert Disk 3 and press **Enter**.
4. When prompted, insert Disk 4 and press **Enter**.
5. Press the **Enter** key.
6. Press the **F8** key to accept the license agreement.
7. If there are any existing partitions, delete them by following the menu option at the bottom of the screen.
8. Create a new partition using the Create Partition option.

9. Format the new partition by selecting the **Format the partition using the NTFS file system** option, and then press **Enter**.
10. After the computer has finished copying files, it will reboot and begin the second half of the installation.

Finishing the Windows 2000 installation

1. Click the **Next** button to begin hardware detection.
2. When prompted, click the **Next** button to confirm the Regional settings.
3. Type your name in the name text box and click the **Next** button.
4. Type the name of your lab workstation provided by your instructor in the computer name text box.
5. Click the **Next** button.
6. Configure the date, time, and time zone as appropriate, and then click the **Next** button.
7. Click the **Custom Settings** toggle button and click the **Next** button.
8. Configure your network setting (IP address, etc.) as specified by your instructor. Then, click the **Next** button.
9. Specify the appropriate domain and workgroup, and click the **Next** button.
10. Click the **Finish** button.
11. The Windows Setup program completes the installation by installing and registering all necessary components, saving the configuration, and removing all unnecessary temporary files.
12. After rebooting your computer, Windows 2000 will boot for the first time.

The Network Identification Wizard

1. When prompted, click the **Next** button.
2. Type the user and domain name as specified by your instructor, and then click the **Next** button.
3. Choose the appropriate access level (per your instructor) and click the **Next** button.
4. Click the **Finish** button.
5. When prompted, type your user name and password to log on to Windows 2000. The installation is now completed.

Verify Device Driver installation

1. Right-click the **My Computer** icon.
2. Click **Manage**.
3. In the Computer Management window, single-click **Device Manager** to highlight it.
4. In the right pane of the Computer Management window, verify that all of the computer's hardware has been properly identified.
5. If a device hasn't been properly identified, or is listed with a question mark, the proper driver must be manually installed. Installing drivers manually will be discussed later in this chapter.

Lab Notes

Windows 2000 and file systems—Windows 2000 is compatible with FAT16, NTFS, and FAT32. The Windows 2000 on-disk version of NTFS has been enhanced to provide new functionality, such as reparse points, disk quotas, encryption, sparse files, and a change journal. (For more information on these functionalities, see the product documentation.) The NTFS on-disk format upgrade is quick and automatic.

Creating the four boot disks for Windows 2000 Professional—To create the four installation boot disks required to install Windows 2000 Professional, use MAKEBOOT.EXE or MAKEBT32.EXE found in the bootdisk directory on the Windows 2000 CD-ROM. The MAKEBT32.EXE program should be used only if you are creating the boot disks using a 32-bit operating system; otherwise use MAKEBOOT.EXE.

Review Questions

Circle True or False.

1. To install Windows 2000 Professional, you must have at least one network interface card. True / False
2. Windows 2000 has a Device Manager utility similar to the Windows 9x utility. True / False
3. Windows 2000 cannot read or write to the FAT32 file system. True / False
4. Windows 2000 Professional requires four installation boot disks, whereas Windows NT requires only three. True / False
5. Which directory can the MAKEBOOT.EXE be found on the Windows 2000 CD-ROM?

____

____

____

____

____

6. What are the minimum hardware requirements for Windows 2000 Professional?

____

____

____

____

____

14

LAB 14.3 WINDOWS 2000—THE COMPUTER MANAGEMENT CONSOLE AND WFP (WINDOWS FILE PROTECTION)

Objective

This lab exercise is designed to provide you an opportunity to explore and understand some of the unique tools provided in the Windows 2000 environment. After completing this lab exercise, you will be able to:

- Describe the various uses of the Computer Management Console.
- Describe the purpose of Windows File Protection (WFP).
- Use the System File Checker to repair system file problems.

Materials Required

- Operating system: Windows 2000 Professional
- Lab workgroup size: 4 students
- Configuration type: modern

Modern Configuration

- 200 Mhz or better Pentium-compatible computer
- 64 MB of RAM
- 2 GB hard drive
- CD-ROM drive
- 1 NIC (Network Interface Card)
- 1 sound card

Additional Devices

- The Windows 2000 installation CD-ROM

Lab Setup & Safety Tips

- Each group of students should have a valid user name and password, and at least Power User rights for their lab workstations.

ACTIVITY

Understanding the Computer Management Console

1. Allow the lab workstation to boot into the Windows 2000 environment.
2. Log on to Windows 2000 (if required).
3. Right-click the **My Computer** icon and click **Manage**.

4. Click one of the snap-ins in the following list, and then press the **F1** key. (The **F1** key is a hotkey for the Help menu. You also can access the same information by right-clicking each snap-in and clicking **Help**.) Use the information provided in the Help menu to write a brief description of each of the following snap-ins:

   - Event Viewer

   - System Information

   - Performance Logs and Alerts

   - Shared Folders

   - Device Manager

   - Local Users and Groups

- Disk Management

- Disk Defragmenter

- Removable Storage

- Services and Applications

5. Close the Computer Management window when you have finished.

Observing WFP (Windows File Protection)

1. Click the **Start** button and click **Run**.
2. Type **cmd** in the textbox and press **Enter**.
3. Type **CD winnt\system32** and press **Enter**.
4. Type **DIR sp*.dll** and press **Enter**.
5. Record the name and file size of each file listed.

6. Type **REN spoolss.dll spoolss.old** and press **Enter**.
7. Type **DIR sp*.dll** and press **Enter**.

8. Record the name and file size of each file listed.

9. On the lines provided, describe how Windows 2000 responded when you renamed the spoolss.dll system file.

10. Type **Exit**, and press **Enter**.

Using the System File Checker

1. Click the **Start** button and click **Run**.
2. In the textbox, type **sfc /scannow** and press **Enter**.
3. If prompted, insert your Windows 2000 Professional CD-ROM.

Lab Notes

The System File Checker—The System File Checker should be used if you suspect that system files have become corrupted or deleted.

Review Questions

Circle True or False.

1. WFP monitors system files and automatically replaces them if it detects any unauthorized changes. True / False
2. Performance alerts can be configured using the Performance Log and Alerts snap-in found in the Computer Management Console. True / False
3. Device Manager, found in the Computer Management Console, can be used to enable and disable services. True / False
4. The System File Checker should be used to detect and repair file problems within the Microsoft Office 2000 suite. True / False
5. Explain what the System File Checker utility does, and describe a scenario in which it should be used.

   ____

   ____

   ____

   ____

   ____

6. You are a helpdesk technician at CCO1.com. Lucy, the customer with whom you are currently working, has described her problem to you but you need more information. Lucy's computer is running Windows 2000 Professional. You would like her to access the Computer Management Console's System Information snap-in so that you can collect the required data to solve her problem. In the lines below, describe to Lucy how to find the System Information snap-in.

   ____

   ____

   ____

   ____

   ____

Lab 14.4 The Windows 2000 Recovery Console

Objective

The objective of this lab exercise is to provide you with experience using the Recovery Console. After completing this lab exercise, you will be able to:

- Start the Recovery Console.
- Create and modify registry values.

Materials Required

- Operating system: Windows 2000 Professional
- Lab workgroup size: 4 students
- Configuration type: modern

Modern Configuration

- 200 Mhz or better Pentium-compatible computer
- 64 MB of RAM
- 2 GB hard drive
- CD-ROM Drive
- 1 NIC (Network Interface Card)
- 1 sound card

Additional Devices

- A set of Windows 2000 installation disks and an installation CD-ROM for each group of students

Lab Setup & Safety Tips

- Each lab workstation should have Windows NT installed and functioning properly.

Activity

Starting the Recovery Console

1. Insert the Windows 2000 installation Disk 1, and allow your system to boot from drive A.
2. When prompted, insert Disk 2 and press **Enter**.
3. When prompted, insert Disk 3 and press **Enter**.
4. When prompted, insert Disk 4 and press **Enter**. Your screen should resemble Figure 14-2.

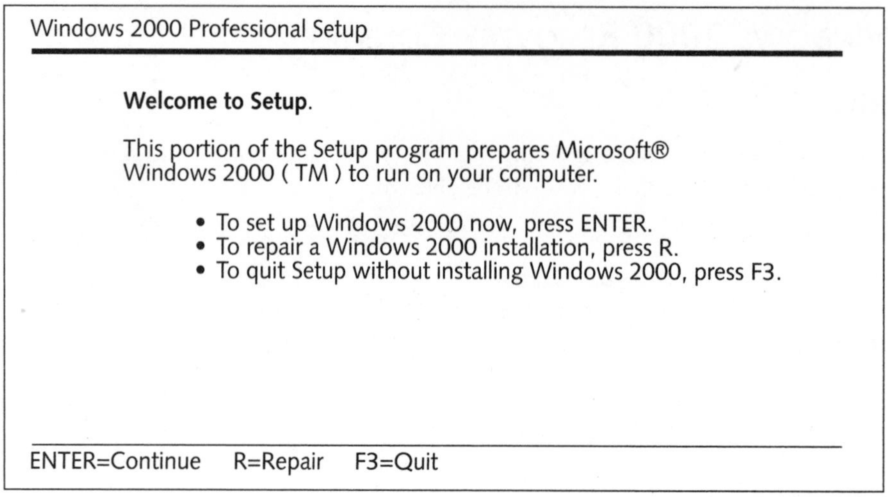

Windows 2000 Professional Setup

Welcome to Setup.

This portion of the Setup program prepares Microsoft®
Windows 2000 (TM) to run on your computer.

- To set up Windows 2000 now, press ENTER.
- To repair a Windows 2000 installation, press R.
- To quit Setup without installing Windows 2000, press F3.

ENTER=Continue R=Repair F3=Quit

Figure 14-2 Use this Windows Setup screen to access the Recovery Console

5. Press the **R** key. Your screen should resemble Figure 14-3.

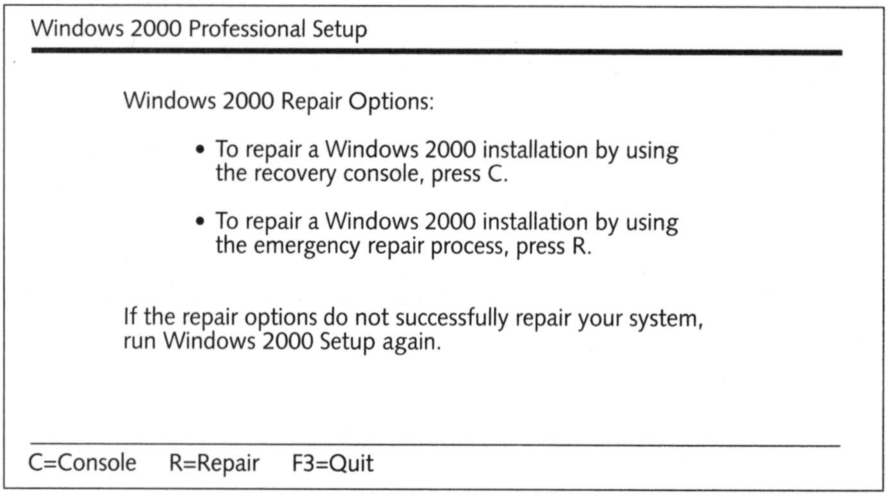

Windows 2000 Professional Setup

Windows 2000 Repair Options:

- To repair a Windows 2000 installation by using the recovery console, press C.
- To repair a Windows 2000 installation by using the emergency repair process, press R.

If the repair options do not successfully repair your system,
run Windows 2000 Setup again.

C=Console R=Repair F3=Quit

Figure 14-3 Windows 2000 offers two repair options

6. Press the **C** key.
7. Type **1** to select the Windows 2000 installation, and press **Enter**.

8. Type the Administrator password and press **Enter**. Your screen should resemble Figure 14-4.

```
Microsoft Windows 2000 ( TM ) Recovery Console.

The Recovery Console provides system repair and recovery functionality.

Type EXIT to quit the Recovery Console and restart the computer.


1: C:\WINNT

Which Windows 2000 installation would you like to log onto
(To cancel, press ENTER)? 1
Type the Administrator password:
C:\WINNT>
```

Figure 14-4 The Windows 2000 Recovery Console command prompt

Viewing and Disabling a service from the Recovery Console

1. Type **Listsvc** and press **Enter**.
2. Record the state of the Alerter service. The state is Enabled, Disabled, Automatic, Boot, Manual, or System.

   ____

3. Type **Disable alerter** and press **Enter**.
4. Type **Listsvc** and press **Enter**.
5. Record the state of the Alerter service.

   ____

14

Set the Alerter Service's state to Manual from the Recovery Console

1. Type **enable Alerter SERVICE_DEMAN_START** and press **Enter**.
2. Type **Listsvc** and press **Enter**.
3. Record the state of the Alerter service.

   ____

4. When finished, remove the floppy disk from drive A and reboot your computer.

Lab Notes

What commands are available from the Recovery Console?—Table 14-1 summarizes many of the useful commands available when you are using the Recovery Console.

Command	Description
Attrib	Changes the attributes of a file or folder: `Attrib -r -h -s filename` This command removes the read, hidden, and system attributes from the file.
Batch	Carries out commands stored in a batch file: `Batch file1 file2` The commands stored in file1 are executed and the results written to file2. If no file2 is specified, results are written to the screen.

Table 14-1 Commands available from the Recovery Console (continued)

Command	Description
Cd	Displays or changes the current directory
Chkdsk	Checks a disk and repairs or recovers the data
Cls	Clears the screen
Copy	Copies a single file: `Copy File1 File2` You can include paths to either file. No wildcard characters are allowed.
Del	Deletes a file: `Del File1`
Dir	Lists files and folders
Disable	Disables a Windows 2000 system service or driver: `Disable servicename`
Diskpart	Creates and deletes partitions on the hard drive. Enter the command with no arguments to display a user interface.
Enable	Enables a Windows 2000 system service or driver: `Enable servicename`
Exit	Quits the Recovery Console and restarts the computer
Expand	Expands a compressed file: `Expand file1`
Fixboot	Rewrites the OS boot sector on the hard drive. If a drive letter is not specified, the system drive is assumed: `Fixboot C:`
Fixmbr	Rewrites the master boot record boot program. This command is the same as FDISK/MBR.
Format	Formats a logical drive. If no file system is specified, NTFS is assumed: `Format C:/fs:FAT32` Uses FAT32 file system `Format C:/fs:FAT` Uses FAT16 file system
Help	Help utility appears for the given command: `Help Fixboot`
Listsvc	Lists all available services
Logon	Allows you to log on to an installation with the Administrator password
Map	Lists all drive letters and file system types
Md or Mkdir	Creates a directory: `MD C:\TEMP`
More or Type	Displays a text file on screen: `TYPE filename.ext`
Rd or Rmdir	Deletes a directory: `RD C:\TEMP`
Rename	Renames a file: `Rename File1.txt File2.txt`
Set	Displays or sets Recovery Console environmental variables
Systemroot	Sets the current directory to the directory where Windows 2000 is installed

Lab Notes (continued)

What about the Registry?—At times, the Recovery Console can be used to overcome a Registry problem. To restore the Registry, follow the procedures outlined in Table 14-2.

Table 14-2 Steps to restore the registry

Command	Description
1. Systemroot	Makes the Windows folder the current folder
2. CD System32\Config	Makes the Windows registry folder the current folder
3. Ren Default Default.save Ren Sam Sam.save Ren Security Security.save Ren Software Software.save Ren System System.save	Renames the five registry files
4. Systemroot	Returns to the Windows folder
5. CD repair\RegBack	Makes the registry backup folder the current folder
6. Copy default C:\WINNT\system32\config Copy Sam C:\WINNT\system32\config Copy Security C:\WINNT\system32\config Copy Software C:\WINNT\system32\config Copy System C:\WINNT\system32\config	Copies the five registry files from the backup folder to the registry folder

Review Questions

Circle True or False.

1. To access the Recovery Console, you must have the fifth Windows 2000 RRC installation floppy disk. True / False
2. The Recovery Console command FIXBOOT will rewrite the OS boot sector on a hard drive. True / False
3. The LISTSVC Recovery Console command will allow you to view all server virtual connections that your computer is actively using. True / False
4. The SYSTEMROOT Recovery Console command will move you to the Windows 2000 systemroot directory. True / False
5. The Recovery Console can never be used to restore the Registry. True / False
6. What are the five files that make up the Windows 2000 Registry, and where are they located?

____

____

____

____

____

CHAPTER

15

PURCHASING A PC OR BUILDING YOUR OWN

LABS INCLUDED IN THIS CHAPTER

- ♦ LAB 15.1 BUILDING A NEW PC: PART 1
- ♦ LAB 15.2 BUILDING A NEW PC: PART 2
- ♦ LAB 15.3 BUILDING A NEW PC: PART 3

LAB 15.1 BUILDING A NEW PC: PART 1

Objective

The objective of this lab exercise is to begin building a PC. This lab exercise combines the skills you have learned in previous exercises and allows you more hands-on practice to further develop your hardware skills. After completing this lab exercise, you will be able to:

- Install a system board.
- Install a CPU.
- Install RAM.

Materials Required

For this lab exercise, students need tools to complete the installation of the following components:

- One PC case
- One Pentium system board
- Two 8 MB SIMMS
- One Pentium CPU
- One CPU cooling fan
- Thermal grease

Additional Devices: None

Lab Setup & Safety Tips

- Always unplug the power cord and properly ground yourself before touching any component inside a computer.
- Students should have documentation that states the correct system board jumper and DIP switch settings for the CPU they are using for this activity.
- Before beginning this activity, students should verify and, if necessary, reconfigure the system board to use the proper jumper and DIP switch settings.

ACTIVITY

Installing the CPU

1. Place the system board on the ESD mat.
2. Remove the CPU from its package and note the blunt end on the processor.
3. Locate the ZIF on the system board and unlatch the lever.
4. Install the CPU by first matching the blunt end of the ZIF with the blunt end of the CPU, and then gently pressing down on the CPU.
5. Don't force the CPU. If it is not moving into place with ease, check for bent pins on the bottom of the CPU. Also verify that you have it lined up properly with the ZIF.
6. Lock the CPU into position using the ZIF lever.
7. Coat the bottom of the CPU fan with thermal grease.
8. Place the CPU fan on top of the CPU.
9. Lock the CPU fan into position.

Installing SIMMS

1. Locate the SIMM banks on your system board.
2. Place the first SIMM at a 45-degree angle and gently slide it into bank zero.
3. Slowly push the SIMM upright until it snaps into position.
4. Repeat Steps 1, 2, and 3 for bank 1.

Installing DIMMS

1. Align the DIMM so that its keying notches line up with the corresponding tabs in the DIMM socket. Make sure the socket's ejector handles are fully open (sitting at a 45-degree angle to the bottom of the socket), as shown in Figure 15-1.

Figure 15-1 Insert the DIMM into the slot by pressing straight down until the supporting arms lock into position

2. Push the DIMM straight down into the socket. The ejector handles will move inward toward the DIMM as it is inserted.
3. Once the DIMM begins to seat, push firmly and simultaneously down on the left and right edge. The DIMM should snap into the socket, and you should then be able to close the ejector handles the rest of the way by gently pushing them against the sides of the DIMM.

Mounting the system board

The process of mounting a system board varies from PC to PC because of the different case designs available. The following Lab Notes discuss some of the similarities between cases.

1. Locate the screws and standoffs necessary for mounting your system board.
2. Line up the system board with the case to determine where the screws and standoffs will be placed.

   Note: Any screws used must be placed within an area on the system board that allows for metal-to-metal contact. If you are unsure, consult the system board user's manual.
3. Install the standoffs.
4. Mount the system board and lock the standoffs into place, if necessary.
5. Secure all screws.
6. Locate the P8 and P9 power connectors.
7. Attach the P8 and P9 power connectors. Be sure the black wires of each connector are placed side-by-side.

Lab Notes

What voltage is my CPU?—Different types of CPUs use different voltage settings. Consult your CPU support documentation for details. *Note:* Some CPUs have the voltage marked on the CPU.

What divisor should I use?—The divisor varies from system to system. Consult your support documentation for the system board and the CPU for more details.

Where is pin one found on a CPU?—You can find pin one on a CPU by locating the flat edge of the processor and aligning it with the flat edge of the ZIF on the system board. When you look at a processor, three of the four edges will be squared, but the fourth will appear flat. The flat corner is pin one.

Review Questions

Circle True or False.

1. System boards are designed to use specific ranges and types of CPUs. True / False
2. You must align pin one when installing a CPU. True / False
3. Use standoffs to keep the system board from touching the case and shorting the entire PC. True / False
4. Power is supplied to AT and Baby-AT style system boards through the P8/P9 power connectors. True / False
5. One of your coworkers, Joe, is installing a CPU. After several attempts, Joe decides to call you for help. Describe to Joe how to identify in which direction the CPU should be installed.

____

____

____

____

____

6. Which memory bank must be populated before a computer will boot?

____

____

____

____

____

Lab 15.2 Building a New PC: Part 2

Objective

The objective of this lab exercise is to continue building the PC you began in Lab 15.1. This lab exercise allows you to further develop your hardware installation and configuration skills. After completing this lab exercise, you will be able to:

- Install COM and LPT ports.
- Install a hard drive.
- Install a CD-ROM drive.
- Install a floppy drive.

Materials Required

The partial lab workstation from the exercise in Lab 15.1

- One cable select data cable
- One hard drive
- One CD-ROM drive
- The COM and LPT ports included with the system board
- One floppy drive
- The tools necessary to complete the installation of the components listed above

Additional Devices: None

Lab Setup & Safety Tips

- Students should have documentation describing the jumper settings for the hard drive and CD-ROM drive prior to starting the activity.
- Always unplug the power cord and properly ground yourself before touching any component inside a computer.

15

Activity

Installing the COM and LPT ports

1. Locate the COM and LPT ports packaged with the system board.
2. Locate two available expansion slots within the case (you will not need any available expansion slots on the system board).
3. Remove any blanks that might be in place.
4. Locate the pins for the LPT cable.
5. Attach the LPT cable to the system board. Be sure that pin one is aligned with the red stripe on the data cable.
6. Slide the LPT port into place and secure it with a screw.
7. Locate the pins for the COM ports.
8. Attach the COM port cables to the system board. Be sure that the pins are aligned correctly.
9. Slide the COM ports into place and secure them with a screw.

Installing the hard drive

1. Locate an available bay for the hard drive.
2. Remove any blanks that might be in place.
3. Slide the hard drive into the bay.
4. Jumper the hard drive to the cable select position.
5. Connect the IDE data cable to the system board. Be sure to verify that the red line on the data cable matches the pin 1 marking on the system board.
6. Connect the IDE data cable and the power connector. Note that the hard drive should be attached to the IDE connector closest to the system board.
7. Mount the hard drive.

Installing the CD-ROM drive

1. Locate an available bay for the CD-ROM drive.
2. Remove any blanks that might be in place.
3. Slide the CD-ROM drive into the bay.
4. Jumper the CD-ROM drive to the cable select position.
5. Connect the IDE data cable and the power connector. Note that the CD-ROM drive should be attached to the IDE connector farthest from the system board. Also connect the audio cable to the sound card.
6. Mount the CD-ROM drive.

Installing the floppy drive

1. Locate an available 3.5-inch drive bay.
2. Remove any blanks that might be in place.
3. Slide the 3.5-inch floppy drive into the bay.
4. Plug in the data cable.
5. Plug in the power connector.

Lab Notes

I/O ports—This lab exercise assumes that both the COM and LPT ports were included with the system board at the time of purchase. Note that this is not always the case and, at times, you may need to purchase a separate I/O card.

Review Questions

Circle True or False.

1. COM ports don't follow the pin one rule. True / False
2. Cable select is the same as master and slave. True / False
3. CD-ROMs must always be slave. True / False
4. A CD-ROM should not be mounted next to a hard drive because it has a magnetic field that could erase data from the hard drive. True / False
5. Floppy drives do not require jumpering in the same manner as does a hard drive. True / False
6. List three ways an IDE CD-ROM could be jumpered to function properly with only one other hard drive present.

____

____

____

____

____

Lab 15.3 Building a New PC: Part 3

Objective

The objective of this lab exercise is to finish building the PC that you began in Labs 15.1 and 15.2. This lab exercise allows you to further develop your hardware installation and configuration skills. After completing this lab exercise, you will be able to:

- Install a video card.
- Install a sound card.
- Install a network card.
- Describe how resources are allocated throughout your PC.
- Complete the final PC configuration steps and describe the value of allowing a system burn-in period.

Materials Required

The partial lab workstation from the exercise in Lab 15.2

- One PCI video card
- One 16-bit ISA sound card
- One network interface card
- The tools necessary to complete the installation of the components listed above

Additional Devices: None

Lab Setup & Safety Tips

- Always unplug the power cord and properly ground yourself before touching any component inside a computer.
- Students should receive documentation describing the jumper settings for the sound card and the network interface card prior to starting the activity.

Activity

Installing the video card

1. Locate the PCI video card.
2. Locate one available PCI expansion slot.
3. Remove any blanks that may be in place.
4. Gently slide the video card into the PCI slot. Be careful not to bend the video card from side to side.
5. Secure the video card with a screw, as shown in Figure 15-2.

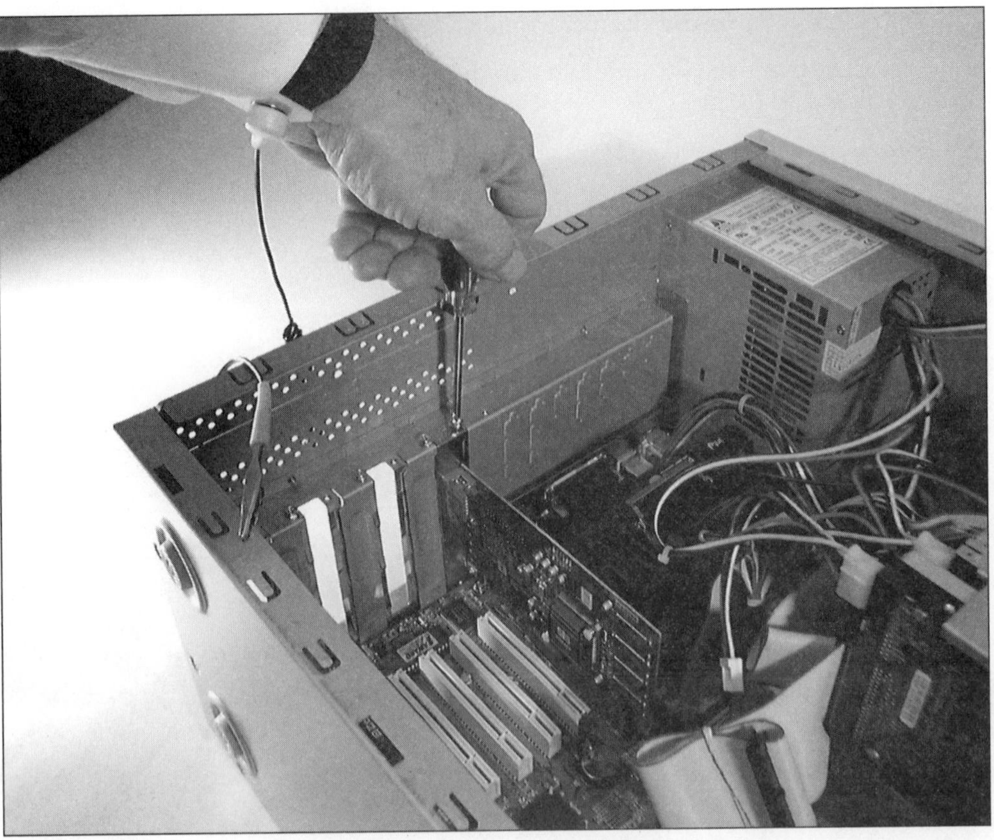

Figure 15-2 Secure the video card in the slot with a screw

Installing the sound card

1. Locate the sound card.
2. Write down your sound card's jumper configuration and verify that it does not conflict with any other devices.

   ____

   ____

   ____

3. Locate one available ISA expansion slot.
4. Remove any blanks that might be in place.
5. Gently slide the sound card into the ISA slot. Be careful not to bend the sound card from side to side.
6. Secure the sound card with a screw, and connect the audio cable to the sound card and the back of the CD-ROM drive, if necessary.

Installing the network interface card

1. Locate the network interface card.
2. Write down your network card's jumper configuration, and verify that it does not conflict with any other devices.

   ____

   ____

   ____

3. Locate one available ISA expansion slot.

4. Remove any blanks that may be in place.
5. Gently slide the network card into the ISA slot. Be careful not to bend the network card from side to side.
6. Secure the network card with a screw.

Completing your resources worksheet

On the lines below, record the resources used by each device.

COM1 ______________________________

COM2 ______________________________

LPT1 ______________________________

LPT2 ______________________________

Sound card ______________________________

Network card ______________________________

Completing the final steps

1. Thoroughly inspect the case. Look for loose wires and any metal (screws, blanks, etc.) that could cause a short.
2. Replace the top to the case.
3. Plug in the monitor.
4. Plug in the keyboard.
5. Plug in the mouse.
6. Secure the LAN line (if available).
7. Connect speakers (if available).
8. Connect all power cords.
9. Power on the PC for the first time.
10. Enter the CMOS Setup program.
11. Set the date and time.
12. Set the correct configuration for each of the hardware components.
13. Save your changes and reboot.
14. Install an operating system.
15. Allow at least 24 hours for a system burn-in period.

Lab Notes

How do I modify the resources of an integrated network card?—When network cards are integrated, you can modify their resources by using the CMOS Setup program.

What is system burn-in?—System burn-in refers to the testing of new hardware. After a PC has been assembled and each component has been tested for functionality, most technicians allow the system at least 24 hours to burn in. During the system burn-in period, the computer is left powered on with an operating system installed and configured properly. Because new hardware components often show any faults during the first 24 to 48 hours of use, the system burn-in period detects these faults before the computer is released to a customer.

Review Questions

Circle True or False.

1. You must always install the video card before the sound card. True / False
2. All network interface cards require DMA 3. True / False
3. PCI video cards are faster than ISA video cards. True / False
4. Before powering on a system, you should always look for loose wires or pieces of metal. True / False
5. Name three CMOS settings that must be modified after a PC is powered on for the first time.

____

____

____

____

____

6. Describe how a system burn-in period affects a product's quality.

____

____

____

____

____

CHAPTER

16

COMMUNICATING OVER PHONE LINES

LABS INCLUDED IN THIS CHAPTER

Lab 16.1 Communications and Windows 9x

Objective

The objective of this lab exercise is to enable you to install and configure all the necessary components to create a functional Dial-Up Networking connection in Windows 9x. After completing this lab exercise, you will be able to:

- Install a modem.
- Install Dial-Up Networking.
- Install a modem device driver.
- Install the dial-up adapter.
- Configure Windows 9x to use a PPP dial-up connection.

Materials Required

- Operating system: Windows 9x
- Lab workgroup size: 2–4 students
- Configuration type: simple

Simple Configuration

- 90 Mhz or better Pentium-compatible computer
- 16 MB of RAM
- 540 MB hard drive
- 1 NIC (Network Interface Card)

Additional Devices

- One jumper-configurable internal ISA modem, and the appropriate documentation

Lab Setup & Safety Tips

- Always unplug the power cord and properly ground yourself before touching any component inside a computer.

Activity

Installing a modem

1. Power off and unplug your lab workstation.
2. Remove the case.
3. Locate an available ISA slot for the internal modem.
4. Remove any blanks that might be in place.
5. Configure the modem's jumpers to use an available COM port.
6. Gently install the modem into the ISA slot. *Warning*: Be careful not to bend the modem from side to side.
7. Secure the modem with a screw.
8. Plug in the lab workstation.
9. Stand clear of the lab workstation and power it on.

10. Enter the CMOS Setup program.
11. Verify that the modem is not conflicting with an existing COM port.
12. If the modem is conflicting with a COM port, disable the COM port.
13. Save your changes and reboot the PC.
14. Power off your lab workstation.
15. Unplug the power cord.
16. Replace the case.
17. Plug in the power cord.
18. Stand clear of your lab workstation, power it on, and allow it to boot into Windows 9x.

Installing Dial-Up Networking

1. Power on your lab workstation and allow it to boot into Windows 9x.
2. Click the **Start** button.
3. Point to **Settings**.
4. Click **Control Panel**.
5. Double-click the **Add/Remove Programs** icon.
6. Click the **Windows Setup** tab.
7. In the list of components, double-click **Communications**.
8. Click the **Dial-Up Networking** check box to select it.
9. Click the **OK** button to close the Communications dialog box.
10. Click the **OK** button.
11. If prompted, enter the path to the installation files.

Installing a modem driver

1. Click the **Start** button.
2. Point to **Settings**.
3. Click **Control Panel**.
4. Double-click the Modems icon. Your screen should resemble Figure 16-1.
5. If you are not prompted to install a modem, click the **Add** button.
6. Click the **Next** button to have Windows 9x search for a modem.
7. Verify that Windows 9x has detected the correct type of modem. You may have to provide a disk if Windows cannot detect your modem.
8. Click the **Next** button.
9. Click the **Finish** button.
10. Click the **OK** button.

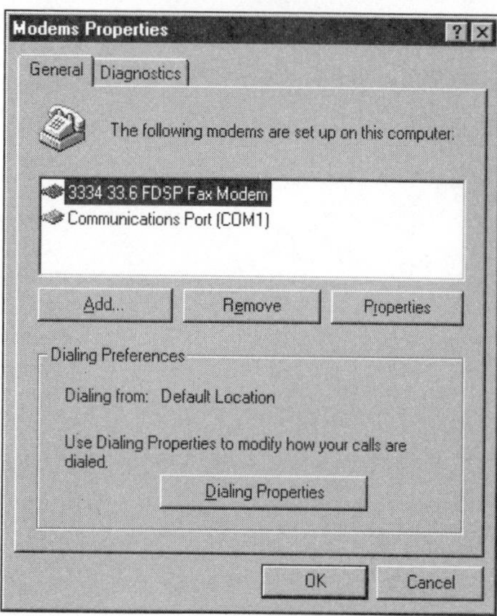

Figure 16-1 The maximum modem speed is often included in the modem name (in this case 33.6 Kbps)

Installing the dial-up adapter

This exercise assumes that you do not have any networking components installed. Prior to beginning this activity, remove any networking components that might be present.

1. Click the **Start** button.
2. Point to **Settings**.
3. Click **Control Panel**.
4. Double-click the **Network** icon.
5. Click the **Add** button.
6. In the type of component list, double-click **Client**.
7. Select **Microsoft** from the Manufacturer list.
8. Double-click the **Client for Microsoft Networks** option.
9. Click **Add** and then double-click **Adapter** in the Type of component list.
10. Select **Microsoft** from the Manufacturer list.
11. In the list of installed network components, double-click the **Dial-Up Adapter** option.
12. Click the **Add** button.
13. In the list of network components, double-click the **Protocol** option.
14. Select **Microsoft** from the Manufacturer list.
15. Double-click the **TCP/IP** option.
16. Click the **OK** button.
17. If prompted, enter the path to the installation files.
18. Click the **Yes** button when prompted to restart your computer.

Creating and configuring a dialer

1. Double-click the **My Computer** icon.
2. Double-click the **Dial-Up Networking** icon.

3. Double-click **Make New Connection**.
4. Type **Lab Dialer** in the Type a name for the computer you are dialing text box, and click the **Next** button.
5. Type **555-5555** in the Telephone Number box.
6. Click the **Next** button.
7. Click the **Finish** button.
8. In the Dial-Up Networking window, right-click the **Lab Dialer** icon.
9. Select **Properties** from the menu.
10. Click the **Server Types** button.
11. Verify that the type of dial-up server is set to the **PPP Windows 95, Windows NT 3.5, Internet** option, or the **PPP: Internet, Windows NT Server, Windows 98** option.
12. Clear the NetBeui and the IPX/SPX check boxes in the Allowed Network Protocols list.
13. Click the **TCP/IP Settings** button.
14. Click the **Specify Name Server Addresses** option button.
15. Type the primary DNS address, provided by your instructor, in the primary DNS box.
16. Click the **OK** button to close the TCP/IP Settings dialog box.
17. Click the **OK** button to close the Server Types dialog box.
18. Click **OK** to close the Lab Dialer dialog box.

Lab Notes

What is the difference between the modem driver and the dial-up adapter?—You install a modem driver using the Modems option in the Control Panel. The modem driver ensures proper communication between the operating system and the modem's hardware. The dial-up adapter is a Dial-Up Networking component that is not necessary to use the modem, but is necessary to connect using some protocols such as PPP.

What is a dialer?—A dialer is a Windows 9x object that contains settings for a particular dial-up connection, such as phone numbers, IP addresses, and allowed protocols. In Windows 9x, you can create and configure multiple dialers, each of which can contain a different configuration.

16

Review Questions

Circle True or False.

1. Dial-Up Networking is installed by using the Add New Hardware option found in the Control Panel. True / False
2. Modem drivers are installed using the Modems option in the Control Panel. True / False
3. All dialers must be configured to dial the same phone number. True / False
4. Dialers are created using the Make New Connection option in the Dial-Up Networking folder. True / False
5. Joy has just purchased and installed a new modem. She has Windows 9x installed on her PC. What should Joy do next so that her operating system will properly communicate with her modem?

____

____

____

____

____

6. List four configurable options in a Windows 9x dialer.

____

____

____

____

____

LAB 16.2 COMMUNICATIONS AND WINDOWS NT

Objective

The objective of this lab exercise is to enable you to install and configure all the necessary components to create a functional Dial-Up Networking connection using the Remote Access Service. After completing this lab exercise, you will be able to:

- Install a modem device driver.
- Install the remote access service (RAS).
- Configure Windows NT to use a PPP dial-up connection.

Materials Required

- Operating system: Windows NT 4.0 Workstation
- Lab workgroup size: 2–4 students
- Configuration type: simple

Simple Configuration

- 90 Mhz or better Pentium-compatible computer
- 16 MB of RAM
- 540 MB hard drive
- 1 NIC (Network Interface Card)

Additional Devices

- One installed modem

Lab Setup & Safety Tips

- Each lab workstation should have one modem installed and functioning properly.
- Each group of students should have the necessary modem drivers for their lab workstations.

16

ACTIVITY

Installing a modem driver

1. Power on your lab workstation and allow it to boot into Windows NT.
2. Log on to your Windows NT system as **Administrator** or an equivalent account.
3. Click the **Start** button.
4. Point to **Settings**.
5. Click **Control Panel**.
6. Double-click the **Modems** icon.
7. If you are not prompted to install a modem, click the **Add** button.
8. Click the **Next** button to have Windows NT search for a modem.
9. Verify that Windows NT has detected the correct type of modem. You may have to provide a disk if Windows cannot detect your modem.
10. Click the **Next** button.
11. Click the **Finish** button.
12. Click the **Close** button.

Installing the RAS

1. Double-click the **My Computer** icon.
2. Double-click the **Dial-Up Networking** icon. The Dial-Up Networking dialog box appears, as shown in Figure 16-2.

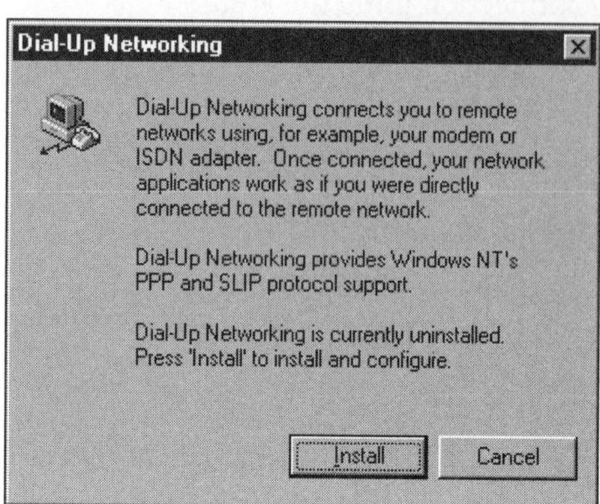

Figure 16-2 Windows NT instructs the user to install Dial-Up Networking before the modem can be used

3. When prompted, click the **Install** button.
4. If prompted, insert the Windows NT CD and enter the path to the installation files.
5. Click the list arrow to select the modem you have previously installed.
6. Click the **OK** button.
7. Click the **Network** button and select the **TCP/IP** check box.
8. Click the **OK** button, and then click **OK** again.
9. Click the **Configure** button.
10. Verify that the **Dial Out Only** option button is selected.
11. Click the **OK** button.
12. Click the **Continue** button.
13. Click the **Yes** button when prompted to restart your computer.

Creating and configuring a RAS connection

1. Double-click the **My Computer** icon.
2. Double-click the **Dial-Up Networking** icon. If necessary, enter location information for your computer, click the **Close** button, and then double-click the **Dial-Up Networking** icon again.
3. Click the **OK** button.
4. Select the **I know all about phonebook entries** check box, and click the **Finish** button.
5. In the phone number box, type **555-5555**.
6. Click the **Server** tab.
7. Click the **TCP/IP Settings** button, and then click the **Specify name server addresses** option button.
8. Type **127.15.8.4** in the primary DNS box (this is a fictional DNS address).
9. Type **127.15.8.5** in the secondary DNS box (this is a fictional DNS address).

10. Click the **OK** button.
11. Click the **Security** tab.
12. Click the **Accept any authentication including clear text** option button.
13. Click the **OK** button.

Lab Notes

How do I uninstall RAS?—To uninstall RAS, access the Network icon through the Control Panel, and then click the Services tab. To completely remove RAS, select RAS by clicking on it and then clicking the Remove button.

Review Questions

Circle True or False.

1. Configuring a dialer in Windows 9x is the same as configuring a dialer in Windows NT. True / False
2. Windows NT will attempt to detect your modem after it has been installed. True / False
3. RAS is used to create and configure Remote Access connections. True / False
4. RAS can be uninstalled by using the Add/Remove Software icon found in the Control Panel. True / False
5. RAS can be configured to dial out or receive calls. True / False
6. A phone book entry is the Windows NT version of a dialer. True / False
7. Neil would like to configure his Windows NT computer to dial into the Internet, but doesn't know where to type the DNS and WINS addresses. Describe where in Windows NT Neil must go to enter the DNS and WINS addresses for his remote connection.

____

____

____

____

____

Lab 16.3 Communications and Windows 2000

Objective

The objective of this lab exercise is to enable you to install and configure all the necessary components to create a functional Dial-Up Networking connection using the Remote Access Service in the Windows 2000 environment. After completing this lab exercise, you will be able to:

- Install a modem device driver.
- Configure Windows 2000 to use a PPP dial-up connection.

Materials Required

- Operating system: Windows 2000 Professional
- Lab workgroup size: 2–4 students
- Configuration type: modern

Modern Configuration

- 200 Mhz or better Pentium-compatible computer
- 64 MB of RAM
- 2 GB hard drive
- CD-ROM drive
- 1 NIC (Network Interface Card)
- 1 sound card

Additional Devices

- One installed modem

Lab Setup & Safety Tips

- Each lab workstation should have one modem installed and functioning properly.
- Each group of students must have a valid Windows 2000 logon with administrative rights.
- Each group of students should have the necessary modem drivers for their lab workstations.

Activity

Installing a modem driver

1. Power on your lab workstation and allow it to boot into Windows 2000.
2. Log on to your Windows 2000 system as **Administrator** or an equivalent account.
3. Click the **Start** button.
4. Point to **Settings**.
5. Click **Control Panel**.
6. Double-click the **Phone and Modem Options** icon.
7. Click the **Modems** tab.

8. Click the **Add** button.
9. Click the **Next** button.
10. If Windows doesn't detect your modem, click the **Next** button. Otherwise, go to Step 15.
11. Insert the modem driver disk provided by your instructor.
12. Click the **Have Disk** button.
13. Click the **OK** button.
14. Choose the appropriate COM port, and click **Next**.
15. Click the **Finish** button.
16. Click the **OK** button in the Phone and Modem Options window.
17. Click the **Start** button and click **Shut Down**.
18. Use the drop-down menu to select **Restart**, and click the **OK** button.

Creating a Dial-up connection

1. Allow your computer to boot into the Windows 2000 environment, and log on using an administrative account.
2. Right-click **My Network Places**, and click **Properties**.
3. Double-click **Make New Connection**.
4. Click the **Next** button.
5. Click the **Dial-Up to private network** toggle key, and click **Next**.
6. If necessary, select your modem by clicking the appropriate check box, and then click the **Next** button.
7. In the phone number box, type **555-5555** and click the **Next** button.
8. Verify that the **For all users** toggle key is selected, and then click the **Next** button.
9. Click the **Finish** button.

Configuring the Dial-up connection

1. In the Connect Dial-up Connection window, click the **Properties** button.
2. Click the **Networking** tab.
3. Click the **Properties** button.
4. Click the **Use the following IP address** toggle key.
5. Type **125.15.8.6** in the IP address box.
6. Type **125.15.8.4** in the Preferred DNS server box (this is a fictional DNS address).
7. Type **125.15.8.5** in the Alternate DNS server box (this is a fictional DNS address).
8. Click the **OK** button.
9. Click the **OK** button in the Dial-up Connection window.
10. You have completed configuring the dial-up connection. To use this dialer, you would enter your username and password in the appropriate text boxes, and then click **Dial**.

Lab Notes

Internet Connection Sharing—Windows 2000 has an option that allows multiple computers to share a single Internet connection. This feature, when configured properly, allows a computer across the network to share your dial-up Internet connection. To enable this feature, right-click your dial-up connection, click Properties, and click the Sharing tab. Then click Enable Internet Connection Sharing for this connection.

Multilink—Combines multiple physical links (typically phones), which increases the total bandwidth of your connection, and dynamically dials and drops multilinked lines as bandwidth is needed. This feature also is configurable through the Dial-Up Connection Properties.

What is ISDN?—ISDN (Integrated Services Digital Network) is a communications standard that can carry digital data simultaneously over two channels on a single pair of wires at almost five times the speed of regular phone lines.

What is ADSL?—ADSL (asymmetric digital subscriber line) is a method of data transmission over phone lines that is digital, allows for a direct connection, and is 50 times faster than ISDN.

How does a cable modem work?—A cable modem transfers data over cable TV lines. This transmission requires a modem and a NIC to send and receive transmissions.

Review Questions

Circle True or False.

1. The Local Area Connections icon, found in the Network and Dial-up Connections window, can be used to configure a Dial-Up Connection. True / False
2. Multilink allows multiple modems to be used at the same time in such a manner that the computer's total bandwidth is increased. True / False
3. ADSL technology utilizes coaxial cable to deliver high-speed Internet access. True / False
4. ADSL is about 10 times faster than ISDN. True / False
5. You are a network consultant for a small firm. The firm has five computers; each computer has access to the LAN. One computer has a modem and Windows 2000 Professional installed. What feature could the Windows 2000 computer invoke to provide Internet access to all the computers on the network, assuming you have one dial-up ISP account?

   ____

   ____

   ____

   ____

   ____

6. Your ISP has recently updated their servers and issued you two new DNS server addresses. The name of your dial-up connection is "My ISP." Describe how to reconfigure the DNS server addresses for the "My ISP" dial-up connection.

   ____

   ____

   ____

   ____

   ____

Lab 16.4 Modem Troubleshooting

Objective

The objective of this lab exercise is to provide you with hands-on practice troubleshooting Dial-Up Networking problems both in Windows 9x and in Windows NT. After completing this lab exercise, you will be able to:

- Troubleshoot modem communications in Windows 9x.
- Troubleshoot modem communications in Windows NT.

Materials Required

- Operating system: Windows NT 4.0 Workstation
- Lab workgroup size: 2–4 students
- Configuration type: simple

Simple Configuration

- 90 Mhz or better Pentium-compatible computer
- 16 MB of RAM
- 540 MB hard drive
- 1 NIC (Network Interface Card)

Additional Devices

- One installed modem

Lab Setup & Safety Tips

- Each lab workstation should be dual booted with the Windows 9x and Windows NT operating systems.
- During the following lab exercises, students are required to dial out using their modems. Note that an analog line for each lab workstation is not necessary. Students must be able to at least make the modem dial by clearing the Wait for dial tone before dialing check box. Note that this option is available in both Windows 9x and Windows NT.
- If students are working in pairs, designate one as Student 1 and the other as Student 2.
- Each lab workstation should have one modem installed and functioning properly.

16

Activity

Troubleshooting modem communications in Windows 9x

The following steps should be performed while Student 2 is away from the lab workstation.

Student 1

1. Power on your lab workstation and allow it to boot into Windows 9x.
2. Click the **Start** button.
3. Point to **Settings**.
4. Click **Control Panel**.
5. Double-click the **System** icon.

6. Click the **Device Manager** tab.
7. Double-click the **Modem** icon.
8. Double-click the installed modem.
9. If you are using Windows 95, clear the **Original Configuration** check box. In Windows 98, clear the **Disable in this hardware profile** check box.
10. Click the **OK** button.
11. Click the **Close** button.
12. Click the **Start** button.
13. Select the **Shut Down** option and restart the lab workstation.

Student 2

1. After Student 1 has reconfigured the lab workstation, answer the following questions and then repair the lab workstation. To repair your lab workstation, you must be able to create and dial out using a dialer configured with the TCP/IP protocol to use the following DNS numbers:

   Primary DNS: 15.8.457.1

   Secondary DNS: 15.8.245.6

   a. Are there any error messages? If so, write them down: ______________________

   ____

   ____

   b. What is the problem? Be specific. ______________________

   ____

   ____

   c. List several possible solutions. ______________________

   ____

   ____

   d. Test your theory (solution) and record the results. ______________________

   ____

   ____

   e. How did you discover the problem? ______________________

   ____

   ____

   f. What would you do differently in the future to improve your troubleshooting process?

   ____

   ____

   ____

   ____

   ____

Troubleshooting modem communications in Windows NT

Student 2

The following steps should be performed while Student 1 is away from the lab workstation.

1. Power on the lab workstation and allow it to boot into Windows NT.
2. Log on to Windows NT.
3. Click the **Start** button.
4. Point to **Settings**.
5. Click **Control Panel**.
6. Double-click the **Network** icon.
7. Click the **Services** tab.
8. Double-click **Remote Access Service**.
9. Click the **Network** button.
10. Clear the **TCP/IP** check box.
11. Select the **NetBEUI** check box.
12. Click the **OK** button.
13. Click the **Continue** button.
14. If prompted, enter the path to the installation files.
15. Click the **Close** button.
16. Click the **Yes** button, and then restart the computer.

Student 1

1. After Student 2 has reconfigured the lab workstation, answer the following questions and then repair the lab workstation. To repair your lab workstation, you must be able to create and use a phone book entry with the TCP/IP protocol configured to use the following DNS numbers:

   Primary DNS: 15.8.457.1

   Secondary DNS: 15.8.245.6

   a. Are there any error messages? If so, write them down: ______________________

   ____

   ____

   b. What is the problem? Be specific. ______________________

   ____

   ____

   c. List several possible solutions. ______________________

   ____

   ____

   d. Test your theory (solution) and record the results. ______________________

   ____

   ____

16

e. How did you discover the problem? ______________________________

____

____

f. What would you do differently in the future to improve your troubleshooting process?

____

____

____

____

____

Lab Notes

If the modem does not respond:

1. Make sure the modem is plugged into the phone jack.
2. If you are using an external modem, make sure it is plugged into the computer, and that the connection is solid.
3. There are two RJ-11 ports on a modem. Check that the phone line from the wall outlet is connected to the line-in port.
4. Plug a phone directly into the wall jack you are using, and make sure that there is a dial tone.
5. If necessary, make sure to instruct the modem to dial an extra character, such as 9 or 8, to get an outside line.
6. During a new installation, check the following:
   - Make sure the modem is set to the same COM port and IRQ that the software is set to.
   - Make sure that no other device is configured to the same COM port or IRQ as the modem.
   - For an internal modem, check that the DIP switches and jumpers agree with the modem properties in the OS.
   - For an internal modem using CMOS setup, disable the COM port that the modem is set to use so that there will be no conflicts. For an external modem, verify that the COM port that the modem is using is enabled.
   - If you are using an internal modem, try installing it in a different expansion slot. If you are using an external modem using a serial port card, move the serial port card to a different slot, and try to install the modem. If you are using an external modem, substitute a known-good serial cable.
   - Check that the software correctly initialized the modem. If you did not give the correct modem type to the software, it may be trying to send the wrong initialization command.

The modem says there is no dial tone, even though you can hear it:

1. Make sure that the phone cord from the wall outlet is plugged into the line jack on the modem.
2. The modem may not be able to detect the dial tone even if you can hear it. Try unplugging any other equipment, such as a fax machine that is plugged into this same phone line.

Review Questions

Circle True or False.

1. RAS can be disabled by using the Modems option in the Control Panel. True / False
2. Windows 9x allows you to create multiple phone book entries. True / False
3. Using Windows 9x, you can view a modem's resources by using the Device Manager. True / False
4. Using Windows NT, you can view a modem's resources by using the Device Manager. True / False
5. Peggy wants to reinstall RAS on her Windows NT computer. Describe how she could complete this task.

   ____

   ____

   ____

   ____

   ____

6. Steve has decided to reinstall his modem driver on his Windows 9x computer. Describe the steps he should take to complete this task.

   ____

   ____

   ____

   ____

   ____

CHAPTER

17

NETWORKING FUNDAMENTALS AND THE INTERNET

LABS INCLUDED IN THIS CHAPTER

Lab 17.1 Network Component Identification & Network Card Installation

Objective

The objective of this lab exercise is to install and configure a network interface card and to familiarize you with the common components of a networked environment. After completing this lab exercise, you will be able to:

- Install a network interface card.
- Identify some common networking components.
- Describe the functions of common networking components.

Materials Required

- Operating system: Windows 9x
- Lab workgroup size: 2–4 students
- Configuration type: simple

Simple Configuration

- 90 Mhz or better Pentium-compatible computer
- 16 MB of RAM
- 540 MB hard drive
- 1 NIC (Network Interface Card)

Additional Devices

- DB-9 cable
- DB-25 cable
- One standard Centronics parallel cable
- RJ-25
- RJ-11
- RJ-14
- RJ-45
- BNC
- BNCT
- PS2/MINI-DIN
- ThickNet
- Unshielded twisted-pair wire
- Shielded twisted-pair wire
- One network interface card designed for use with both an RJ-45 connector and a BNC connector

For demonstration purposes, the instructor can use the following:

- One hub
- One router
- One switch
- Fiber-optic cable and connectors

To demonstrate advanced networking devices, the instructor must provide the following:

- Network sniffer
- Protocol analyzer
- Time domain reflector
- Any type of ISDN devices

Lab Setup & Safety Tips

- The instructor should label each network and wiring component.
- Always unplug the power cord and properly ground yourself before touching any component inside a computer.

Activity

Identifying network components

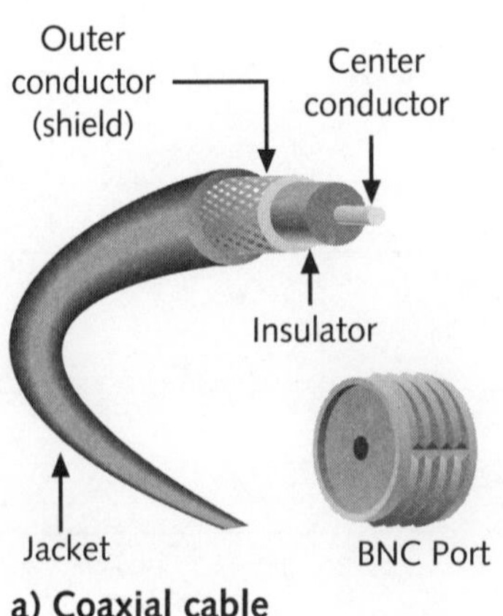

a) Coaxial cable

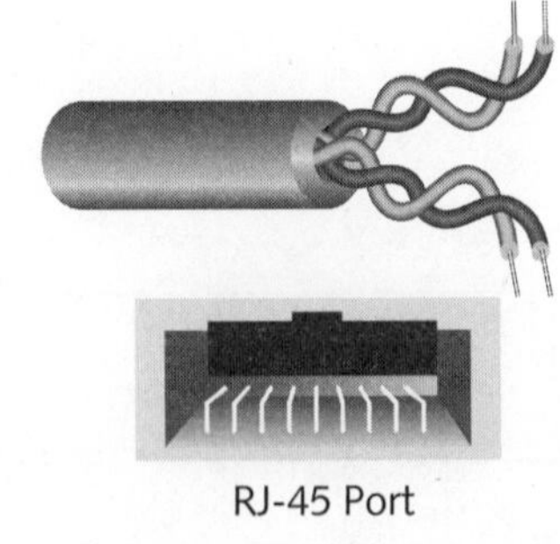

b) Unshielded twisted pair (UTP)

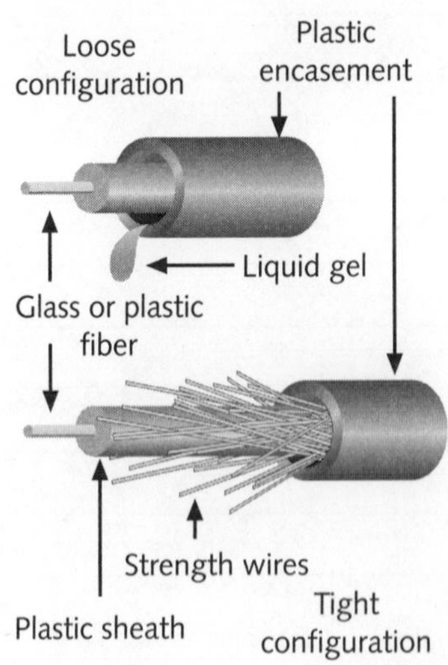

c) Fiber-optic cables with tight and loose sheaths

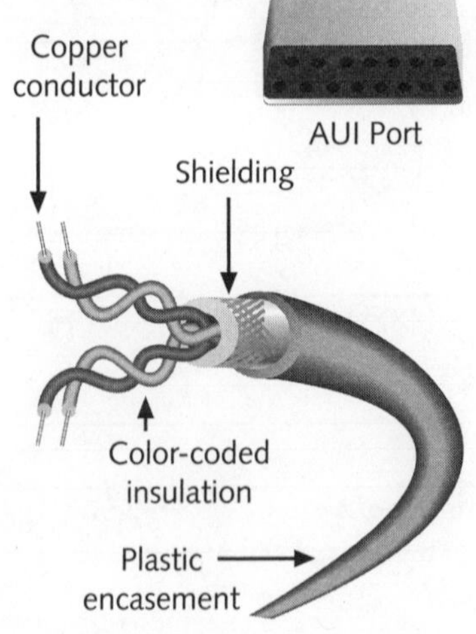

d) Shielded twisted pair (STP)

Figure 17-1 Networking cables

1. Observe the cables in Figure 17-1. Then, describe the function of each of the following items, and explain how each could be used in a networked environment:

   a. DB-9 cable

   ____

   ____

   ____

17

b. DB-25 cable

____

____

____

c. Centronics parallel data cable

____

____

____

d. RJ-25

____

____

____

e. RJ-11

____

____

____

f. RJ-14

____

____

____

g. RJ-45

____

____

____

h. BNC

____

____

____

i. BNCT

____

____

____

j. PS2/MINI-DIN

____

____

____

k. ThickNet

l. Unshielded twisted-pair wire

m. Shielded twisted-pair wire

n. Network interface card

o. Hub

p. Router

q. Switch

r. Fiber optics

s. Network sniffer

t. Protocol analyzer

____

____

____

u. Time domain reflector

____

____

____

v. ISDN devices

____

____

____

Installing the network interface card

1. Unplug the power cord.
2. Remove the case.
3. Locate an available slot where you will install the network interface card.
4. Using the documentation provided, verify that the network interface card is configured to use the predetermined I/O address and has an available IRQ.
5. Gently install the network interface card into the slot. *Warning*: Don't bend the card from side to side; move the card only back and forth from end to end.
6. Screw the mounting screw into place.
7. Replace the top of the case.
8. Plug in the system unit.
9. Power on the lab workstation and allow it to boot into Windows 9x.
10. If the workstation fails to boot properly, power cycle the PC, and when prompted, choose Safe Mode.

Lab Notes

What does RJ stand for?—RJ stands for registered jack.

What does LAN stand for?—The term LAN stands for local area network. LAN normally refers to a small or midsized network that is contained within a small geographical area.

What does WAN stand for?—The term WAN stands for wide area network. WAN normally refers to a network that is spread across a large geographical area.

What is a MAN?—The term MAN stands for metropolitan area network. MAN is normally used to refer to a small or midsize network that is contained within a metropolitan area.

Review Questions

Circle True or False.

1. An RJ-11 connector is commonly used as telephone wire. True / False
2. RJ stands for registered jack. True / False
3. RJ-45 connectors are often used in a LAN environment. True / False
4. BNC connectors are most commonly used to connect UTP. True / False
5. Describe the difference between UTP and STP.

____
____
____
____
____

6. Describe the difference between a router and a hub.

____
____
____
____
____

Lab 17.2 Networking and Windows 9x

Objective

The objective of this lab exercise is to provide you with hands-on networking experience in the Windows 9x environment. After completing this lab exercise, you will be able to:

- Install network interface card drivers.
- Configure Windows 9x to communicate on a LAN.
- Share resources in a networked environment.
- Map a network drive.
- Configure the TCP/IP protocol in the Windows 9x environment.

Materials Required

- Operating system: Windows 9x
- Lab workgroup size: 2–4 students
- Configuration type: simple

Simple Configuration

- 90 Mhz or better Pentium-compatible computer
- 16 MB of RAM
- 540 MB hard drive
- 1 NIC (Network Interface Card)

Additional Devices: None

Lab Setup & Safety Tips

- Each lab workstation should have one network interface card installed, but not configured to communicate on a network.
- The classroom should be wired for network communications.
- The instructor will provide an IP address for each lab workstation prior to the start of activities. *Note*: All IP addresses issued should be on the same subnet unless the classroom supports other configurations.
- The instructor will provide computer names for each lab workstation before the activities are completed.

Activity

Installing network interface card drivers

The following lab exercise assumes that your lab workstation is not configured with any networking components. If your lab workstation does have networking components installed, remove them all, and reboot your system before proceeding.

1. Power on your lab workstation and allow it to boot into Windows 9x.
2. Click the **Start** button.
3. Point to **Settings**.
4. Click **Control Panel**.

5. Double-click the **Network** icon.
6. Click the **Add** button.
7. In the list of network components, double-click **Client**.
8. In the list of manufacturers, click **Microsoft**.
9. In the list of network clients, double-click **Client for Microsoft Networks**.
10. In the list of manufacturers, click **NIC**.
11. Double-click the correct NIC driver.
12. Click the **Add** button.
13. Double-click the **Protocol** option.
14. In the Manufacturers list, click **Microsoft**, as shown in Figure 17-2.
15. Double-click the **TCP/IP** option.
16. Click the **Identification** tab.
17. Type the computer name specified by your instructor.
18. Click the **OK** button.
19. If prompted, enter the path to the installation files.
20. Click the **Yes** button when you are prompted to restart your computer.

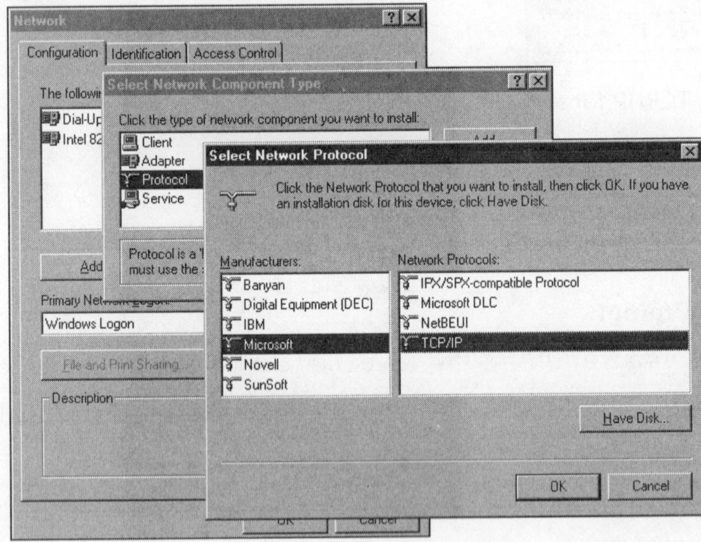

Figure 17-2 Installing TCP/IP from the Network window of the Control Panel

Configuring the TCP/IP protocol

1. Click the **Start** button.
2. Point to **Settings**.
3. Click **Control Panel**.
4. Double-click the **Network** icon.
5. Double-click the **TCP/IP** protocol.
6. Click the **Specify an IP address** option button, as shown in Figure 17-3.
7. Type the IP address issued to your lab workstation.

8. Enter any additional information your instructor requires.
9. Click the **OK** button to close the TCP/IP Properties dialog box.
10. Click the **OK** button to close the Network dialog box.
11. Click the **Yes** button when prompted to restart your computer.

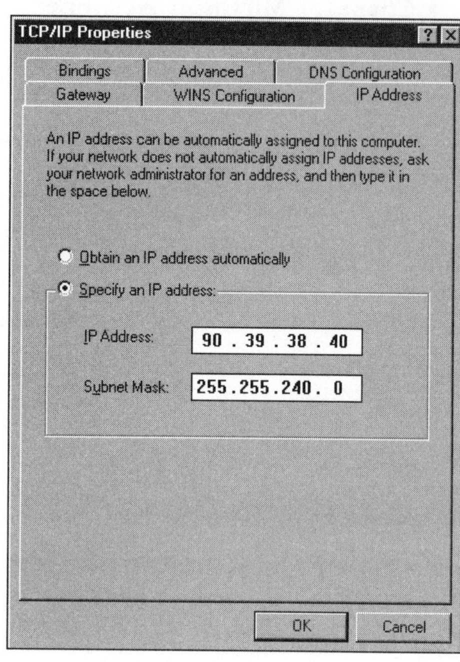

Figure 17-3 Configuring TCP/IP for static IP addressing

Using the PING command to test the network

1. Click the **Start** button.
2. Point to **Programs**.
3. Click **MS-DOS Prompt**.
4. Type **PING** ###.###.###.### (### represents your lab workstation's IP address).
5. Type **PING** ###.###.###.### (### represents the IP address of your neighbor's lab workstation).

Enabling resource sharing

1. Click the **Start** button.
2. Point to **Settings**.
3. Click **Control Panel**.
4. Double-click the **Network** icon.
5. Click the **File and Printer Sharing** button.
6. Click both check boxes to check them and allow the lab workstations to share resources.
7. Click the **OK** button to close the File and Printer Sharing dialog box.
8. Click the **OK** button to close the Network dialog box.
9. Click the **Yes** button when prompted to restart your computer.

Sharing your C drive

1. Double-click the **My Computer** icon.
2. Right-click the icon for your C drive.
3. Select **Properties** from the shortcut menu.
4. Click the **Sharing** tab.
5. Click the **Shared As** option button.
6. Click the **Full** option button.
7. Click the **OK** button.

Connecting to a shared resource

1. Right-click the **Network Neighborhood** icon.
2. Select the **Map Network Drive** option.
3. Click the Drive list arrow and then click the drive letter **G**.
4. Type ***COMPUTERNAME**SHARENAME*** in the path box (the computer and share name should be your neighbor's).
5. Click the **OK** button.

Lab Notes

PING (Packet Internet Groper)—The PING command is a useful diagnostic tool that can be used to test network connectivity. Devices on networks communicate as shown in Figure 17-4. PING sends a signal to a remote computer specified using the computer's name or IP address. If the computer is online, it will respond; otherwise, the command will timeout.

UNC (Universal Naming Convention)—In a networked environment, the UNC is a way to identify a shared file located on another computer without having to know the storage device on which it is located.

In the Windows environment, the UNC format is as follows:

\\computername\sharename\path\filename

In this lab, you connect using this format:

\\computername\sharename

What is a protocol?—A protocol is a generally agreed upon set of rules that computers use to communicate in a networked environment.

What is bandwidth?—In the networking environment, bandwidth refers to the amount of data that can be sent or received over a given type of transmission medium (copper wire, fiber-optic cable, radio or satellite channel, and so on) at any given time. Bandwidth is usually expressed in bits per second (bps), kilobits per second (Kbps), or megabits per second (Mbps).

What is a gateway?—A gateway is a device or process that connects networks with different protocols. A router often is used as a gateway.

What is DNS?—DNS stands for Domain Name System or Domain Name Service. A DNS is a database on a top-level domain name server that keeps track of assigned domain names and their corresponding IP addresses.

17

Lab Notes (continued)

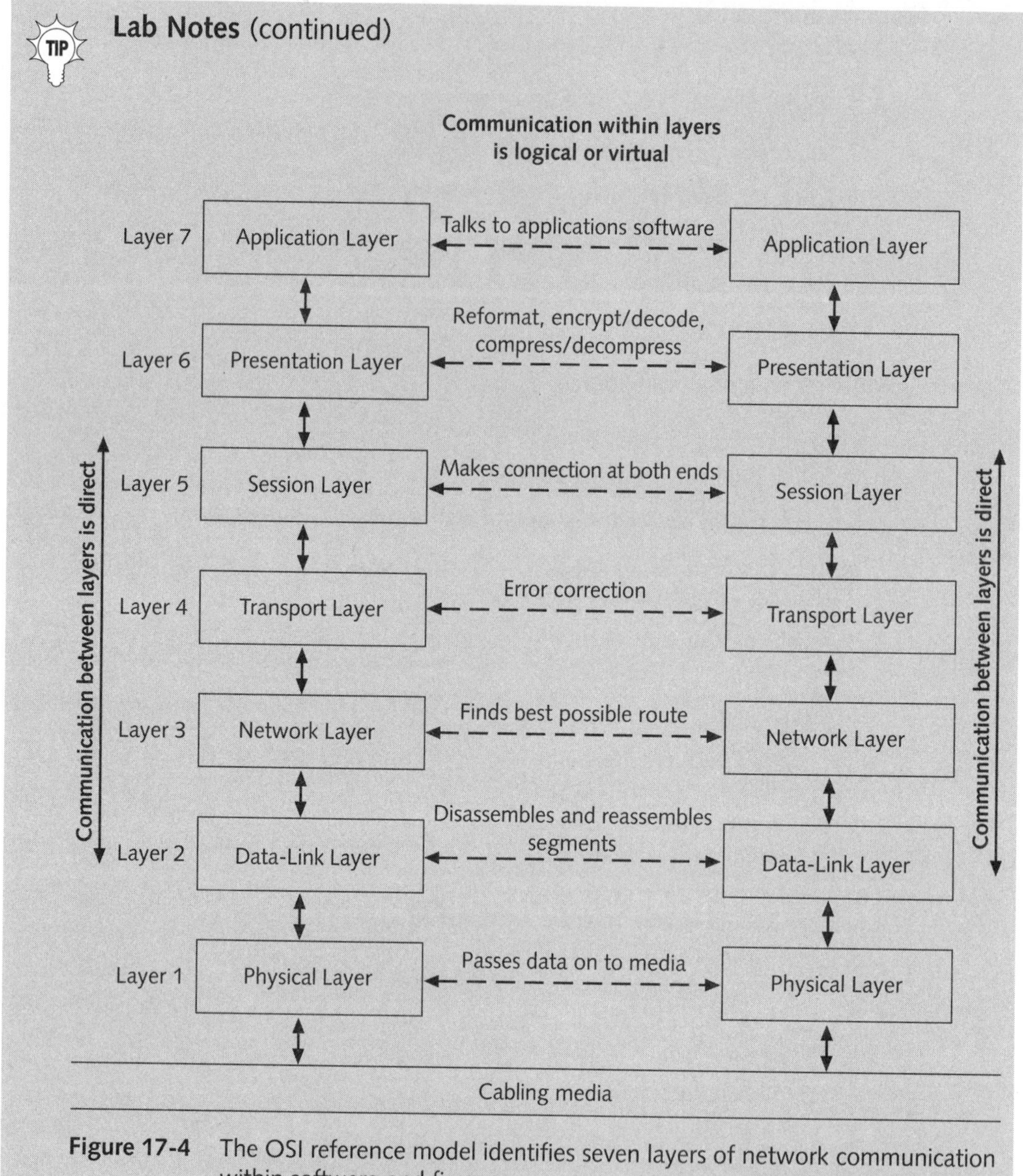

Figure 17-4 The OSI reference model identifies seven layers of network communication within software and firmware

Review Questions

Circle True or False.

1. You can configure Windows 9x to use an IP address by using the Control Panel Network option. True / False
2. You can use the PING command to share network resources. True / False
3. All network drives that map from a Windows 9x PC to a Windows 9x PC must be mapped as drive G. True / False
4. Melanie can access the network properties on her Windows 9x computer by right-clicking the My Computer icon and selecting Properties from the shortcut menu. True / False
5. Roy would like to enable file and printer sharing on his Windows 9x laptop. He has already installed TCP/IP and can share resources on the network, but is unable to share any files. Describe the steps that Roy should take to enable file and printer sharing.

____
____
____
____
____

6. Where do you specify a computer and workgroup name in Windows 9x?

____
____
____
____
____

LAB 17.3 NETWORKING AND WINDOWS NT

Objective

The objective of this lab exercise is to provide you with hands-on networking experience in the Windows NT environment. After completing this lab exercise, you will be able to:

- Install network interface card drivers.
- Configure Windows NT workstation to communicate on a LAN.
- Share resources in a networked environment.
- Map a network drive in the Windows NT environment.
- Configure the TCP/IP protocol in the Windows NT environment.

Materials Required

- Operating system: Windows NT 4.0 Workstation
- Lab workgroup size: 2–4 students
- Configuration type: simple

Simple Configuration

- 90 Mhz or better Pentium-compatible computer
- 16 MB of RAM
- 540 MB hard drive
- 1 NIC (Network Interface Card)

Additional Devices: None

Lab Setup & Safety Tips

- The classroom should be wired for network communications.
- Each lab workstation should have one network interface card installed, but not configured to communicate on a network.
- The instructor will provide an IP address for each lab workstation prior to the start of activities. *Note*: All IP addresses should be on the same subnet unless the classroom supports other configurations.
- The instructor will provide computer names to each lab workstation before the activities are completed.
- Each student or group of students will require a local administrative Windows NT account.

ACTIVITY

Installing network interface card drivers and configuring TCP/IP

1. Power on your lab workstation and allow it to boot into the Windows NT environment.
2. Click the **Start** button.
3. Point to **Settings**.
4. Click **Control Panel**.
5. Double-click the **Network** icon.

6. Click the **Adapter** tab.
7. Click the **Add** button.
8. Select the correct NIC driver from the list.
9. Click the **OK** button.
10. If prompted, enter the path to the installation files.
11. Click the **Protocol** tab.
12. Click the **Add** button.
13. Select **TCP/IP Protocol** from the list provided, as shown in Figure 17-5.

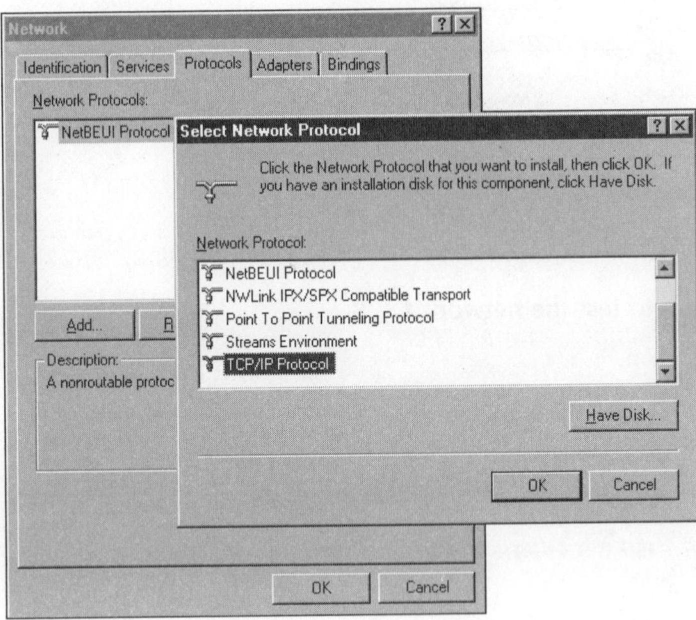

Figure 17-5 For Windows NT, install TCP/IP from the Network window of the Control Panel

14. Click the **OK** button. If you see a message asking if you want to use dynamic binding, click **No**.
15. In the Protocol list, click **TCP/IP**, and then click the **Properties** button.
16. Type the IP address issued to your lab workstation.
17. Enter any additional information your instructor requires. Your screen should resemble Figure 17-6.
18. Click the **Close** button.
19. Click the **Yes** button when prompted to restart your computer.

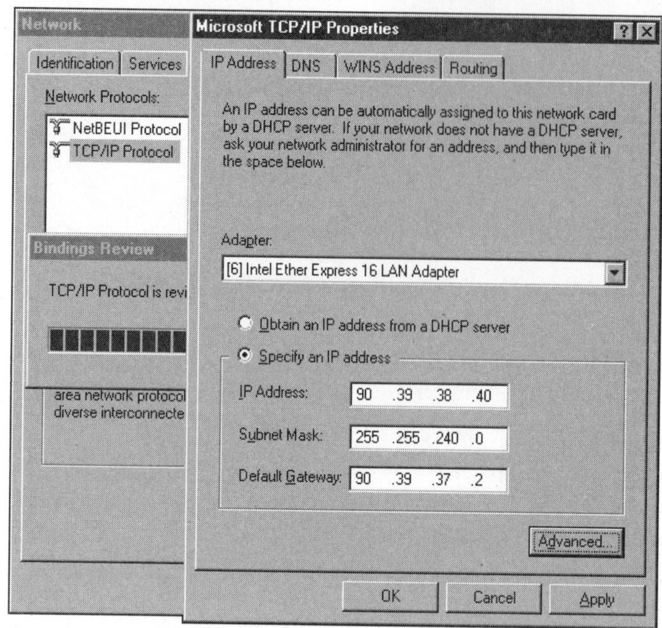

Figure 17-6 Configuring TCP/IP for Windows NT for static IP addressing

Using the PING command to test the network

1. Click the **Start** button.
2. Point to **Programs**.
3. Click **MS-DOS Prompt**.
4. Type **PING** ###.###.###.### (### represents your lab workstation's IP address).
5. Type **PING** ###.###.###.### (### represents the IP address of your neighbor's lab workstation).

Sharing your C drive

1. Double-click the **My Computer** icon.
2. Right-click the icon for your C drive.
3. Select **Properties** from the shortcut menu.
4. Click the **Sharing** tab.
5. Click the **Not Shared** option button.
6. Click the **Apply** button.
7. Click the **Shared As** option button.
8. Click the **OK** button.

Connecting to a shared resource

1. Right-click the **Network Neighborhood** icon.
2. Select the **Map Network Drive** option.
3. Click the Drive drop-down arrow and choose the drive letter **G**, if available.

4. Type *COMPUTERNAME**SHARENAME* in the path box (the computer and share name should be your neighbor's).

5. Click the **OK** button.

Lab Notes

TIP

How is the default gateway used?—The client uses the default gateway to send data packets to an IP address on a different network. Examine Figure 17-7 for more information.

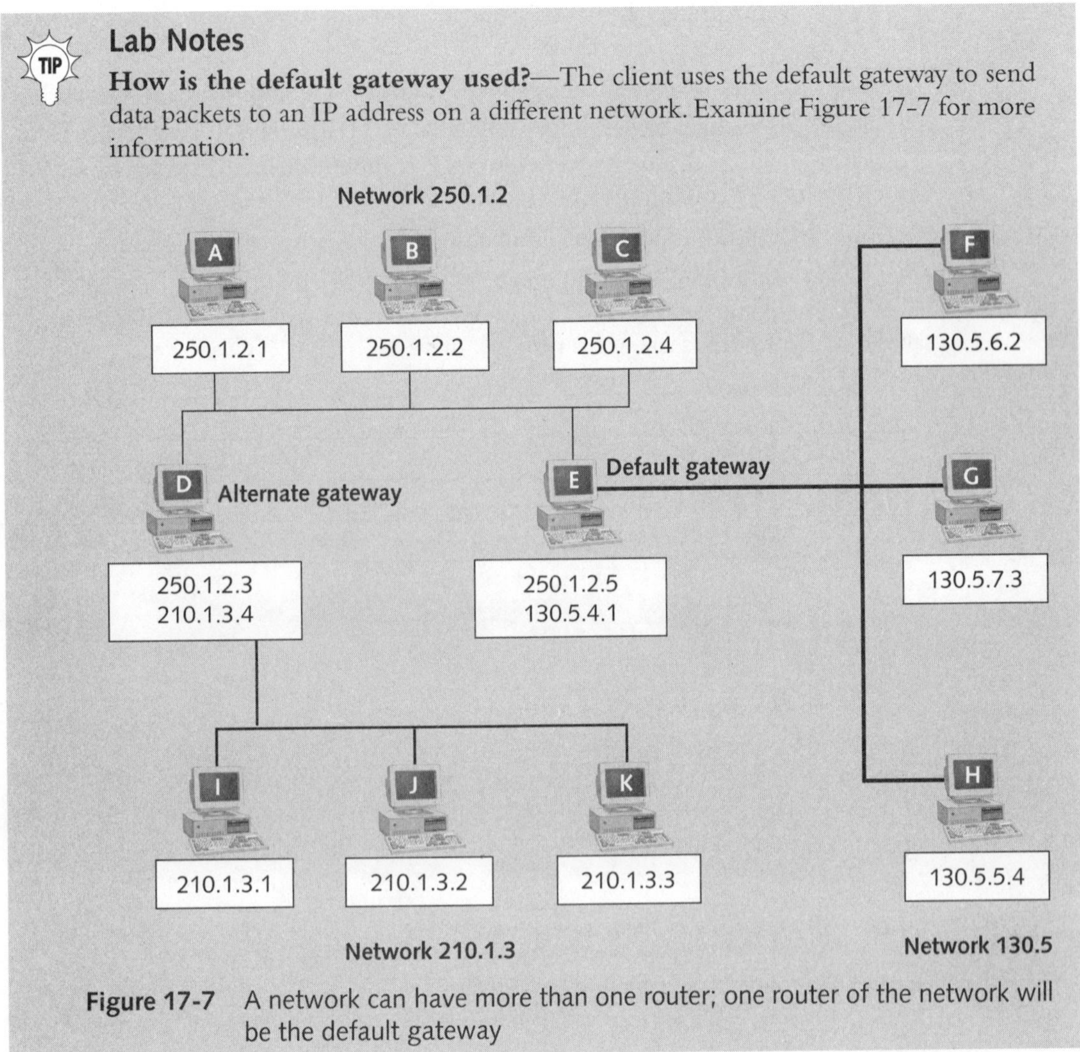

Figure 17-7 A network can have more than one router; one router of the network will be the default gateway

Review Questions

Circle True or False.

1. Windows NT does not allow you to share your C drive. True / False
2. The PING command serves the same function in both Windows 9x and Windows NT. True / False
3. To install a protocol in the Windows NT environment, you must view the Network properties, choose the Protocol tab, and click the Add button. True / False
4. Roxy would like to change her Windows NT computer name. To complete this task, Roxy can open the Network properties window and choose the Bindings tab. True / False
5. Windows NT allows you to share and connect to different network resources. True / False
6. Max would like to connect his Windows NT computer to a UNIX share. Max wants the UNIX share to appear as drive N in his My Computer window. Describe the steps Max will take to map a UNIX share as his network drive N.

____

____

____

____

____

Lab 17.4 Networking and Windows 2000

Objective

The objective of this lab exercise is to provide you with hands-on networking experience in the Windows 2000 environment. After completing this lab exercise, you will be able to:

- Uninstall network interface card drivers.
- Install network interface card drivers.
- Configure Windows 2000 Professional to communicate on a LAN.
- Share resources in a networked environment.
- Map a network drive using Windows 2000.
- Configure the TCP/IP protocol.

Materials Required

- Operating system: Windows 2000 Professional
- Lab workgroup size: 2–4 students
- Configuration type: modern

Modern Configuration

- 200 Mhz or better Pentium-compatible computer
- 64 MB of RAM
- 2 GB hard drive
- CD-ROM Drive
- 1 NIC (Network Interface Card)
- 1 sound card

Additional Devices: None

17

Lab Setup & Safety Tips

- The classroom should be wired for network communications.
- Each lab workstation should have one network interface card installed and configured to communicate on a network using TCP/IP.
- Each student or group of students will require a local administrative Windows 2000 account.

Activity

Recording the TCP/IP configuration

1. Power on your lab workstation and allow it to boot to Windows 2000 Professional. Then log on, if necessary.
2. Click the **Start** button.
3. Point to **Settings**.
4. Click **Control Panel**.
5. Double-click the **Network and Dial-up Connections** icon.

6. Right-click **Local Area Connection** and click **Properties**.
7. Click **Internet Protocol (TCP/IP)** to highlight it.
8. Click the **Properties** button.
9. Record all of the following information found on the Internet Protocol (TCP/IP) property sheet. (You will need this information to configure TCP/IP later in this activity.)

   IP address: ______________________________

   Subnet mask: ______________________________

   Default gateway: ______________________________

   Preferred DNS server: ______________________________

   Alternate DNS server: ______________________________
10. Click **OK** when finished.
11. Click the **OK** button in the Local Area Connection property sheet.

Uninstall the NIC driver

1. Right-click **My Computer** and click **Manage**.
2. In the left pane of the Computer Management window, click **Device Manager**.
3. In the right pane, double-click **Network adapters**.
4. Right-click the installed **NIC driver**, and click **Uninstall**.
5. Click **OK** when prompted to confirm the operation.
6. Close the Computer Management window.
7. Click the **Start** button and click **Shut Down**.
8. Use the drop-down menu to select **Restart** and click **OK**.

Viewing the adapter

1. If necessary, log on to your lab workstation. Then, right-click **My Computer** and click **Manage**.
2. In the left pane of the Computer Management window, click **Device Manager**.
3. In the right pane, double-click **Network adapters**.
4. In most cases, Windows 2000 automatically redetects your NIC when the computer is rebooted and will reinstall the appropriate driver.
5. If the driver wasn't automatically reinstalled, use the Add/Remove Hardware applet found in the Control Pannel to reinstall the network adapter.
6. Windows may prompt you for a driver disk or the Windows 2000 installation CD-ROM.

Configuring TCP/IP

1. Click the **Start** button.
2. Point to **Settings**.
3. Click **Control Panel**.
4. Double-click the **Network and Dial-up Connections** icon.
5. Right-click **Local Area Connection** and click **Properties**. Note that the Local Area Connection icon won't be available if the driver isn't installed properly.

6. Single-click **Internet Protocol (TCP/IP)** to highlight it.
7. Click the **Properties** button.
8. Click **Use the following IP address** toggle key.
9. Type the information that you recorded at the beginning of this exercise.
10. Click the **OK** button when finished.
11. Click the **OK** button in the Local Area Connection property sheet.
12. Click the **Start** button and click **Shut Down.**
13. Use the drop-down menu to select **Restart** and then click **OK**.

PATHPING (ping + route tracing)

1. Allow your computer to boot into the Windows 2000 environment, and log on using an administrative account.
2. Click the **Start** button.
3. Click **Run**.
4. Type **CMD** in the textbox and press **Enter**.
5. Type **PATHPING** ###.###.###.### (### represents your lab workstation's IP address).
6. Record the results: ____________________
7. Type **PATHPING** ###.###.###.### (### represents the IP address of your neighbor's lab workstation).
8. Record the results: ____________________
9. Type **EXIT** when finished.

Sharing your C drive

1. Double-click **My Computer**.
2. Right-click the C drive **icon**.
3. Select **Properties** from the shortcut menu.
4. Click the **Sharing** tab.
5. Click the **Do not share this folder** option button.
6. Click the **Apply** button.
7. Click the **Share this folder** option button.
8. Click the **OK** button.

17

Connecting to a shared resource

1. Right-click the **My Network Places** icon.
2. Select the **Map Network Drive** option.
3. Click the Drive drop-down arrow and choose the drive letter **Z**, if available. If it is not available, you should use a drive letter provided by your instructor.
4. Type ***COMPUTERNAME******SHARENAME*** in the path box (the computer and share name should be your neighbor's).
5. Click the **Finish** button.

Lab Notes

TRACERT—TRACERT is a command-line utility used to trace the route that data is traveling between two network devices.

PATHPING—PATHPING is a new command-line utility introduced by the Windows 2000 suite. PATHPING was designed to combine the functionality of ping and tracert. PATHPING sends packets to each router on the way to a final destination, and does so over a period of time. It then computes the results based on the packets returned from each hop.

Review Questions

Circle True or False.

1. Similar to Windows 9x, Windows 2000 automatically attempts to detect new hardware. True / False
2. The PATHPING command serves the same function in both Windows NT and Windows 2000. True / False
3. The Dial-up Networking Connection icon is used to change a NIC IP address. True / False
4. If Windows 2000 doesn't automatically detect hardware, Device Manager can be used to detect hardware changes. True / False
5. Write a scenario question with only one correct answer that utilizes the PATHPING utility.

____
____
____
____
____

6. Write a brief network installation and configuration comparison between Windows 2000 Professional and Windows NT.

____
____
____
____
____

Lab 17.5 Using the Internet

Objective

The objective of this lab exercise is to develop your Internet skills. These skills include the installation and configuration of Internet software, as well as the browsing for and downloading of information from the Internet. After completing this lab exercise, you will be able to:

- Install Netscape Communicator 4.04 or later.
- Configure a Netscape profile.
- Use the HTTP protocol to connect and view Web sites.
- Use the FTP protocol to download files from an FTP site.

Materials Required

- Operating system: Windows 9x
- Lab workgroup size: 2–4 students
- Configuration type: simple

Simple Configuration

- 90 Mhz or better Pentium-compatible computer
- 16 MB of RAM
- 540 MB hard drive
- 1 NIC (Network Interface Card)

Additional Devices

- Netscape Communicator 4.04 standard edition or later
- One installed modem

Lab Setup & Safety Tips

- Each lab workstation should have access to the Internet and have Windows 9x installed and functioning properly.
- Each lab workstation should have the Netscape Communicator installation files on drive C before starting the activity.

17

Activity

Installing Netscape Communicator 4.04 standard edition

Note: The following steps have been tested and verified as accurate for Netscape Communicator 4.04. Steps may vary for other versions of Netscape Communicator.

1. Power on your lab workstation and allow it to boot into Windows 9x.
2. Double-click the **Netscape Installation** icon to start the Setup program.
3. Click the **Next** button.
4. Click the **Yes** button.
5. Click the **Next** button.
6. Click the **Yes** button.

7. Click the **Next** button.
8. Click the **Install** button.
9. Click the **No** button.
10. Click the **OK** button.

Configuring your Netscape profile

1. Click the **Start** button.
2. Point to **Programs**.
3. Point to **Netscape Communicator**.
4. Click the **Netscape Messenger** icon.
5. Click the **Next** button.
6. Type *your name* in the Full Name box.
7. Type *your e-mail address* in the Email address box.
8. Click the **Next** button.
9. Type *your name* in the Profile Name box.
10. Click the **Next** button.
11. Type the name of your SMTP server in the Outgoing Mail (SMTP) Server box.
12. Click the **Next** button.
13. Type your mail server user name in the Mail Server User Name box.
14. Type the name of your POP or IMAP server in the Incoming Mail Server box.
15. Click the correct option button to specify either a POP3 server or an IMAP server.
16. Click the **Next** button.
17. Type the name of your news server in the News (NNTP) server box.
18. Click the **Finish** button.
19. Click the **Do not perform this check in the future** check box to select it.
20. Click the **Yes** button.
21. Close Netscape Messenger.

Using the HTTP protocol

1. If necessary, connect to the Internet.
2. Start **Netscape Communicator**.
3. If you already know of a Web site that you want to visit, type the URL for it in the Location box and press Enter. Otherwise, you can visit *www.intel.com* or *www.microsoft.com*.
4. Press **Enter**.

Using the FTP protocol

1. Start **Netscape Communicator**.
2. In the location box, type **ftp://ftp.intel.com**.
3. Click the **Readme** link to see the readme file.

Configuring the Netscape Communicator browser to use a proxy server

In the following section you will configure your Web browser to use to use a sample proxy server for the HTTP and FTP services called WEB-PROXY.LAB.TEST.COM:8088.

1. Start **Netscape Communicator**.
2. Click the **Edit** menu.
3. Click **Preferences**.
4. In the Category text box, click the **Advanced** option.
5. Click **Proxies**.
6. Click the **Manual Proxy configuration** option button.
7. Click the **View** button.
8. In the HTTP box, type **web-proxy.lab.test.com**, press **Tab**, and type **8088**.
9. In the FTP box, type **web-proxy.lab.test.com**, press **Tab**, and type **8088**.
10. Click the **OK** button.
11. Click the **OK** button.

Lab Notes

What is an ISP?—ISP stands for Internet Service Provider. ISPs are used as connection points to the Internet. When at home, most people dial into an ISP network that is connected to the Internet. This gives home users access to the Internet.

Review Questions

Circle True or False.

1. Netscape Communicator is a Web server software package. True / False
2. The HTTP protocol is used when viewing Web pages such as *www.microsoft.com*. True / False
3. You can download a file from the Internet by clicking the link to the file and pressing the Save button. True / False
4. Netscape Communicator does not support proxy servers. True / False
5. Describe the steps you take to connect to an FTP site.

____

____

____

____

____

6. List three examples of domain names.

____

____

____

____

____

CHAPTER

18

PRINTERS

LABS INCLUDED IN THIS CHAPTER

Lab 18.1 Understanding Laser Printers

Objective

The objective of this lab exercise is for you to inspect and understand the function of each component within a laser printer. After completing this lab exercise, you will be able to:

- Describe the function of each internal laser printer component.
- Describe the laser printing process.

Materials Required

- Operating system: N/A
- Lab workgroup size: 2–4 students
- Configuration type: N/A

Additional Devices

- One functional laser printer for each lab workstation
- One disassembled printer cartridge
- Labels for each lab laser printer

Lab Setup & Safety Tips

- The instructor should be familiar with the lab laser printers.
- Always unplug the power cord before touching any component in the printer.

Activity

Inspecting and labeling a laser printer cartridge

1. Using Figure 18-1 as a guide, identify each component in the disassembled laser printer cartridge, and describe its function on the lines provided.

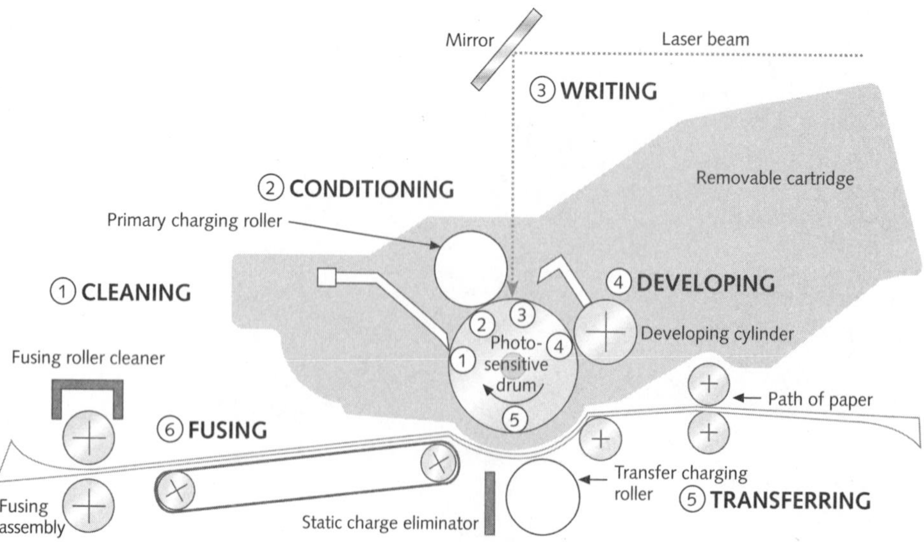

Figure 18-1 The six progressive steps of laser printing

Primary charging roller ______________________________

____

____

____

Photosensitive drum ______________________________

____

____

____

Developing cylinder ______________________________

____

____

____

Inspecting and labeling a laser printer

Although all laser printers follow the same printing process, each has a different design. Your instructor will show you how to disassemble your lab workstation's laser printer so you can complete the following exercise.

1. Power off and unplug your laser printer.

   (If your laser printer has been used recently, allow it to cool before proceeding.)

2. Open your laser printer.
3. Identify each of the following laser printer components and describe its functionality:

   Fusing components ______________________________

   ____

   ____

   ____

   Paper path ______________________________

   ____

   ____

   ____

   Primary charging roller ______________________________

   ____

   ____

   ____

   Transfer charging roller ______________________________

   ____

   ____

   ____

Power supply ____

____

____

____

Sensors (all) ____

____

____

____

Expansion slots ____

____

____

____

Logic boards (all) ____

____

____

____

Lab Notes

The Six Steps of Laser Printing:

Step 1: Cleaning

The printer uses the cleaning blade to scrape leftover toner from the previous image off the drum. It removes the previous electrostatic image from the drum with an erase lamp.

Step 2: Conditioning

The primary charging roller applies a uniform negative charge (-600 volts) to prepare the drum for the new image. *Warning*: Do not expose the drum to light.

Step 3: Writing

- The PC sends the image to the formatter.
- The PC formatter sends the image to the DC controller.
- A laser beam is initiated and directed toward the scanning mirror.
- The laser beam reflects off the scanning mirror and is focused by the focusing lens.
- The laser deflects off the mirror and is projected through a slit into the removable cartridge.

Note that the speed of both the drum motor and the scanning mirror motor are synchronized so that the laser beam completes one scan line and returns to the beginning of the drum.

Step 4: Developing

The electrostatic image develops into a visible image when toner from a developer cylinder is transferred to the discharged (-100 volt) areas of the drum. The developer cylinder has a magnetic core that attracts the iron in the toner. As the cylinder rotates, the doctor blade keeps the toner at a uniform height. The toner acquires a negative charge by rubbing against the developer cylinder. This negative charge causes the toner to be attracted to the relatively positive (-100 volt) areas of the drum that have been exposed to the laser light.

Lab Notes (continued)

Step 5: Transferring

The transfer charging roller produces a positive charge (+600 volts) on the back of the paper that pulls the toner off the drum and onto the paper. Once the toner is on the paper, a static charge eliminator reduces the paper's charge.

Step 6: Fusing

The toner is held on the paper by gravity and a weak electrostatic charge until it reaches the fuser assembly. Heat (180° C/356° F) and pressure applied by the fuser rollers melt the toner into the paper and produce a permanent image. Because the photosensitive drum is 3.75 inches in circumference, the print cycle must be repeated several times to print one sheet of paper. If the temperature rises above 410° F, the printer automatically shuts down to cool off the fuser.

What about ink jet printers?

As the print head moves across the paper, an electrical pulse flows through thin resistors at the bottom of all the chambers that the printer uses to form a character or image. The resistor in each chamber heats a thin layer of ink to more than 900° F to form a vapor bubble. As the vapor bubble expands, it pushes ink through the nozzle to transfer a drop of ink to the paper. A typical character is formed by an array of ink drops arranged in a pattern that is 20 across by 20 high.

Review Questions

Circle True or False.

1. The photosensitive drum is always housed within the printer cartridge. True / False
2. The primary charging roller is always housed within the fuser. True / False
3. During the printing process, mirrors are used to control the movement of a tiny laser beam. True / False
4. What are the six steps of the laser printing process?

____

____

____

____

____

5. Describe how to replace the fuser in your lab workstation.

____

____

____

____

____

Lab 18.2 Inkjet Printer Maintenance and Cleaning

Objective

The objective of this lab exercise is to provide experience performing maintenance duties for an inkjet printer. After completing this lab exercise, you will be able to:

- Disassemble an inkjet printer.
- Clean an inkjet printer.
- Assemble an inkjet printer.

Materials Required

- Operating system: Windows 9x
- Lab workgroup size: 2–4 students
- Configuration Type: simple

Simple Configuration

- 90 Mhz or better Pentium-compatible computer
- 16 MB of RAM
- 540 MB hard drive
- 1 NIC (Network Interface Card)

Additional Devices

- One inkjet printer for each group of students
- Distilled water
- Cotton swabs
- Manufacturer printer instructions (if available)

Lab Setup & Safety Tips

- A Hewlett Packard DeskJet 672C was used to write this lab exercise. The instructor may need to slightly modify some steps if an HP DeskJet printer isn't used in the lab.
- The instructor should be familiar with the lab inkjet printers.
- Always unplug the power cord and properly ground yourself before touching any components inside a computer.

Activity

Removing the print cartridge

1. If necessary, use your lab workstation or a key combination to instruct the printer to move the print cradle to the print cartridge add/remove position.
2. Power off your printer, and then study the diagram in Figure 18-2.
3. Unplug the power cable.
4. Open the top panel of the printer so that you can access the print cradle.
5. If necessary, remove the paper load tray.

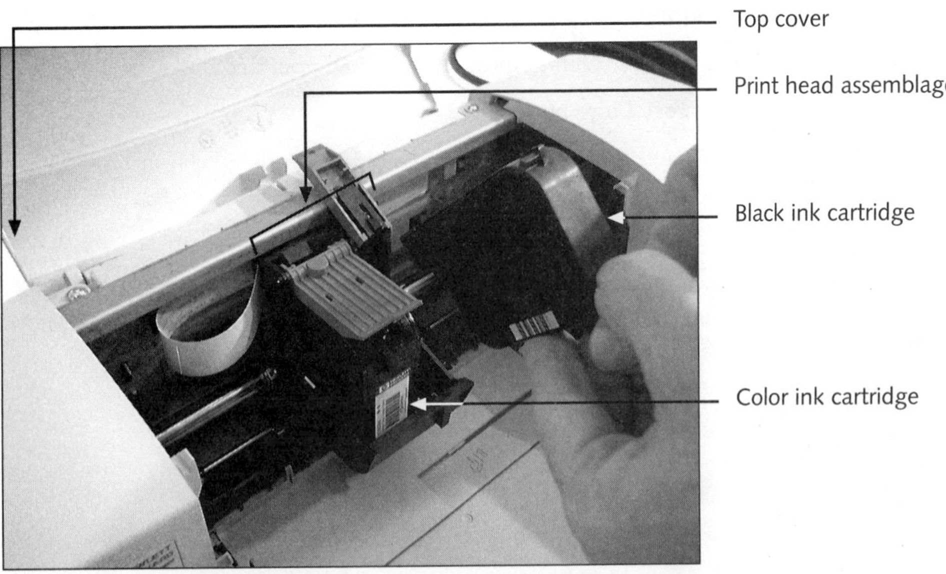

Figure 18-2 Removing the ink-jet printer cartridge

6. Move the print cradle latch to the open position.
7. Remove the print cartridge, making sure not to touch the print cartridge faceplate.

Clean the print cradle

1. Wet a cotton swab with distilled water.
2. Using the cotton swab, gently rub the underneath edges of the print cartridge. If the printer is have problems with ink streaks, it is normally because of build-up under the print cradle. Use as many cotton swabs as necessary.

Clean the rollers

1. With a clean cotton swab, scrub the printer roller. Note that with most printers, you will only be able to see a small portion of the roller at a time.
2. Not all rollers can be moved. Check your product documentation before attempting this step. After cleaning the visible portion of the roller, gently roll the roller forward and repeat Step 1 with a new cotton swab. Cleaning the roller will help if the printer is having problems gripping the paper or if rollers are leaving dirty marks on the paper.

18

Install the print cartridge

1. With the print cradle latch in the open position, place the printer cartridge into the print cradle (faceplate down).
2. Close the print cradle latch to secure the print cartridge. *Warning:* Don't force it. If it won't easily close, it may be jammed or the print cartridge may not be seated properly.

Finishing up

1. If necessary, replace the paper tray.
2. Close the top of the printer.
3. Plug in the power cord.

Testing your work

1. Allow your lab workstation to boot into the Windows environment.
2. Double-click **My Computer**.

3. Double-click **Printers**.
4. Right-click the icon for your printer and click **Properties**.
5. Click the **Print Test Page** button.
6. Check your test page to confirm that it printed correctly.

Lab Notes

How do I fix a paper jam?—If paper becomes jammed inside a printer, find the location of the paper jam and pull gently and evenly to remove the paper. Always check the printer documentation for specifics before you clear a paper jam.

Review Questions

Circle True or False.

1. The print cradle can cause ink streaking. True / False
2. An ink cartridge faceplate should never be touched; doing so will cause it to become damaged or dry out. True / False
3. Ink-speckled paper is a symptom of a dirty roller. True / False
4. Some printers require that a sequence of buttons or a software program be activated before you can replace the ink cartridge. True / False
5. In your own words, briefly describe how to clear a paper jam.

____

____

____

____

____

6. Write a scenario question, with only one correct answer, that depicts an inkjet printer with some type of a roller problem.

____

____

____

____

____

Lab 18.3 Installing and Sharing Local Printers

Objective

The objective of this lab exercise is to install a printer, load the proper drivers, and share the printer on the network. After completing this lab exercise, you will be able to:

- Install a local printer.
- Install printer drivers.
- Share a local printer.

Materials Required

- Operating system: Windows 9x
- Lab workgroup size: 2–4 students
- Configuration type: typical

Typical Configuration

- 166 Mhz or better Pentium-compatible computer
- 24 MB of RAM
- 800 MB hard drive
- CD-ROM Drive
- 1 NIC (Network Interface Card)

Additional Devices

- One functional laser printer for each lab workstation
- The cords and cables necessary to connect each laser printer to its respective lab workstation
- One Windows 9x CD for each lab workstation

Lab Setup & Safety Tips

- Each lab workstation should be configured to communicate on the network.
- The instructor should be familiar with the lab laser printers.

Activity

Installing a Local Printer

1. Power off your lab workstation.
2. Locate the parallel cable for your printer.
3. Attach the appropriate end of the cable to the back of the printer.
4. Attach the other end of the cable to the back of your lab workstation.
5. Plug in the power cord for the printer.
6. Power on your lab workstation and allow it to boot into Windows 9x.

Installing a printer driver

1. Double-click the **My Computer** icon.
2. Double-click the **Printers** folder.

3. Double-click **Add Printer**.
4. Click the **Next** button.
5. Choose the **My Computer** option, and click the **Next** button.
6. Choose whether you want to install a local or networked printer. Then choose the correct printer driver by selecting the appropriate manufacturer and the printer model. Click the **OK** button when you are done.
7. Select the appropriate printer port, and click the **Next** button.
8. In the Printer Name text box, type **PRINTER1**.
9. Click the **Yes** toggle key to select this printer as your Windows default.
10. Click the **Next** button.
11. Click the **Yes** toggle key and then click the **Finish** button to print a test page.
12. Close the Printers folder by clicking the **Close** button.
13. Close the My Computer window by clicking the **Close** button.

Installing file and print sharing for Windows 9x

1. Click the **Start** button, point to **Settings**, and choose **Control Panel**.
2. Double-click the **Network** icon.
3. On the **Configuration** tab, click the **File and Print Sharing** button.
4. In the File and Print Sharing window, click the **I want to be able to allow others to print to my printer(s)** check box.
5. Click the **OK** button.
6. Click the **Next** button in the Network Properties window.
7. Insert the Windows 9x CD, if prompted, and then click **OK**.
8. Click **Yes** when prompted to restart your computer.

Sharing a local printer

1. Click the **Start** button, point to **Settings**, and then click **Printers**.
2. In the Printers window, right-click the **PRINTER1** print object.
3. Choose **Properties** from the shortcut menu.
4. Click the **Sharing** tab, as shown in Figure 18-3.
5. Click the **Shared As** option button.
6. Notice that the printer name (in this case PRINTER1) has appeared in the Share Name text box. Use this text box to specify the share name of the printer.
7. Click the **OK** button to begin sharing the printer.

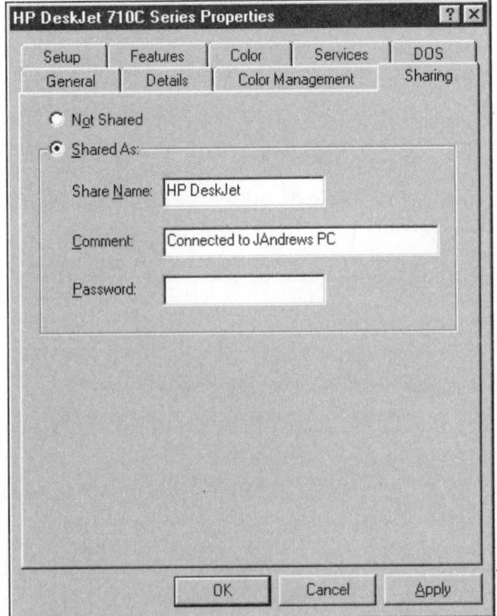

Figure 18-3 When using Windows 98, use the printer Properties window to share a connected printer with other computers on the network

Lab Notes

Are serial connections used with printers?—Although serial connections are less frequently used with printers than with parallel connections, they are still found on specialized units such as pen plotters or printers used for creating bar code labels or credit card receipts. There are also many items of electronic test equipment that include a serial printer port for purposes such as data logging. If there is a need to use a serial connection to drive a printer you're working with, and the printer does not directly support such an option, you can work around it either by purchasing a serial interface kit from the printer's manufacturer (if available) or by using a serial-to-parallel converter.

What about preventive maintenance?—Check the documentation provided with the printer. Some manufacturers sell PM (Preventive Maintenance) kits that include the parts that receive the most wear and tear.

How do I prevent white streaks from appearing when I print a document?—When streaks or speckles appear on documents, you should first check your print cartridge. Remove the cartridge and then tap or gently shake the toner cartridge to redistribute the toner. If the problem persists, check the printer manual for specific parts that may need attention.

Review Questions

Circle True or False.

1. You can use either a serial or parallel cable to connect to some printers. True / False
2. Parallel printing is faster than serial printing. True / False
3. You can enable File and Print Sharing in Windows 9x by double-clicking the Network icon in the Control panel to open the Network dialog box. True / False
4. In Windows 9x, you first must install File and Print Sharing to allow other people to print to your local printer. True / False
5. You install printer drivers using the Add New Hardware icon in the Control Panel. True / False
6. Angie is trying to share her local printer so that Bart can print to it. When she views the properties of the installed printer, she doesn't see a Sharing tab. Explain why Angie doesn't have a Sharing tab for her printer, and describe the steps she needs to take to share her printer with Bart.

____

____

____

____

____

Lab 18.4 Troubleshooting Shared Printers

Objective

The objective of this lab exercise is to give you experience both in printing to a network printer and troubleshooting printing in a networked environment. After completing this lab exercise, you will be able to:

- Connect to a shared printer.
- Print to a shared printer.
- Troubleshoot network printing.

Materials Required

- Operating system: Windows 9x
- Lab workgroup size: 2–4 students
- Configuration type: simple

Simple Configuration

- 90 Mhz or better Pentium-compatible computer
- 16 MB of RAM
- 540 MB hard drive
- 1 NIC (Network Interface Card)

Additional Devices

- One functional laser printer for each lab workstation
- The cords and cables necessary to connect each laser printer to its respective lab workstation

Lab Setup & Safety Tips

- Each lab workstation should be configured to communicate on the network.
- The instructor and students should be familiar with the lab laser printers.
- Each lab workstation should be configured so a local laser printer can be installed correctly and shared on the network as Printer1.
- The instructor should designate groups, two pairs of students to a group.
- Each pair of students will assume a role, Student 1 or Student 2.

18

Activity

Connecting to a Shared Printer

Student 1

1. Power on your lab workstation and allow it to boot into Windows 9x.
2. Click the **Start** button, point to **Settings**, and then click **Control Panel**.
3. Double-click the **Network** icon and then use the Identification tab to identify Student 2's lab workstation.
4. Click the **Start** button, point to **Settings**, and then click **Printers**.
5. Double-click the **Add Printer** icon and then click the **Next** button.
6. Click the **Network Printer** option button.
7. Click the **Next** button. Your screen should resemble Figure 18-4.

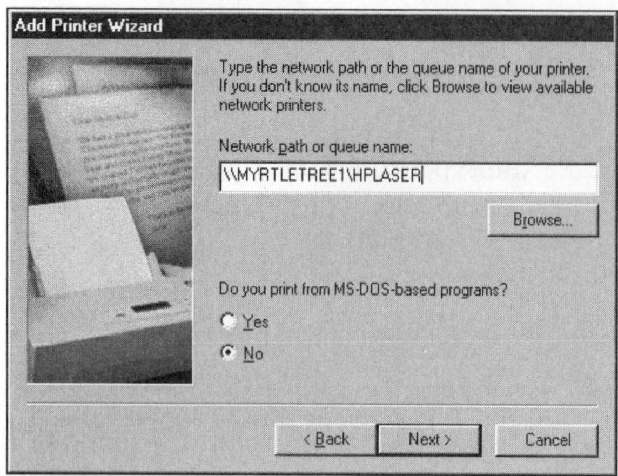

Figure 18-4 To use a network printer under Windows 9x, enter the host computer name followed by the printer name

8. In the **Network printer or queue name** text box, type ***Student 2's computer name*\Printer1**.
9. Click the **Next** button.
10. If both lab workstations are using the same operating system, the printer driver will automatically be installed. You then can click the **Finish** button. If this isn't the case, complete Steps 11-12.
11. From the list, choose the appropriate manufacturer and printer type, and then click the **Next** button.
12. Click the **Finish** button.

Creating problem 1

Student 2

While Student 1 is away from the workstation, proceed with the following steps:

1. Click the **Start** button, point to **Settings**, and then click **Printers**.
2. Click the **PRINTER1** icon.
3. Click the **File** menu.
4. Click the **Work offline** option to check it.
5. Close the Printer window.

Troubleshooting and resolving problem 1

Student 1

After Student 2 has reconfigured one or both of the lab workstations, answer the following questions and repair the network printing function.

Are there any error messages? If so, write them down. ______________________________

____

____

____

____

____

What is the problem? Be specific. ____

____

____

____

____

____

List several possible solutions (if applicable). ____

____

____

____

____

____

Test your theory (solution) and record the results. ____

____

____

____

____

____

How did you discover the problem? ____

____

____

____

____

____

What would you do differently in the future to improve your troubleshooting process?

____

____

____

____

____

Creating problem 2

Student 1

While Student 2 is away from the workstation, proceed with the following steps on Student 2's lab workstation:

1. Click the **Start** button, point to **Settings**, and then click **Printers**.
2. Right-click the **PRINTER1** icon and choose **Sharing** from the shortcut menu.
3. In the **Share Name** text box, type **PRINTER2**.

4. Click the **Apply** button.
5. Click the **OK** button.
6. Click the **OK** button.
7. Close the Printer window.

Troubleshooting and resolving problem 2

Student 2

After Student 1 has reconfigured one or both of the lab workstations, answer the following questions and repair the network printing function.

Are there any error messages? If so, write them down. ______________________________

What is the problem? Be specific. ______________________________

List several possible solutions (if applicable). ______________________________

Test your theory (solution) and record the results. ______________________________

How did you discover the problem? ______________________________

What would you do differently in the future to improve your troubleshooting process?

____

____

____

____

____

TIP

Lab Notes

Can I share my C drive like I share a printer?—Yes. Sharing your C drive is similar to sharing a printer. First you must use the Network applet in the Control Panel to enable the File Sharing service. Next locate the directory or drive that you want to share, and then click the Sharing tab on the Network Properties sheet to configure drive sharing service.

What is the Work Offline setting used for?—The Work Offline feature in Windows 9x is designed for users that are not always connected to a network or a printer. When you select the Work Offline feature, Windows allows you to spool print jobs, but will not attempt to print them until you deselect Work Offline. This allows remote users to print a document the next time a printer becomes available.

Review Questions

Circle True or False.

1. When a device is configured to work offline, it will queue print jobs, but will not attempt to print them until it is brought back online. True / False
2. A printer's share name is always the same as the printer name. True / False
3. UNC syntax is typically used when mapping to a shared print device. True / False
4. Jacob has shared an HP LaserJet 4 printer on the network. Jacob gave you the following information and told you to set up the printer on your workstation:

   Computer Name: Jacob1

   Printer Name: HPLJ4

   In the lines provided, describe how to connect to Jacob's HP Laser Jet 4 and print a document.

   ____

   ____

   ____

   ____

   ____

5. Alice has an HP LaserJet 6L at her desk. She telephones you because it won't print. She says that there is a yellow light flashing on the front panel and it is just sitting there. List at least three things you would have Alice check to resolve her printing problem.

   ____

   ____

   ____

   ____

   ____

18

CHAPTER

19

VIRUSES, DISASTER RECOVERY, AND A MAINTENANCE PLAN THAT WORKS

LABS INCLUDED IN THIS CHAPTER

- LAB 19.1 VIRUS PROTECTION
- LAB 19.2 CREATING AND MAINTAINING BACKUPS
- LAB 19.3 DESIGNING A PREVENTIVE MAINTENANCE PLAN

Lab 19.1 Virus Protection

Objective

The objective of this lab exercise is to identify virus symptoms and learn how to use antivirus software to detect and disinfect viruses. After completing this lab exercise, you will be able to:

- Scan for viruses using antivirus software.
- Name some of the most common types of viruses.
- Describe the effects of several types of viruses.

Materials Required

- Operating system: Windows 9x
- Lab workgroup size: 2 students
- Configuration type: simple

Simple Configuration

- 90 Mhz or better Pentium-compatible computer
- 16 MB of RAM
- 540 MB hard drive
- 1 NIC (Network Interface Card)

Additional Devices

- Cheyenne Antivirus
- Nuts & Bolts software
- Access to the Internet

Lab Setup & Safety Tips

- Each lab workstation should have the Cheyenne Antivirus software and the Nuts & Bolts software installed prior to beginning the activities.

Activity

Scanning for viruses

1. Power on your lab workstation and allow it to boot into Windows 9x.
2. Click the **Start** button.
3. Point to **Programs**, and then point to **Nuts & Bolts**.
4. Click **Cheyenne Antivirus Scanner**.
5. In the Scanning box, type **c:**.
6. Click **Advanced**.
7. Verify that both the Boot Sector and the Files options are selected.
8. Click the **File Types** tab.
9. Verify that the **All Files** option is selected.
10. Click the **OK** button.
11. Click the **Start** button.

Researching viruses and describing their symptoms

1. Observe Figure 19-1 and discuss how you or your classmates might react to the depicted scenario. Then, in each of the following categories, list five different types of viruses and describe their symptoms. Use the Internet as a research tool.

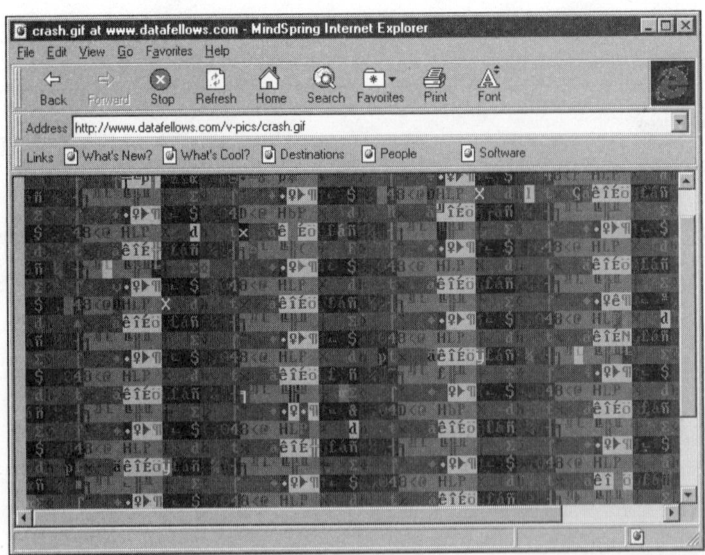

Figure 19-1 The crash virus appears to be destructive, making the screen show only garbage, but does no damage to the hard drive data

a. Boot sector viruses ______________________________

____

____

____

____

____

b. Worm ______________________________

____

____

____

____

____

c. Trojan horse ______________________________

____

____

____

____

____

19

d. Macro viruses ____

e. Multipartite viruses ____

f. Stealth viruses ____

g. Partition table viruses ____

h. Virus hoaxes ____

Lab Notes

Where do viruses come from?—All viruses are written by programmers. You can contract a virus through many different forms of communication, such as disks, file downloads, e-mail, and even Web sites.

Review Questions

Circle True or False.

1. All viruses can cause fatal damage to your operating system. True / False
2. If your PC often freezes, you probably have a virus. True / False
3. Some viruses are designed to infect specific types of files such as Word 97 or Excel 97 documents. True / False
4. Currently there are only 990 viruses in existence. True / False
5. Name three common ways viruses are contracted.

____

____

____

____

____

6. List two things you can do to help prevent the spread of viruses.

____

____

____

____

____

Lab 19.2 Creating and Maintaining Backups

Objective

The objective of this lab exercise is to provide the hands-on experience necessary to properly install, configure, and execute a full backup in the Windows NT environment. After completing this lab exercise, you will be able to:

- Install an external tape backup device.
- Configure Windows NT workstation to use an external tape backup device.
- Use the Windows NT backup program.

Materials Required

- Operating system: Windows NT 4.0 Workstation
- Lab workgroup size: 2 students
- Configuration type: simple

Simple Configuration

- 90 Mhz or better Pentium-compatible computer
- 16 MB of RAM
- 540 MB hard drive
- 1 NIC (Network Interface Card)

Additional Devices

- One external tape backup drive and the appropriate cables
- One tape for the backup drive

Lab Setup & Safety Tips

- Each lab workstation should have one network interface card installed.
- Always unplug the power cord and properly ground yourself before touching any component inside a computer.
- Students should have the documentation and drivers necessary to install and configure the tape backup drive.

Activity

Installing a tape backup drive

1. Power off your lab workstation.
2. Plug the parallel cable into the back of the tape drive.
3. Attach the parallel cable to the LPT1.
4. Plug in and power on the tape drive.
5. Power on your lab workstation and allow it to boot into Windows NT.

Installing the tape backup drive's device drivers

1. Click the **Start** button.
2. Point to **Settings** and click **Control Panel**.
3. Double-click the **Tape Devices** icon.
4. Click the **Drivers** tab.
5. Click the **Add** button.
6. Insert the disk containing the tape drive device drivers.
7. Click the **Have Disk** button.
8. Click the **OK** button.
9. Select the correct drivers for your tape drive.
10. Click the **OK** button.
11. If prompted, enter the path to the Windows NT installation files.
12. Click the **Close** button.
13. Click the **Yes** button to restart your computer.

Using the Windows NT backup program

1. Insert a tape into the tape backup drive.
2. Click the **Start** button.
3. Point to **Programs** and then click **Administrative Tools**.
4. Click the **Backup** option.
5. In the Backup program window, click the **Operations** menu.
6. Select the **Hardware Setup** option.
7. Verify that the proper tape backup device is shown in the Hardware Setup box.
8. Click the **OK** button.
9. Click the check box next to the C: drive to check it.
10. Click the **Operations** menu.
11. Click **Backup**.

Lab Notes

What is a differential backup?—A differential backup only backs up files that have changed or have been created since the last full backup.

What is an incremental backup?—An incremental backup only backs up files that have been changed or files that have been created since the last incremental or full backup.

Review Questions

Circle True or False.

1. The Windows NT Backup program allows you to back up files to either a floppy drive or a tape drive. True / False
2. You can install a tape drive device driver by using the Control Panel Add New Hardware icon. True / False
3. To begin a backup using the Windows NT Backup program, launch the Backup program, click the Tools menu, and then click Backup Now. True / False
4. Windows NT supports full, incremental, and differential backups. True / False
5. The Windows NT Backup program automatically backs up the PC nightly, unless otherwise specified. True / False
6. Joy has decided to back up her hard drive. She understands how to execute the back-up process but is unsure what kind of backup she should perform (incremental, differential, or full). Explain below which type of backup Joy must use and why.

____

____

____

____

____

LAB 19.3 DESIGNING A PREVENTIVE MAINTENANCE PLAN

Objective

The objective of this lab exercise is to create a preventive maintenance plan for a small business network. After completing this lab exercise, you will be able to:

- Design a preventive maintenance plan.
- Name some common preventive maintenance tasks for networked computers.
- Understand and describe the importance of maintenance delegation.

Materials Required

- You will not require any additional materials for this exercise.

Additional Devices: None

Lab Setup & Safety Tips

- Your instructor will discuss some common preventive maintenance procedures.

ACTIVITY

Developing a PC preventive maintenance plan

Table 19-1 Guidelines for developing a PC preventive maintenance plan

Component	Maintenance	How Often
Inside the case	• Make sure the air vents are clean. • Use compressed air to blow the dust out of the case. • Ensure that chips and expansion cards are firmly seated. • Clean the contacts on expansion cards.	Yearly
CMOS setup	• Keep a backup record of setup (for example, use Nuts & Bolts rescue disk).	Whenever changes are made
Floppy drive	• Only clean the floppy drive head when the drive does not work.	When the drive fails
Hard drive	• Perform regular backups. • Automatically execute a virus scan program at startup. • Defragment the drive and recover lost clusters regularly. • Don't allow smoking around the PC. • Place the PC where it will not get kicked or bumped.	• At least weekly • At least daily • Monthly
Keyboard	• Keep the keyboard clean. • Keep the keyboard away from liquids.	• Monthly • Always
Mouse	• Clean the mouse rollers and ball (see Chapter 7).	Monthly
Monitor	• Clean the screen with a soft cloth.	At least monthly
Printers	• Clean out the dust and bits of paper. • Clean the paper and ribbon paths with a soft cloth. • Don't re-ink ribbons or use recharged toner cartridges.	At least monthly

Table 19-1 Guidelines for developing a PC preventive maintenance plan (continued)

Component	Maintenance	How Often
Software	• If so directed by your employer, check that only authorized software is present. • Regularly remove files from the Recycle Bin and \Temp directories. • Remove any temporary files in the \DOS directory.	At least monthly
Written record	• Record all software, including version numbers and the OS installed on the PC. • Record all hardware components installed, including hardware settings. • Record when and what preventative maintenance is performed. • Record any repairs done to the PC.	Whenever changes are made

1. Observe the ideal maintenance activities in Table 19-1. You are the network administrator for a 75-user network. Your employer has asked you to create a preventive maintenance plan for all of the hardware components connected to the network. You have started this project by creating the following list, which contains each of the hardware components that should be included in the preventive maintenance plan. Using the table above for reference, write at least two preventive maintenance tasks for each of the listed hardware components. Be sure to state how often the preventive maintenance task should be completed and who should be responsible for completing the tasks (that is, yourself or the user). Remember that you are the only network administrator and will not realistically be able to complete every preventive maintenance task necessary to maintain a network of this size.

   a. **System unit**

      i. PM Task 1 ____

      ____

      ____

      ____

      ii. PM Task 2 ____

      ____

      ____

      ____

   b. **CMOS setup**

      i. PM Task 1 ____

      ____

      ____

      ____

      ii. PM Task 2 ____

      ____

      ____

      ____

   c. **Floppy drive**

      i. PM Task 1 ____

      ____

      ____

      ____

ii. PM Task 2 ______

d. **Hard drive**

i. PM Task 1 ______

ii. PM Task 2 ______

e. **Keyboard and mouse**

i. PM Task 1 ______

ii. PM Task 2 ______

f. **Monitors**

i. PM Task 1 ______

ii. PM Task 2 ______

g. **10 Laser printers**

i. PM Task 1 ______

ii. PM Task 2 ______

h. **7 Inkjet printers**
   i. PM Task 1 ______________________________
   ____
   ____
   ____

   ii. PM Task 2 ______________________________
   ____
   ____
   ____

Lab Notes

What is a PM kit?—PM kits, or preventive maintenance kits, are designed to keep printers in good working order. A PM kit normally is administered during off-business hours to refresh and revitalize printer components that receive the most wear.

Review Questions

Circle True or False.

1. PM kits are designed to minimize printer downtime. True / False
2. Shaking the dust out of a system unit is considered an excellent preventive maintenance task that should be completed once a month. True / False
3. Smoking around a hard drive can shorten its life. True / False
4. If all client computers are using the Windows NT operating system, you will not need to create a preventive maintenance program. True / False
5. Write a scenario using the information in the preventive maintenance plan that you created in the previous activity. Your question must have only one correct answer.

   ____
   ____
   ____
   ____
   ____

CHAPTER

20

THE PROFESSIONAL PC TECHNICIAN

LABS INCLUDED IN THIS CHAPTER

- ♦ LAB 20.1 TELEPHONE SUPPORT
- ♦ LAB 20.2 ON-SITE SUPPORT
- ♦ LAB 20.3 DOCUMENTING YOUR WORK

Lab 20.1 Telephone Support

Objective

The objective of this lab exercise is to simulate a technical support call. After completing this lab exercise, you will be able to:

- Troubleshoot both hardware and software problems over the phone.
- Describe the advantages and disadvantages of supporting PCs over the phone.
- Understand the importance of listening to your customer.

Materials Required

- Operating system: Windows 9x
- Lab workgroup size: 2 students
- Configuration type: simple

Simple Configuration

- 90 Mhz or better Pentium-compatible computer
- 16 MB of RAM
- 540 MB hard drive
- 1 NIC (Network Interface Card)

Additional Devices

- One modem

Lab Setup & Safety Tips

- The modem should be installed and functioning properly prior to beginning the activity.
- During this lab exercise you will be simulating a telephone support call. For the most realistic results, the student in the role of the technician should not be able to see what his or her customer is doing on the lab workstation.
- Students should be working in pairs; designate one as Student 1 and one as Student 2.
- Always unplug the power cord and properly ground yourself before touching any component inside a computer.

Activity

Student 2 (Customer)

In this activity, you will delete the currently installed modem. After restarting your computer, you then will call your customer support line.

1. Power on your lab workstation and allow it to boot into Windows 9x.
2. Right-click the **My Computer** icon.
3. Select **Properties** from the shortcut menu.
4. Click the **Device Manager** tab.
5. Click **Modem**.
6. Select the installed modem, press the **Delete** key, and then click the **OK** button.
7. Click the **Close** button.

8. Click the **Yes** button when prompted to restart your computer.
9. Call the customer support line, and explain that you have installed a modem but can't get it to dial.

Student 1 (Technician)

The only resources you should have during this simulation are a pen and a piece of paper. After providing telephone support to your customer, answer the following questions.

Were there any error messages? If so, write them down: ______________________________

What was the problem? ______________________________

List several (at least three) clues that helped lead you to the problem (include the customer dialog): ______________________________

What would you do differently in the future to improve your troubleshooting process?

____

Student 1 (Customer)

You are calling customer support (Student 2) because you recently purchased some memory, but you are not sure how to install it.

1. Power off your lab workstation and unplug it.
2. Remove the case.
3. Remove all the RAM.
4. Call the customer support line, explain that you have removed the case, and you now want to install your new memory (use the memory you removed as the new memory).

Student 2 (Technician)

The only resources you should have during this simulation are a pen and a piece of paper. After providing telephone support to your customer, answer the following questions:

Were there any error messages? If so, write them down: ______________________________

____

____

____

____

____

What was the problem? ____

____

____

____

____

____

List several (at least three) clues that helped lead you to the problem (include the customer dialog): ____

____

____

____

____

____

What would you do differently in the future to improve your troubleshooting process?

____

____

____

____

____

Lab Notes

Listening to your customers—While working through this lab exercise, you probably discovered the importance of listening to your customer. At the beginning of a support call it is a good idea to allow your customer to describe the problem in detail and explain each step he or she has taken prior to the call. A good technician listens to the customer and at times even allows the customer to troubleshoot the problem. Some customers already know the answer to their problem, but lack the confidence to follow through.

Maintaining control of a call—Although it is important to listen to your customers, don't lose control of the conversation or situation. If you feel you are losing control, ask your customer any questions you need answered and then reiterate what they say to you. At this point explain to the customer the next step to resolving their problem, and make sure that this is acceptable.

Review Questions

Circle True or False.

1. As a technician you should always be sensitive to your customer's situation. True / False
2. Always tell your customers what to do. True / False
3. Customers often can provide clues to their problem. True / False
4. What do you think are the three most important personality traits a help desk technician should have?

____

____

____

____

____

Lab 20.2 On-Site Support

Objective

The objective of this lab exercise is to simulate a desktop PC support call. After completing this lab exercise, you will be able to:

- Troubleshoot both hardware and software problems while communicating with a customer.
- Describe the advantages and disadvantages of desktop support.

Materials Required

- Operating system: Windows 9x
- Lab workgroup size: 2 students
- Configuration type: simple

Simple Configuration

- 90 Mhz or better Pentium-compatible computer
- 16 MB of RAM
- 540 MB hard drive
- 1 NIC (Network Interface Card)

Additional Devices

- One DOS system disk

Lab Setup & Safety Tips

- If students are working in pairs, designate one as Student 1 and one as Student 2.

Activity

Student 2 (Customer)

You have called a technician out to your desk because your system won't boot and is giving you the error message "Invalid or missing command interpreter: command.com." Complete the following steps while Student 1 is away from the lab workstation.

1. Insert a system disk in drive A.
2. Power on your lab workstation and allow it to boot from the system disk.
3. At the A prompt, type **C:** and press **Enter**.
4. Type **REN C:\COMMAND.COM C:\COMMAND.OLD**.
5. Press **Enter**.
6. Type **REN C:\MSDOS.SYS C:\MSDOS.OLD**.
7. Press **Enter**.
8. Reboot your lab workstation and verify that you receive the error message "Invalid or missing command interpreter: command.com."
9. Ask your technical support person for help. Explain that you just installed some registry cleaning software and now nothing works right.

Student 1 (Technician)

The only resources you should have during this simulation are a pen and a piece of paper. After providing on-site support, answer the following questions:

Were there any error messages? If so, write them down: ______________________________

What was the problem? ______________________________

List several (at least three) clues that helped lead you to the problem (include the customer dialog): ______________________________

What would you do differently in the future to improve your troubleshooting process?

____

Student 1 (Customer)

You will reposition the RAM so your system won't boot. Complete the following steps while Student 2 is away from the lab workstation.

1. Power off and unplug the lab workstation.
2. Remove the case.
3. Unplug the data cable to the hard drive.
4. Change the jumper to the slave position.
5. Reposition the RAM and move it into the wrong banks.
6. Replace the case.
7. Power on the lab workstation and enter the Setup program.

8. Remove the hard drive from the Setup program.
9. Save the changes and exit.
10. Ask your technical support person for help. Explain that you didn't touch anything except the memory because you just installed new memory.

Student 2 (Technician)

The only resources you should have during this simulation are a pen and a piece of paper. After providing on-site support, answer the following questions:

Were there any error messages? If so, write them down: ______________________

____

____

____

____

What was the problem? ______________________

____

____

____

____

List several (at least three) clues that helped lead you to the problem (include the customer dialog): ______________________

____

____

____

____

What would you do differently in the future to improve your troubleshooting process?

____

____

____

____

____

Lab Notes

Safe Mode—Safe Mode is a Windows 9x troubleshooting mode. When Windows 9x is started in Safe Mode, it will load only a minimal set of drivers that are necessary to load Windows. You can boot Windows 9x into Safe Mode by pressing the F8 key during the boot process.

Review Questions

Circle True or False.

1. You can use Safe Mode to troubleshoot Windows 9x. True / False
2. You can enter Safe Mode by pressing the F8 key during the boot process. True / False
3. Windows 9x doesn't need the COMMAND.COM or MSDOS.SYS files. True / False
4. Troubleshooting the Windows NT environment is similar to troubleshooting the Windows 9x environment. True / False
5. Describe how a Windows 9x repair disk can be used to repair the Windows 9x startup environment.
6. Lesa has decided to clean some files off her hard drive but isn't sure which files are safe to delete. Make Lesa a list of five files that she should not delete.

____

____

____

____

____

Lab 20.3 Documenting Your Work

Objective

The objective of this lab exercise is to document your work from the previous lab exercises. After completing this lab exercise, you will be able to:

- Complete a standard service call report form.
- Complete a standard help desk call report form.
- Describe the values of A+ certification.

Materials Required

- You will not require any additional materials for this lab exercise.

Additional Devices: None

Lab Setup & Safety Tips

- To complete the following activity, you must have already completed Labs 20.1 and 20.2.

Activity

Documenting your help desk call (from Lab 20.1)

1. Complete the following Help Desk Report Form with the information from the activities in Lab 20.1.

Help Desk Call Report Form

INITIAL CALL

Caller: ____________________ Date: ______________ Time: ______________

Location: ______________________________ Phone: ______________________

Received by: ____

Description: ____

CALL NOTES: ____

____

____

____

____

FOLLOW-UP CALL ON: ______________________ BY: ______________

____

FOLLOW-UP CALL ON: ______________________ BY: ______________

____

CALL RESOLUTION: ____

____

____

____

____

Documenting your PC support call (from Lab 20.2)

1. Complete the following Service Call Report Form with the information from the activities in Lab 20.2.

Service Call Report Form

INITIAL REQUEST

Requested by: ____________ Date: ____________ Time: ____________

Location: ____________ Phone: ____________

Received by: ____________

Problem Description: ____________

INITIAL ACTION

Advice: ____________

Appointment Made:

By: ____________ Date: ____________ Time: ____________

Directions: ____________

____

DETAILED PROBLEM DESCRIPTION: ____________

____

____

____

____

SERVICE CALL RESOLUTION: ____________

____

____

____

____

NOTES: ____________

____

____

____

____

Lab Notes

What are the advantages of A+ certification?—A+ certification is an industry-recognized proof of competence and will greatly improve/increase your job opportunities.

What are your copyright responsibilities?—You are responsible for complying with the license agreement of the software package you are installing. It is also your responsibility to purchase only legitimate software packages that are properly licensed. You should report any software piracy issue by calling 1-888-NOPIRACY.

20

Review Questions

Circle True or False.

1. Copyright protection is everyone's responsibility. True / False
2. One of your customers, John, asked you several weeks ago to create a shortcut to File Manager for him. He has now called you back in frustration because the shortcut you made has stopped working. Describe the best way to diffuse this situation.

   ____
   ____
   ____
   ____
   ____

3. List at least three reasons why call report forms are used.

   ____
   ____
   ____
   ____
   ____

4. Cindy has no previous experience working on a PC. To complete her job duties, she must be able to use Microsoft Word. List five or more things you would teach Cindy to help her get started successfully.

   ____
   ____
   ____
   ____
   ____